Don't Kill the Cow Too Quick

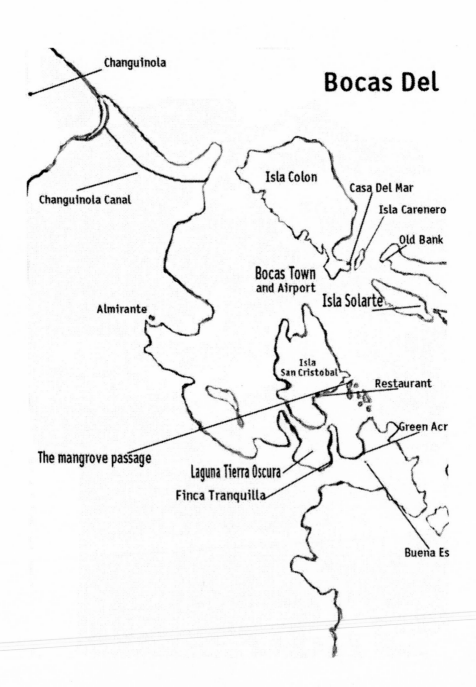

Toro Islands

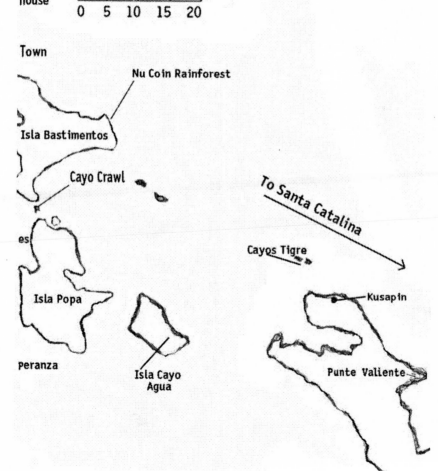

Approximate Distance
In Kilometers

house

0 5 10 15 20

Town

Nu Coin Rainforest

Isla Bastimentos

Cayo Crawl

To Santa Catalina

es

Cayos Tigre

Isla Popa

Kusapin

peranza

Isla Cayo
Agua

Punte Valiente

Don't Kill the Cow Too Quick

◆

An Englishman's Adventures Homesteading in Panama

Malcolm Henderson

iUniverse, Inc.

New York Lincoln Shanghai

Don't Kill the Cow Too Quick
An Englishman's Adventures Homesteading in Panama

iUniverse, Inc.

For information address:
iUniverse, Inc.
2021 Pine Lake Road, Suite 100
Lincoln, NE 68512
www.iuniverse.com

ISBN: 0-595-31949-1

Printed in the United States of America

For my children whose misfortune it has been to have a maverick father.

Contents

Part III   The Turn Of The Tide

Acknowledgements

The support of others has made the self-indulgence of writing this book possible. I thank my wife, Patricia Buckley Moss, for her patience, my son Jaik Henderson and friends Bonnie Stump and Marlyn de Waard for corrections to my spelling and punctuation. Tricia Miles for further perceptive editing and her tireless entering of the corrections, Clyde Stephens for contributing to the Notes to Chapter One on the subject of the cultural mix of Bocas del Toro, and Tito Thomas for correcting my Spanish spellings. I am also grateful to Richard Paris, Karen Jones and Lilia Gutierrez for encouraging me to complete the writing marathon. Lastly my grateful thanks to iUniverse and its Road Map to Publishing, which rescued me from the seemingly endless pursuit of an agent and brought the professional touch to the book's final form.

Introduction

The dream of retiring to a tropical island passes through the minds of many faced with the pressures of First World life. Inexpensive beach front living, cool sea breezes, no winter heating bills, domestic help at wages affordable by pensioners and margaritas sipped beneath palm trees as the sun sets all combine to stimulate desires for change. For most, the dream remains a dream.

My impulsive decision to force change at the moment when the desire was at its height led to the purchase of a house on one island and a rainforest on another. It was a selfish act committed at the end of our first full day in Bocas del Toro and without the prior approval of my wife. However it may well have saved our lives.

My wife, Pat Buckley Moss, is an artist, one of those few artists who make a healthy income from the sale of their paintings and prints. In 1997, I was her manager. Together we traveled the United States promoting her art and benefiting local charities by her presence at fundraising events. Often we drove long distances after late night receptions. We were riding a carousel that we seemed powerless to stop. We were at risk of a stroke or a major road accident.

With an unexpected week to spare, we headed to Costa Rica to visit members of an indigenous Indian tribe, hoping they would show us the path to a tranquil life. Diverted by a washed out road, our journey took us to the archipelago of Bocas del Toro in the Republic of Panama. It was here the adventures of the next six years began.

In much of the first half of my life, I had lived in exotic places—the New Terrorizes of Hong Kong, the Highlands of Kenya, the Nilgris Hills of Southern India, and the foothills of Mount Trodos in the Mediterranean island of Cyprus—lands and peoples that I came to love. Panama was to become my final destination and the most loved of them all.

I was in my fifties before I first visited the Caribbean. On the island of Carriacu that belongs to Grenada Pat and I found a hilltop cooled by the ever-present trade winds. Our interest in purchasing the land and building a second home ended when the Californian owner jumped the price four-fold.

By then I was hooked on the Caribbean with its easy access from the United States, its sea breezes, clean air, abundance of fish and fresh fruit and a cost of living a fraction of that in the First World. It took another fifteen years for me to arrive at the point of purchase.

The lesson learned over the six years covered by this book came from practical experience. Many are lessons on what not to do and as such are helpful to those whose dreams are in the formative stage or those who are beginning the experience of adapting to life in a Latino country. The building of an unusual house and the gradual conversion of a neglected property into a self-sufficient organic farm were challenges that took me close to breaking point. The support of my new Panamanian friends carried me through the roughest times.

The depth to which ex patriots immerse themselves in local culture ranges from those who live amongst their own kind in gated communities, with little social interchange beyond their walls, to those who live among the locals and absorb their customs. As this book reflects, my path led me into some invaluable friendships outside of the foreign community. These friendships have changed my perception as to what are the true rewards of life.

Like most of the world's less developed countries, Panama has held to practices that sadly have become diluted or lost in the busy lifestyles of the peoples of the wealthiest nations. Here the extended family tradition is still strong, ensuring that few go without food and shelter and that the elderly are cared for within the family home. There is time to smile and to converse with a stranger. Eye contact is not considered to be harassment and is returned in kind. Conversations are sincere and forthright and, although at first they can be a little disconcerting, one soon appreciates the frankness. Amongst the indigenous peoples, the understanding of Nature's needs and of mankind's dependence on her bounty, remains both practical and spiritual.

Although this is a small country, it has a distinctive personality that manifests itself in the friendliness of its people. It is a country in which the stranger soon feels comfortable and unafraid to ask for help.

About the size of South Carolina, Panama today has a population of approximately three million. The country forms a lateral land bridge linking the continents of North and South America. Its Northern shores are Caribbean and its Southern border the Pacific. High mountains run most of its length, creating distinctly different climatic conditions on either side. The diversity of habitats gives Panama a vast variety of animal and plant life, some of which is not yet catalogued.

Bocas del Toro is on the North Coast, an hour's flight or a nine-hour drive from Panama City, the nation's capital, and twenty miles from Costa Rica. When

Pat and I first arrived, Bocas was a sleepy backwater, visited only by those tourists seeking the road less traveled and unknown to most Panamanians.

Malcolm Henderson
Bocas Del Toro, May 2004

PART I
Getting Acquainted

1

Taking a Chance

Cool water flowed over my shoulders and down the front of my sweat-laden shirt. I was sitting in a rock chair sculpted by the passage of a jungle stream. Beyond the sound of the falling water, silence extended indefinitely. On either side, dense foliage formed an impenetrable barrier.

I breathed deeply, filling my lungs with virgin air unsoiled by man. The sun's rays filtered through the canopy, creating patterns of light on leaves the size of elephant ears.

I listened to the silence, imagining eyes watching through gaps between leaves, observing me, as an inquisitor observes his prisoner. I became nervous. If attacked, no one would hear my cry.

When my eyes had adjusted to the dim light, details appeared in the shadows. On a leaf, within arm's reach, sat a red frog no bigger than the nail of my smallest finger. He was facing me, motionless, apparently unafraid, though I was, in all probability, the first human he had seen. I stared back, waiting for him to move but he felt no need to do so.

"If this frog has no fear, why am I nervous?" I asked myself and finding no valid reason, relaxed.

"Thank you for being here," I said to Frog. "I am pleased to have someone to share this moment."

Frog disdained to comment. This was his time for meditation.

"I am sorry," I said.

Following Frog's example, I focused on the chant of the cascading water. I tried to meditate, but many thoughts kept erupting in my mind.

Five days ago, Pat and I had flown to San Jose, Costa Rica.

"We have a free week. I want us to fly to Costa Rica and visit the Bribri Indians. We need their help," I had told Pat one evening in Virginia.

"What for?" she had asked.

3

"We need them to teach us how to jump off this runaway carousel before it kills us."

"Whatever you say, darling, I'll go along with you. You usually know what's best."

Pat and I have been married for fifteen years. She is a successful artist. Her medium is watercolor and her talents have brought her wide recognition across the United States. Along with this recognition, and the fact that she is a dyslexic success story, had come demands for appearances at galleries and charity fund-raisers. I had been her escort and manager. Together, we had driven from gig to gig, often traveling late at night after exhausting public appearances.

We had reached our mid-sixties, and although we had said it would never happen to us, age was beginning to sap our energies. We were on the fast track to either a road accident or a stroke. We needed to adjust our priorities, but we did not know how.

We had arrived in San Jose to find the rainy season had begun earlier than usual. After a night of listening to thunderous rain beating on the tin roof of our modest hotel, we prepared to catch the bus to Puerto Viejo and the start of our walk to join the Indians. Pat already had her rucksack in the passage when the telephone rang.

"Forget it! Don't answer it!" Pat had called as she headed down the corridor. "Forget it, or we'll miss the bus."

I was in one of my moods in which I do the opposite to whatever Pat says.

I picked up the phone. A man's voice informed me the road to Puerto Viejo was washed out. It would be several days before it became passable.

"Can we go home early?" Pat asked. "There is no point in sitting here in the rain."

"It isn't raining in Panama," I said.

"Where is Panama?" asked Pat.

"Next door," I replied. "I have read about a place called Bocas del Toro, 'The Mouths of the Bull.' I want to check it out."

"We only have four days left," said Pat.

"Fine. One day to get there, two days to explore and one day to come back."

"Whatever you say, my love," said Pat resignedly.

We flew south along Costa Rica's Pacific coast. To our left I got a clear view of the Continental Divide. At the summer reunion of my army buddies, a retired general and I had boasted that next year we would walk from the Atlantic to the Pacific. We should have known better. The map we were studying had told us nothing of the series of steep ridges that run parallel to the chain of mountain peaks. From six thousand feet above, it was clear that we would have suffered an ignominious defeat.

Soon after crossing the Panamanian border we landed at David, the second largest city in Panama and the capital of the province of Chiriqui, the province in which Noriega had built the power base that enabled him to eventually take control of the country.

As we climbed out of the plane, we were hit by a wall of hot humid air and before reaching the shade of the little airport, my shirt was wet with sweat. We had six hours to wait for the thirty-minute flight that would lift us over the Continental Divide and down into Bocas del Toro.

We took a taxi into town and wandered aimlessly around uninspiring shops before sitting on a concrete bench in the small rectangular park that forms the center of the city. Pat lay down, and I cradled her head on my lap. The hours passed slowly.

Back at the airport, we found a table in a shaded outdoor café. Nearby sat a young girl in a neat blue uniform.

"There is a lot to be said for school uniforms," Pat remarked.

It appeared the three of us were the only passengers for the flight to Bocas. Pat and I were the first into the little plane. We took the two front seats and were adjusting our belts when the girl passed by and entered the cockpit, taking the seat next to the pilot.

"Probably the pilot's girlfriend," I remarked.

"More like his daughter," was Pat's comment.

Through the open door we could see the girl in the co-pilot's seat. She was playing with the instruments.

"Can you imagine that being allowed back home?" I asked.

"Quaint," said Pat.

"She's starting the engine," I said as the single prop struggled into life.

"Hey, remember, you got us into this," said Pat with a trace of nervousness.

We started down the runway gaining momentum. The girl pulled back on the joystick and we rose rapidly above the fertile coastal plain looking down on fields of wheat, barley and rice.

Moments later we were over the foothills of the Continental Divide and below us were fenced farms with cattle and horses. Continuing our climb toward clouds that shrouded the mountaintops, the scene below changed yet again and we were above steep hillsides of neatly regimented coffee trees. This side of the divide the rainfall is moderate and, depending on the altitude, a variety of crops flourish. I had read that the province of Chiriqui is the breadbasket of Panama.

The girl took us into a steep climb, lifting into thick cloud. The ride became a nightmare, with the little plane bouncing about like a cork in the eddy of a waterfall. I felt Pat's hand tighten its grasp on mine. A curtain of gray covered the windows. In a fleeting gap we caught a glimpse of the summit of Volcan Baru, Panama's highest mountain, above us and to the left but then it was gone.

"How does she know how high to go?" asked Pat.

"Instruments," I answered through clenched teeth.

We both closed our eyes.

"Please, God, get us out of this one," I begged.

God heard me and took pity. We began to descend and dropped down into crystal clear weather and our first sight of the archipelago with its five major islands and myriad of surrounding islets. We were in awe of its beauty. Bathed in the soft tones of evening light and encased in the pinks of a spectacular sunset, the scene immediately won a place in our hall of favorite memories.

The girl achieved a feather bed landing and we relaxed our grip on each other's hand.

"Wonderful flight!" I called through the open door of the cockpit. "Wouldn't have missed it for anything."

The girl smiled. I don't know if she understood me.

"Gracias," she said and continued with a rapid stream of Spanish that I think was an apology for the bumpy ride.

I came back to the present. Frog had moved to the forward edge of his leaf and was basking in a circle of sunlight. I should have left at that point and followed the stream to the beach where Pat and Peter Kent, a fellow Englishman and the owner of this property, were swimming. Instead I stayed, loathing to leave the present and commit this magic to the lesser joy of memory.

We had met Peter, a six-foot-three, blue-eyed Adonis, last night over supper and had accepted his invitation to show us Bocas and its surrounds during our two remaining days. We had each been served a handsome sized king mackerel, grilled to perfection by Alberto Barbarossa, an Italian who with his wife Marcela owned the Todo el Mundo Restaurant. A leaking roof and a stream of water crossing the floor had failed to suppress our good humor. We were delighting in the relaxed atmosphere of this sleepy tropical town.

After dinner we left Peter's company and walked down the main street, Calle Rev. Ephraim Alphone. The street was wide and once had a center garden of trees and plants running the quarter mile of its length. There being only ten cars on the island, pedestrians ruled the road. The drivers of the cars had to navigate their way cautiously around each strolling group.

"This reminds me of the main street in Perugia," Pat said, referring to one of our favorite Italian cities. "Everyone is out parading."

We adjusted to the general pace of the evening stroll, walking alongside families of Ngobe Indians, Afro-Antilleans and Chinese. The smallest of the Ngobe children rode on the hips of older siblings. The Afro-Antilleans, taller than the Indians, walked with the rhythm of the Caribbean, always about to break into dance. The Chinese were gracious and more reserved.

There were many faces that told of mixed parentage, faces that had taken the best features of each race and molded them into a work of beauty. Later, we were to learn that the name for those of mixed color, particularly of Indian and white parentage, is mestizos.[1]

We had only been in the town a few hours but felt at ease. There was gentleness and a respect in the way greetings were exchanged at every opportunity.

"Buenas noches," we responded to smiles and eye contacts that assured us of welcome.

"Enjoying this, darling?" I asked Pat.

"I am glad we came here," she said, squeezing my hand. "It feels good to be here."

We were lulled to sleep by the gentle lapping of the sea beneath our bedroom floor. Our nine-dollar-a-night hotel room, with its headless shower spigot and its tattered linoleum floor, was a romantic adventure and worth twenty times its price.

In the morning, Peter had brought his boat to the hotel verandah and carried us to Isla Carenero, an island a quarter of a mile from the town. There he showed us two houses he had recently built.

The first house won our hearts. Made of local hardwoods, it had a tree trunk for a center pole and a reception room large enough to host dinner for twenty and out of each window, views to the ocean.

I watched Pat. She cannot enter a house without embarking on the mental exercise of deciding the furniture she would choose and the theme of the decoration.

"Do you feel a good karma?" I asked.

"Yes, and you, too. I can tell."

"Where would you paint?"

"No problem. We would build a separate studio."

---

1.   For an explanation of the racial and cultural mix of Bocas del Toro, see page 223, Notes to Chapter 1.

From the house on Isla Carenero, Peter had brought us in his boat to this waterfront property at Punta Viejo, on the far end of Isla Bastimentos. It consists of twenty-five acres of virgin rainforest and a beach of soft golden sand.

It was time to go, but still I had not resolved the question in my mind. Should I buy the house and this rainforest and be sure of saving our lives, or should I go back to the States and discuss the idea rationally with Pat and the children?

"Which should I do?" I turned to ask Frog, but he was no longer there. Was this an omen?

I looked for Pat on the beach. She was swimming, still wearing her hat as protection from the noontime sun. I took photographs of her against a backdrop of white surf where waves that originated far across the ocean smashed onto coral. She called to me but her voice was drowned by the surf's continual roar, the roar of a freight train passing between tall warehouses but never receding into the distance. I swam to her.

"It's heaven," she said. "And all this just for us."

I kissed her. "It has possibilities," I said.

"Shame Peter's here," she smiled. "It does have possibilities."

It was time to leave. Peter headed the boat for the only gap in the reef. There the waves passed through the barrier unbroken, alarmingly tall and menacing. He judged the moment. With surf high on either side, we slapped our way into and over the next wave. It was exhilarating and when safely on the open sea, I felt a sense of achievement, as if I had been at the helm.

On our way back to Bocas, we stopped at a thatched restaurant over the water on the edge of a small island called Cayo Crawl that lies between Isla Bastimentos and Isla Popa. There we took a late lunch of fried red snapper, rice and plantains.

Fish of brilliant crimson, yellow and aquamarine swam beneath us. A two-foot barracuda lay motionless and menacing. We scraped the scraps from our plates in their direction, igniting a feeding frenzy that lasted only moments before the scene returned to the peacefulness of a hot afternoon. Before leaving, we snorkeled, having our first experience of the wondrous shapes and colors of the surrounding coral.

We were both tired when Peter headed the boat for town and our hotel. Along the way we passed many small islands of mangrove trees, some of which had sufficient dry land for a few palms to grow. The palms towered high above and apart from the mangroves which had their roots anchored in the sea.

We encountered several dugout canoes, known locally as cayucus, traveling away from Bocas, bound for distant communities. Powered by outboard motors, they were the equivalent of the country bus. Each was heavily laden with passengers, baggage and supplies and looked ready to be swamped by the next big wave.

When we arrived at the hotel, Pat was the first out of the boat.

"I am going to take a shower and then a rest," she announced.

"I want to take another look at the house," I said. "I won't be long."

Back on the island, I asked Peter for the use of his phone. I called our accountant Bill Speakman at his home in St. Michaels, Maryland. I asked God to let him be there. I needed a quick answer. We had one day left before returning to San Jose.

"Well, hello, Malcolm. Where are you, for goodness sakes? I never know where you and Pat are, you keep hopping around so." Ann, Bill's wife, had answered the phone.

"Ann, I am in Panama. Is Bill there?"

"In Panama. Oh my goodness. What is the weather like? Pat isn't there with you, is she?" asked Ann.

"It is hot and sticky. Yes, Pat is here with me. Ann, is Bill there?"

"Give Pat my love and tell her to be careful. Isn't Panama Noriega Country?"

"It was once," I admitted. "Ann, it is important that I speak to Bill now and besides I am using someone else's phone. Is Bill there?"

"I'd better call him for you," said Ann, reluctant to end our conversation. "He's outside building a hoist for his new boat."

I waited patiently while visualizing the message being passed to Bill, and Bill laying down his tools and walking to the house. In my mind I traveled the course twice at a conservative pace but still no further sound at the other end. I was about to give up when I finally heard Bill's voice.

"How much do you need?"

"How do you know what I am calling about?" I asked amazed.

"I know you. You want me to tell you can have one hundred and forty thousand."

"Bill, you are incredible! One hundred and thirty will do."

"As long as it is not Pat's money, go ahead and spend it."

"You don't think I am mad?"

"Yes! But you are old enough to make your own decisions without me telling you what you should do."

"Thanks, Bill. Standby to transfer the money."

By the time Peter and I headed to the hotel, an hour had elapsed. As we approached, I saw Pat on the verandah. She looked refreshed and glamorous and was talking with a redheaded man, somewhat younger than us. The two of them watched our arrival.

"Hey, darling, what have you been up to? What's that smile all about?" asked Pat.

"I have bought that beach where you swam this morning and the twenty-five acres of rainforest."

"You're still smiling. What else have you done?"

"I bought the house."

"See what I mean?" Pat said to her companion. "He dances to his own tune and doesn't consult me. Not even on the matter of a house."

"Malcolm, this is Jeff. He is an international equestrian judge. He owns a lot on Isla Carenero and after what you've just done, it looks as though we'll be neighbors."

At dinner that evening Peter was more than willing to pick up the check. In the four years he had been buying and selling property in the Bocas, this was the best day he'd ever had.

"Malcolm, do you mind if I ask what made you make such a quick decision?" Peter asked.

"It was a matter of life or death."

"I see. But could you explain it bit more. I'm delighted, of course, but I've never known anyone to make up his mind so quickly."

"Peter, if we were to go home uncommitted, our children would promptly rationalize us out of buying property in Panama. We would be pounded with reasons why doing so would be lunacy. It would be our age, Noriega's legacy, disease and lack of first rate medical facilities, crime, responsibilities to our grandchildren. It would be an odds on bet that you would never hear from us again."

"That is what happens nine times out of ten," admitted Peter.

When Pat and I arrived back in Mathews, Virginia, I e-mailed my four sons with the news that I now owned property in Panama. Three were too shocked to comment. The fourth, Dougal, who lives in Brisbane, Australia, responded with, "Good on you, Dad. You did right."

Two days later there was a second message from Dougal. "Dad, did you forget that when I was eighteen and hitching to Peru, Olivier and I spent three or four days in Bocas before walking over the mountains to David?"

I had forgotten, but then I recalled Dougal telling me of how he and a French school friend had come upon an island paradise on the Caribbean coast of Panama. That had been in the 1980s when Bocas was truly an isolated community with no road connection to the rest of the country.

Relieved to have someone not think me crazy, I called Dougal.

"We had come down the coast from Costa Rica and took a break to swim and just relax in the little town," he told me. "There were only two ways to go from there. We could either wait a week for the boat that would take us along the coast to Colon or we could walk over the mountains to David and the Pan American Highway. We did the latter to save both time and money."

"The journey took four days," he continued. "The first day we hired an Indian to take us in his cayucu across the lagoons to Chiriqui Grande. The second day we walked along a banana railway track to the foothills. That was hard going because the sleepers were unevenly spaced and we had to keep changing our strides. We spent that night with an Indian family whose finca (farm) was close to a glorious rock pool where we swam and bathed. By the second night we were on the top of the mountain ridge where we pitched our tents next to another Indian's home. The third day of walking brought us to David."

Dougal is the adventurer amongst my four sons. After becoming bored with working in the financial sector of the City of London, he and three friends from his days at Oxford University bicycled from London to Australia. For each country they crossed, their sponsors donated to The Red Cross. It took them a year and some risky moments to complete their journey. The informality of the Australian business world appealed to Dougal and he stayed, eventually taking Australian citizenship.

The knowledge that Dougal had trod these parts caused me to wonder if others with our genes were once here. Could one of our forebears have been amongst the early Scottish settlers? Could this be why I felt at ease with these people? Perhaps some were distant cousins whose highland genes had long intermingled with those of forebears of darker color.

2

Getting My Feet Wet

Two months later, Pat and I returned to Bocas for an extended stay stretching from Christmas to Easter. We had expected Peter to be at the airport. We were greeted instead by a black girl with a warm smile and confident manner.

"Senor Malcolm and Senora Patricia, welcome. My name is Virginia and Senor Peter asked me to look after you. He did went to New Zealand for two months to see his parents."

Virginia had a taxi waiting, and in no time we were back on the verandah of the Las Brisas Hotel, looking down on a new fiberglass boat.

"Senor Malcolm, this is your boat and this is Evan Castil. He work for Peter," said Virginia, introducing a man in his early thirties, whose name and features evidenced his mix of racial genes.

I looked down at the boat, an eighteen-foot fiberglass skiff with a pointed bow and a shallow "V." A forty HP Yamaha engine was mounted on the transom. There was no center consol with wheel and no electric start. The throttle was in the steering arm and to start you cranked the engine with a pull cord.

Evan was stowing our baggage while Pat was climbing aboard. Virginia handed me the safety key and with an air of confidence that was not in keeping with my nervous feelings, I set about starting the engine.

There being only four miles of hard top road in Bocas and everywhere the sea, a boat is as essential as a car back home. It would be a poor beginning to admit I am a strictly a car and motorcycle man and have never driven an outboard or helmed anything bigger than a Sunfish. I had asked Peter to order us a boat just like his, but I had expected him to teach me how to use it.

"We'll see you over there," said Virginia. "Evan and I will follow. Ramon, the caretaker, is waiting on the dock to carry the baggage."

I pulled the starting cord. The engine turned over but did not fire. I pulled again with increased vigor and nothing happened. I kept pulling. The sun was directly overhead and I felt its intensity on the back of my neck. Sweat ran from my forehead into my eyes. I took a rest, mopping the sweat with my handkerchief. My eyes were stinging. I heard Evan whisper to Virginia. I looked up.

"Senor Malcolm, have you put the key in?" asked Virginia. "You have to put the key I give you round that red button there."

The red button located and the key inserted, I pulled again but by then my strength was gone.

"Senor Malcolm, I think it best if Evan and I come with you," said Virginia and the two of them came aboard.

We crossed to the island with Evan at the helm, and I feeling a failure. I was the owner of this boat, but not the captain. I wondered if I would ever be able to handle it. For the first time, I had doubts as to whether we belonged here.

Our house exceeded in beauty the images that had lived with us those past months. Virginia had placed flowers in every room, great bursts of red and yellow blooms from plants we had not encountered before but whose names we had heard or read somewhere in the past. A sea breeze cooled our bodies. We walked from room to room, looking out of windows. To the front of the house was the sea, to the back the jungle, green and beckoning.

"I stock the fridge with sufficient food for you for today," said Virginia as she opened the refrigerator door to reveal a variety of essentials. "Peter has left you his pots and pans, china and knives and forks to use until you get your own. There is no hurry because he will not be back soon. You can buy more food at the market in the morning."

We tried to think if there was anything else we needed that night but it seemed that Virginia had thought of everything.

"Right. I'll leave you then," said Virginia. "Here is your boat key. Remember to insert it before trying to start."

Soon after Virginia left, a neat, diminutive white skinned lady of our own age appeared at the door dressed in a sarong and sporting a red flower in her hair.

"Welcome. I am Joan. Ron and I live two doors down. We are here for another two weeks. We spend half the year here and the other half at our home in Alabama. I thought you might like this cake."

We thanked Joan profusely, delighted by this show of friendship and the knowledge that for two weeks at least, we had a source to turn to for advice; Ron and Joan were four-year veterans of Isla Carenero.

"Ron would have come with me but he has a man working with him building a new dock. When you are settled in we will have you come over for supper."

Ron, a compulsive engineer whose hands can never be idle, had discovered Bocas a quarter of a century earlier when working for the Agency of International

Development on a feasibility study for the future road over the mountains to the Pan American Highway. With children and grandchildren matching ours, they had purchased the first house Peter built.

That evening, finding homes for our belongings, we felt like newlyweds. We ate at the dining table made by Peter's workers from a design sent by Pat. Pat had also designed the dining room chairs and our king-size bed.

Pat's design of the chairs had shown the intended height of the backs measured from the floor but instead, the carpenter had measured from the seat-level, giving us chairs whose backs reached up to the top of our shoulders. The effect was both elegant and unique and to be the subject of comment by every new visitor.

We watched the flames of candles sway in the eddy of the fan and we breathed the scent of the flowers. The Chilean wine was surprisingly pleasing and the simple meal became a gourmet delight. Our mattress was hard to the degree we both like and our night in our new house was one of absolute contentment.

In the morning we ventured to cross the water to visit Andino's store. Pat stood in the bow with bowline in hand, ready to jump ashore and make fast the boat. I had spent the first part of the morning practicing nautical maneuvers under the tutelage of Ramon, Indian caretaker, a man of amazing tact and patience.

As we approached the market, I saw several men standing on the dock with apparently nothing to do but watch our arrival. Their presence distracted my concentration and I forgot Ramon's caution to reduce speed early and come in slowly.

I was barraged by instructions shouted from the watching group.

"Cut it, Mister."

"Take it slow, Capt'n," and, "Put in reverse, for Christ's sake, Mon."

I followed the last suggestion and thrust the gear lever straight into reverse, completely forgetting to pause in neutral. There was an unhappy sound of grinding gears and then silence. The engine had stalled and I was left without stopping power. While I looked back at the engine in disgust, we continued forward till the bow hit the concrete dock head on with an ominous sound of splitting fiberglass.

Pat was thrown forward into the arms of a black Hercules.

"Nice catch, Mon. Now put the lady down," advised one of the spectators.

Pat thanked her savior and then turned to glare at me.

"Do that again, and I'm going home," she said with justification.

Andino's supermarket was our first surprise. It measured only some sixty feet by twenty. With two center displays, the aisles were barely shoulder width apart, making it often impossible to pass other people without bodily contact. The alternative was to move at the leisurely pace of the person in front or to go into reverse and approach from another aisle. The range of foods and necessities was utilitarian and geared to local tastes and needs.

In spite of Virginia's efforts to keep us safe from harm, it was not long before my first visit to the emergency room at the Bocas hospital.

On the fourth day, I came back from town carrying a carton piled high with groceries over which I could not see. I was walking to the house, keeping to the center of the dock by looking down at my feet.

As I neared the shore, I caught sight of a movement to my right. Looking up, I saw a young white boy walking the beach. I was taken aback. I did not know there was anyone other than Joan and Ron on this part of the island. Still looking at the stranger, I veered to the right and fell off the dock into the sea. My left foot caught the edge of the dock and was wrenched backwards.

Groping to catch floating oranges and to salvage bags of coffee and sugar, I was aware of acute pain in my ankle.

During a sleepless night of throbbing agony, my ankle grew to the size of my thigh. I called Virginia early in the morning and she organized my rescue from the island and delivered me by taxi to the hospital.

X-rays, pain pills, and a plaster cast cost me eleven dollars. I was almost sorry to hear I had not broken my ankle. It seemed unjust to have to suffer intense pain for just a sprain.

"The doctor said it is an extremely bad sprain," I told fellow members of the Gringo (foreign) community, but Gringos are not sympathetic to one who walks off his own dock. I hobbled around town, miserable about the snorkeling I imagined I would have been doing.

Soon after my accident, I appointed Virginia to be our agent. I started paying her a monthly retainer to do her best to keep us out of trouble. She took her duties seriously, even to the extent of trying to keep me clean and smart looking.

"Senor Malcolm, you look all raca taca. Your shirt has spots on it. You have not shaved properly and your socks don't match."

"I am sorry!" I said. "It is all because of this leg of mine."

"You should be ashamed of yourself," she reprimanded me, ignoring my plea of mitigation.

"Have you done your homework?" she would often ask. Spanish classes had become part of our daily routine.

In the mornings, Pat painted at the dining room table and drew the plans for the building of a more practical easel, additional furniture and the studio Peter would build after our return to the States. Occasionally, she took time off to play cards with Joan.

My office was one-half of the downstairs bedroom. At first, I found the jungle's close proximity a distraction. I would start e-mails to folks battling winter storms up north with an account of the view from my window and the mention that when work was over I would be windsurfing. I found working from a distance to be productive. I got more done in less time without the distraction of visitors or verbose phone calls. Often, I would fire off an e-mail to our staff at the start of their workday, just to let them know I was still on the team.

Virginia was teaching at the high school and in the afternoons when school was over, she came to teach Spanish to Pat and me. I am unable to roll my "r's" and that put me at a disadvantage, but I loved the language. I made good progress, even though my pronunciation would never amount to much.

In my own school days, I was hopeless at languages, along with every other subject except geography, where my painstakingly drawn maps won praise. Now, I found myself enjoying learning for the first time.

Virginia and I started a program in the Isla Carenero Elementary School to teach English to the Indian children. With fewer fish in the sea and tourists coming to visit the islands, the tourist industry was becoming an alternative to fishing. A knowledge of English would greatly improve the chance of employment.

Historically, the Bocas man's role had been to fish and the woman's to have babies and take care of them. Many of the Indian girls started producing babies in their mid-teens, some even earlier. It was not unusual for a woman to bear ten or more children, often sired by more than one man.

Another consideration that made us sure of the necessity for our program was the growing dominance of the English language on the World Wide Web. If any of our students were to continue their education beyond high school, the ability to read English and access information from the Internet would be invaluable.

We began a practice of going around the classrooms asking the children, "What would you like to be when you leave school?"

At the start of our program, most seemed surprised by the question, as if there was an alternative to fishing and producing babies. We told them that through hard work at school and staying free from drugs and alcohol, they could qualify for jobs that would earn a regular wage and give their family security.

A change was not long in coming. Soon we had children aspiring to become teachers like Virginia, whom they much admired. Others talked of being nurses, carpenters, tourist guides and chefs. Ramon's oldest daughter set her heart on becoming a veterinarian, an ambition that may be within her reach judged by her results in high school.

News of our English program reached The P. Buckley Moss Society, whose membership consists of collectors of Pat's paintings and prints and whose mission includes helping Pat in charitable endeavors. The Society adopted the English program and has provided much of its funding.

The combination of being a Gringo[1] and having a leg in plaster made me a subject of interest to the locals. On a day when nothing much was happening, the sight of this elderly man weaving his way on crutches through the maze of pot-holes was worthy of comment.

I knew that two men who were sitting on one of the benches by the park were talking about me. I imagined their conversation:

"He from Carenero," informed Porfilio. "He the mon what went buy da house."

"What him call himself?" asked his friend, Eladio.

"Me no know," said Porfilio. "Me forget ask Evan, but Evan say he good mon."

Porfilio and Eladio, Afro-Antilleans in their mid-thirties, were in front of the Palazio, the once grand building that is home to the provincial government, the judiciary, the local government and the post office. Like the plaster on my leg, the outside of the building had long been in need of cleaning.

"What he gone do his leg then?" asked Eladio

"He did went in de sea."

"How he do that?"

"Evan say he did went walk off de dock," Porfilio said.

Although the two can speak Spanish, they prefer to converse in English.

Word of my accident had spread quickly. For those who asked, Virginia and Evan told them that I was known as Senor Malcolm.

Senor, or Senora in the case of a woman, is a respectful title used when addressing an older person or when speaking about that person. In Bocas, with its English language heritage, Mister and Miss are also used, as they still are in some rural parts of the States, including the County of Mathews, Virginia, our State-side abode.

---

1.   The word Gringo refers only to those foreigners whose native tongue is English; however, in Bocas the term is often used to describe all foreigners of Caucasian origin. For simplicity I have followed this colloquial use throughout the book and ask those of other tongues to forgive me.

Pat, therefore, is known as Senora Patricia or Miss Patricia. Patricia spoken in Spanish, with each symbol distinctly pronounced is a much prettier sound than the English equivalent. It takes longer to say and requires greater lip movement but it is worth the extra effort, Pa-tri-ci-a, with the "i" letter pronounced "e." The lips are forward for "Pa," then pulled far back for "tri," halfway forward for "ci" and forward for the final syllable, "a."

Because of the spectacle of this old man with his injured leg, I was becoming something of a celebrity. Unlike the Gringos, who considered I had let down the side by doing something stupid, the Bocatoranians have a different view. They saw me as one in need of help and as being unlikely to tell them how things should be done, a common failing of those Gringos who want to bring Californian methods and habits to Bocas.

By now, my plaster was in an advanced state of decay, brought on by frequent contact with water. It was the wet season and monsoon-like rains descended at frequent intervals. At Pat's urging, I wore a plastic trash bag over the plaster. At first it had seemed a logical solution and in any other climate it would have been. Here, with the temperatures in the 90's and the humidity close to 100, the effect was to both steam cook my leg and soften the plaster.

The plaster was rapidly unraveling itself from the toes up and had developed an unpleasant odor. There were still four days until I was to have the plaster removed, but unless I were to sleep at the end of the dock there was no way I could continue to be at home. I headed up the road to the emergency room.

I did not have to wait my turn to see a doctor. By unanimous agreement of all present, I was moved to the front of the line. The doctor's judgment was swift and made without consulting my medical notes. As he retreated, a nurse handed me a pair of wire cutters.

"Here, you cut it off," she said moving back to a safe distance.

I cut down the side of the plaster and peeled it away, like peeling a banana. I revealed a leg that was sickly white and prune wrinkled.

"Here, take this bag and put the plaster in it," the nurse told me.

I did as I was told and stood to test the leg.

The nurse handed me a walking stick.

"You will need this until your leg regains strength. When you have finished with the stick, hand it back at the front office."

I left the emergency room and walked to the front of the hospital. There I handed in the walking stick and took a taxi back to the boat.

3

A Purpose Revealed

"What is your connection with Panama?" I asked the man in the aisle seat.

The dinner trays had been removed. Delta flight 363 was halfway to Panama. I had downed two dry martinis and was starting my second glass of Cabernet. Pat was asleep, her head pillowed against the window.

The alcohol had encouraged me to put aside my Spanish language tapes and find what was to be learned from my neighbor.

"I am an environmental scientist," the owlish man told me.

"Consulting in Panama or vacationing?" I asked with genuine interest.

"Neither. I am attending a symposium." He returned to the papers he had been studying. I decided it was worth another attempt.

"Are we winning?" I asked.

"Winning what?" He sounded irritated.

"I mean are we going to be able to dispose of all our garbage before we pollute everything to death?"

"In one word: No!"

"Oh," I said reaching for my glass. "That's not reassuring."

"From your point of view, no," he conceded. "But for the long-term health of this planet, yes. It is all part of evolution."

"Sounds like devolution to me."

"The devolution of the present and the genesis of the future."

"Does the future include mankind?" I asked.

"It is hardly likely."

"I suppose the roaches will be top dog," I said with a nervous laugh.

"You are probably right," he said. "They are equipped to survive."

"When will this happen?" I asked.

"A lot sooner than you think."

I had not thought but now he had me thinking. He had taken out a pen and was drawing a graph on the backside of his paper.

"The world population growth over the past 250 years looks like this."

The graph showed an almost imperceptible climb for three quarters of its way across the scale. It then began to curve upwards, accelerating rapidly and in its final years looked as though it was already on a vertical path.

"You know what happens to a colony of bacteria after reaching this point?" he was indicating the tip of the line.

"No, I don't," I said.

"It dies, poisoned by the accumulation of its own excrement. Nature takes it back to square one. That is the fate of mankind."

I left the environmentalist to his work.

"It won't happen in what is left of my lifetime," I told myself, but found little comfort in this. I have worked hard to have money to educate my children and to help with their children's education. The future of my grandchildren is of greater importance than my own.

"Maybe Nature does not have to do a total job of it. She could keep some humans alive to continue the species," I mused.

Further thought brought the fear that this is hardly likely.

"We humans have eliminated many thousands of species. God is hardly likely to view our case kindly," I told myself.

"Well, God is benevolent and there are those of us who have spoken out against the rape of the planet. Maybe He will be selective and save us good guys."

The debate within my head was getting nowhere and I switched to contemplating death. My main concern about dying is not about what will happen to me when my spirit leaves my body, but about the temporary matter of pain at the time of my departure.

Death is a one-time experience, and I don't want to be distracted by suffering pain. I remember reading of Doctor Timothy Leary's death in his New York Soho loft, with his friends gathered round watching his peaceful transition.

I came near to that point soon after the first visit Pat and I made to Panama. Three days after leaving Bocas, I thought I was starting the flu.

"I will take myself off to the guesthouse and get over this on my own," I told Pat. "With all that you have to do in the next month, the last thing we need is you getting sick."

I lay on the sofa in the guesthouse beneath a pile of blankets, alternating between bouts of sweating and attacks of shivering. I had a splitting headache and my bones were aching.

"How are you doing, love?" asked Pat that evening from the safety of the doorway.

"Fine!" I said. "I am sweating it out. I'll be back to normal in the morning."

"I am leaving a bowl of chicken soup on the table. When I am gone, get up and eat it. It will do you good."

That night the dreams started. Each was short by clock time but insufferably long in dreamtime. Between each dream I awoke disturbed in my mind and fearful of falling asleep again, knowing that I would return to the nightmares. I struggled to stay awake, not rising from the couch except to stagger to the bathroom.

In my fitful sleep, I found myself back in the army. Not in my time, but in my father's when he was a medical officer in France in the First World War. Each Christmas when I was in my early teens, I would accompany him on a visit to a patient who had also fought in the trenches. At home, my father never spoke of his war. Only when he and Sir Charles Clee had bettered most of a bottle of scotch did the tales begin.

On graduating from Aberdeen University, my father, one of thirteen children of a Scottish highland family, had been appointed medical officer to an infantry battalion of the South Staffordshire Regiment. Sir Charles's son John and I listened to the tales of courage, fear, carnage, sickness and madness. The images became etched in my mind.

"You didn't drink your soup," I heard Pat's voice coming from afar.

This time she came into the room and was standing beside the couch, her hand feeling my forehead.

"You've got a fever," she announced. "What's your temperature?"

"I don't know," I said. "I don't have a thermometer."

"I think I had better take you to see Michael."

"What time is it?" I asked.

"Ten o'clock. I didn't come over earlier because I thought I would let you sleep. Nancy will have a thermometer. I'll get it."

My temperature was 105. Half an hour later we were headed for Washington, DC, and the offices of Doctor Michael Newman, our internist. To keep my mind focused and clear of nightmares, I concentrated on thinking about Michael.

Michael and I had been windsurfing buddies for several years. We had flown to Aruba on a number of occasions to catch the strong trade winds that blow across the low-lying island. We would take an apartment at Sail Board Vacations and spend the daylight hours riding the ocean, the evening talking and the nights in exhausted sleep.

It has always surprised me that Michael and I are such good friends. He is an intellectual, who reads and retains his information and is seldom found to be wrong on any of his vast store of facts. I am the opposite, with a lack of the ability to remember detail.

Since he is our internist, Pat and I are sure to see Michael at least once a year for our physicals. Prior to our coming to Panama, we would dine twice a year with him and Marion, his equally intelligent wife.

I recalled sitting in front of his desk waiting to receive my annual reprimand for being overweight. Michael was recording my statistics on a dictaphone.

I tried not to appear apprehensive. I studied photos of Marion and their two daughters and then picked up a photo album. It contained numerous shots of Michael climbing Mount Kilimanjaro by the most difficult route. He had shown it to me twice before, a reminder that I had not been to the top of Africa's highest mountain.

Michael stopped dictating and looked at me with a serious face.

"Malcolm, you are in good shape for your age. Your prostate is the size of a forty-year-old."

I am eight or so years older than Michael, and he has to tell me I am doing well because he knows my sailing ability is at least equal to his.

"I am concerned about your weight, though. You need to lose at least ten pounds." He handed me his latest diet printout.

"And how much do you need to lose, Michael?" I asked.

"The same as you," he said, still looking serious. "We both have a weight problem."

"How much are you drinking these days?" he asked, looking back down at my file.

"One glass a day or so," I said unconvincingly.

"One glass of what?" Michael asked.

"It depends," I replied evasively.

"Malcolm, that is not what I want to hear."

Six days later, when we arrived in Aruba, we went directly from the airport to the supermarket to buy our week's supplies.

"Malcolm, you take your cart and go down those two lines. Buy what you think we need. I will start on this side. We will meet in the middle." Michael always likes to take charge.

I worked my way down my allotted aisle, conscious of last week's reprimand. I picked out saltines, fat-free Philadelphia cream cheese, nonfat yogurt, oatmeal, sardines and nonfat milk.

Arriving at the meeting point, I became impatient waiting for Michael. This was to be a quick shop so we could catch an hour or two on the water before sunset.

Michael eventually appeared, his head barely visible behind a cart stacked with two cases of beer, several bottles of wine, French bread, cheeses, butter and a ham.

"You know the saying," he said. "Do as I say and not as I do."

The journey from Mathews County to downtown Washington takes three hours with Pat at the wheel and three and a half if I am driving. Naturally, Pat was in the driver's seat. I was in agony beside her, feeling as though my back was trying to force its way out through my chest.

Michael had told his receptionist to send us straight in.

"When did you get back from your visit to Costa Rica?" asked Michael handing me a blown up photo of him carving a near perfect jibe on his windsurfer.

"Two days ago," Pat answered for me.

After taking my temperature, Michael broke the news that I had malaria. He had blood pulled from me. Rather than await the laboratory analysis of the samples, he started the treatment immediately.

The drugs eased my pain and fever but made me as weak as a rag doll. That night Pat left me in the basement apartment of her daughter Becky's Washington home and returned to her studio in Mathews.

The following afternoon Michael called for more blood samples. The lab report had come back negative.

"This can happen," he assured me. "Sometimes the malaria never shows in a person's blood."

The next day I gave more samples. I was beginning to doubt the malaria theory. There was no malaria in Bocas.

"Maybe you got bitten in San Jose," Pat said over the phone. "You remember the stagnant pool of water just outside our hotel window."

I was now too weak to care. For three days, I lay on the bed in the darkened basement, hardly touching the soup Becky brought me. This was a time of reflection. Too weak for anything but thought, my mind traveled the course of my life and what it saw along the way it did not like.

I have much to be ashamed of and, as I took inventory of my destructiveness, I ceased to care whether I lived or died. I wasn't an asset to anyone. I flushed the remainder of my malaria treatment pills down the toilet.

"Your voice sounds so weak," Pat said two days later when she called me by phone. "I think I had better come up to Washington."

"No, don't bother. I will be better tomorrow."

"I will leave in an hour," Pat said, putting down the phone before I could protest.

I lay back defeated.

"God, I am ready to die," I said, believing now this was God's will.

I felt no fear. "I am in Your hands, do whatever You like."

At that moment of giving up, I felt a presence of total love surrounding me. I knew that life's failures and disappointments were of no account in this new world in which all was understanding and forgiveness. I drifted contentedly into peaceful sleep. An hour later, I awoke to the realization that my pains were gone. My mind was clear for the first time since the start of my illness.

I sat up and drank the cold soup.

When I recounted my experience to Michael, he told me I had been hallucinating under the effect of the drugs. I did not tell him I had ended the treatment two days previously.

As the plane started its descent, I took the risk of being snubbed and asked the environmentalist, "If a plague was sweeping the world, where would one have the best chance of surviving?"

"In the rainforests of the equator would be my choice," he said.

This gave me the start of the idea of owning a farm in the tropics that could support all members of my family if disaster, natural or man-made, caused widespread havoc in the developed regions of the world. I started to look for a suitable corner of Bocas in which to develop a subsistence farm. Meanwhile, life in Bocas continued to be an adventure.

4

It's a Man's World

Evan Castillo, Peter's number one, is an avid fisherman. His favored method of fishing is with the spear gun. If I am visiting my rainforest property on Isla Bastimentos on a weekend and Evan is not working overtime for Peter, he likes to accompany me, knowing that after inspecting the property we will go to his favorite hunting ground. Part Spanish, part Indian and part West Indian, Evan is an intelligent and handsome man.

Our first fishing trip was to an isolated area of coral that lies a mile or so outside the main reef off Old Point. Here the coral rises to about five feet from the sea's surface. The weather was calm and we rode the swell with ease, heading east along the north shoreline of Bastimentos.

"I feel today is my lucky day, Mister Malcolm. Today I get a shark."

Evan was watching my face for a reaction. I hoped he could not see the flicker of fear his enthusiasm created. I imagined an irate shark, wounded by this intrepid hunter, directing its fury at me.

"Right!" I said. "After our inspection, we will hunt sharks."

Our inspection was perfunctory. Evan is not a jungle man. As I have an exaggerated fear of sharks, Evan has a fear of the jungle. When I started to walk up the creek to the waterfall, he began to lag behind. That day I did not linger waiting for my friend, Frog, to appear.

I could hear no sound of Evan following me, and I knew he had turned back to the safety of the beach. I imagined him sitting on the trunk of a fallen tree, gazing out beyond the reef, willing the shark to be there.

"It is time we fish, Mister Malcolm."

"We have plenty of time, Evan, the day is still young."

"Maybe we need plenty time to find the shark," he said.

I helmed the boat out through the gap in the reef and Evan took up a stance at the bow, holding the bowline taut to brace himself against the swell. He was giving me hand signals to go left or right and eventually to slow down. He stared into the water, looking for a place to drop anchor without damaging the coral.

The anchor set and the engine stopped, a silence surrounded us. There was no other boat in sight. Somber dark clouds were gathering further out to sea. My imagination ran high.

"What if Evan encounters a shark and comes off the worst for it? How would I get an injured Evan back into the boat? How would I stem the flow of blood?"

I wished then that Peter were with us.

I have always suffered from an uncontrollable imagination that has needlessly tormented me. When I was a cadet at the Military Academy, I had entered my name for parachute training because not to do so would have put my strength of character in question. The chances of being selected were one in ten. My fear and imagination kicked in the moment I learned I had been chosen.

In 1950, the British army did not jump with a reserve chute. If your chute should fail to open, you had only moments more to live. To most cadets this chance only seemed to heighten the adventure and they sang a song whose refrain included, "And they scraped him off the tarmac like a case of strawberry jam."

Throughout my first days of training, I thought of the girl packing my chute. What if she had just busted up with her boyfriend? One fold in wrong sequence and I would be hurtling to the ground in what is called a Roman Candle, the silk of the chute entangled and devoid of air.

Evan was the first to have his flippers on and spear gun ready. He was sitting on the gunwale set to somersault backwards into the water.

"You go ahead," I said. "I'll follow you in a minute."

Evan was a hundred yards from the boat before I gingerly lowered myself over the side. Deep fissures reaching into darkness intersected the coral bank below. I held my spear gun at the ready, not for the purpose of hunting but for self-defense. I did not move far from the boat and after a few tentative explorations, climbed back on board and made myself comfortable as I waited for Evan.

Sitting relaxed in the silent emptiness of the sea, I gave thought to fear.

Usually my fear before an action has been greater than the fear during it. When the lift webs of my parachute tangled in a low level night jump, leaving me little time to release a light machine gun strapped to my side and adjust my chute, I had remained calm and methodical.

I looked at the fear I had felt in the water and knew I needed to exorcize it before leaving. I put my mask back on and went to join Evan.

Although we searched for a couple of hours, we did not see a shark or any fish that justified shooting. Since then, I have had no hesitation in hunting with Evan, though we have yet to find our shark.

Pat declined to accompany us on these excursions. She had learned to swim in the fast moving currents of the Delaware River where Pennsylvania, New York and New Jersey meet. She is a strong swimmer and, early in our knowing each other, had challenged me to a race, unaware that I, too, had swum competitively. She was surprised when I beat her, but I was equally surprised by the narrow margin of my victory.

Swimming over shallow coral reefs is fine for Pat; but, when the water gets deeper and she can no longer see what is beneath, she is off back to shore, her arms and legs flailing the water in her haste to reach safety. I sympathize with her, because that is how I was before overcoming the fear.

If we had come to Panama at a younger age, I am sure that Pat would have joined me in these mini adventures; but, in her mid-sixties, the peace and security of her studio were of greater appeal than accompanying her maverick husband on rough sea voyages or following him along jungle paths deep in mud. Pat stayed at the house awaiting my return and when lonely called the children back home.

"It's fine for the men," said Marilyn Johnson who, with husband Jerry, had found Bocas shortly after our first visit. "The men have all the fun doing their thing, while we are left behind to see that whoever is working on the house or the yard does not slack off or steal the contents of the bodega (store room)."

Marilyn gave up her Mercedes and an award-winning real estate agency in Sacramento, California, to accompany Jerry on the fulfillment of his dreams. A well-preserved blonde who had never allowed the sun's rays to touch her face, Marilyn's years of selling real estate had instilled for life the discipline of always looking your best and always projecting an air of super efficiency.

Jerry, a roundish man of moderate height with dancing eyes and a smile that seldom left his face, was the senior of two partners in an insurance brokerage business, specializing in commercial truck insurance. In between days trolling for tuna beyond the reef, he continued his brokerage work from the spare bedroom of their house on the shores of the jungle.

Before long, Marilyn had opened a real estate office in the front half of the Buena Vista Bar and Restaurant in partnership with Jim McLarn who, with wife, Summayaha, owned the restaurant. With no apparent need for licenses, several Gringos were setting themselves up as brokers, advertising on the Internet their own properties and the properties of other Gringos.

As the one person in town who had qualifications and experience, only Marilyn knew the disciplines and procedures of brokerage. In Bocas, where the caution "buyer-beware" could seldom have been more appropriate, Marilyn's reputation for professionalism soon brought success to her new business.

Jerry meanwhile emerged as the leader of the Gringo community. I called him the Gringo Mayor. A central player in any social happening, Jerry had the communication skills of the salesman and used them well to orchestrate the social interchanges, ensuring that no one was excluded and each had a share of his personal attention.

Jerry's quick wit invariably left me scrambling for an adequate response and seldom finding one that halfway equaled his. Jerry and Marilyn became friends, and with them Pat and I made our first sortie to the other side of the mountain.

Renting a car in David, we ventured into a world very different from tropical Bocas. Once out of the city and climbing into the foothills, the temperature dropped rapidly and the humidity disappeared. Both the climate and the scenery were reminiscent of the highlands of Kenya in colonial times; wide vistas, manicured rows of well-tended coffee trees and the huts of the workers contrasting with the spacious homes of the owners.

"I could live here very happily," said Pat. "I've always loved the mountains."

"Maybe one day we will find something this side and split our time between the two," I suggested.

"I know," said Pat, "You must have the sea to play on."

We stayed two nights at the Panamonte in Bouquete, a charming 1920s colonial-style hotel with a fire burning in the lounge.

At dinner Jerry chose the wines. I had learned that when sharing a meal with a Californian, it is a mistake to take the initiative on the subject of wines.

"Go on, Jerry. You are from wine country. You choose," I offered.

Jerry gave the wine list a perfunctory study and chose a Chilean Merlot. There was little alternative.

5

The Learning Process

The Gonzales family was our neighbor. Ramon was Peter's caretaker for the four houses he had built and also for the lots he had to offer further along our shoreline. He cut the grass with his machete, provided security and helped those of us who had trouble starting our boats, which, more often than not, was me.

Like most Indians Ramon is short of stature. From the age of two he has paddled cayucus, at first in play in shallow waters around his home and then in the fetching and carrying of people and supplies. The frequent upper body exercise of paddling has given him broad shoulders and a strength that far outstrips his stature.

"There are ten of them."

Pat was at the window of our main room. She was using binoculars to watch the family start the quarter mile journey to town. "Another person and the canoe would be under water. It's a good thing it's not blowing hard."

"They are headed for church," I said. "The Church of God has its service on Saturday evenings."

Ramon was sitting in the back of the canoe. His eldest son Evan was in the bow. Both had long wooden paddles. In unison they stretched forward to maximize the length of their pull. The canoe moved easily through the water.

Between the two sat the other eight members of the family. Abelina, the mother, was cradling the new baby. The other children were in pairs along the length of the canoe.

"How can Abelina dress them so beautifully?" Pat questioned without expecting an answer.

The family lives in a twenty by twenty foot wooden house over the water. At that time, the house had no electricity and no running water. The girls were in party dresses. The oldest daughter Eva had yet to reach puberty. Evan, a year older than Eva, was wearing a white shirt and black trousers. They were as well turned out as any young Virginian family headed for Sunday worship.

Pat passed me the glasses, and I watched the canoe's progress until it was safely at the supermarket dock. It will be dark long before they return, I thought, and said a silent prayer for the weather to stay calm.

Already we were becoming attached to this family. The children, with their black shining eyes and trusting affection, won our hearts on the first day they helped with our luggage. From their house, they could see our dock and whenever we returned from town with more than we could carry, they would come running to our aid.

I learned the hard way the relative strength of the Indians to those of us who exercise in a gym. Pat had suggested I obtain some black earth to enrich our flowerbeds. I negotiated with Daniel, the head Indian on the Island of Solarte. We agreed on a price of a dollar a sack, and one dollar fifty cents for each sack of chicken manure with which to further enrich the soil.

When I arrived in my boat to pick up the sacks, they were lined up along the shore. I took the boat in as close as the tide would permit and jumped into the shallows. Daniel was waiting for me and so were his children and grandchildren, all of whom were watching from his house.

"You stay with your boat, Mister Malc. Let me carry the sacks," Daniel said.

"Nonsense," I replied, standing head and shoulders above him. "We will share the work."

I reached down to take hold of the first sack and swing it on to my shoulder. It would not move. I stood up, pulled in my stomach muscles and made a second supreme effort. I got the sack off the ground and up to waist height, but no further. Clutching it to my stomach as if it were a sack of gold, I staggered unevenly toward the boat, barely able to advance one foot in front of the other.

By the time I dropped my sack over the side of the boat, Daniel was beside me with his second sack. Gingerly, I stood up straight and leaned backwards, my back aching throughout its length. I turned and looked across at the spectators' gallery. Young and old alike were unable to contain their laughter. I made a deep bow, sweeping my hat from my head and collapsed onto my knees in the water.

Daniel stood beside me. "Mister Malc, you carry the chicken shit. I carry the earth."

His decision was a good one. The chicken manure was a quarter the weight of the black earth.

By the end of January, I had improved my nautical skills but was still capable of the ridiculous.

Every Wednesday morning the ferry from the mainland used to bring the vegetable lady with her fresh broccoli, cauliflower, onions, lettuce and tomatoes, grown in the cooler and drier climate of the Pacific side.

As the slow-moving ferry approached the island, a crowd would gather in the shade of The Chiriqui Land Company dock, where the vegetable lady set out her produce. In those days, this lady was the only vendor of fruits and vegetables, and her arrival was a time of tension born of the desire to secure the best of the week's offerings. The hotel and B and B owners were in competition with the residents and felt their needs should come before those of us who were not in business.

One Wednesday, Pat and I arrived by boat as usual. I moored alongside the dock, below where the vegetable lady was already set up and about to give the signal for the fray to begin.

"Go for a cauliflower," Pat ordered. "I'll get a papaya."

I entered the scrimmage around the cauliflowers, but came up a loser, returning to our corner empty-handed.

"You should have been able to get one," Pat admonished me.

"Go for the tomatoes," she ordered.

I was successful this time. There were plenty of tomatoes.

Pat was talking to Lili, a tall, elegant black girl whose graceful movements brought to mind the Somali women I admired from afar when soldiering in Northern Kenya. Lili was the hostess of the Buena Vista. To her, everybody was "sweetie" or "handsome." Loyal to her boyfriend Barry, our wives did not mind Lili's ubiquitous flirting, even though Barry spent most of the time working in the oil fields of Saudi Arabia.

"I wanted a cauliflower, but Malcolm didn't get one for me," Pat bemoaned.

"Don't worry, sweetie," said Lili. "I get you a cauliflower."

Ten minutes later we were standing by our pile of fruits and vegetables waiting for the vegetable lady to tally us. Next to our papaya and tomatoes sat the magnificent cauliflower.

Lili came over. "You like it, honey?" she asked Pat.

"You bet I do. How'd you get it?"

"Don't ask, honey. It yours now," said Lili. Then, unable to keep her own secret, said, "I take it from Swan Cay Hotel. They don't need it."

"I think we should give it back," I said.

"No, sweetie. I never speak to you again if you give it back," Lili promptly threatened.

Pat and Lili departed to search for paint for Pat. I was standing, waiting my turn to pay, when I saw the Italian owner of Swan Cay Hotel looking at my cauliflower. I tried to give an impression of legitimate ownership while perspiration was breaking out all over. He did nothing, but I felt I was now a marked man.

I was loading up the boat when I spotted Irma. The daughter of a wealthy German family, Irma dressed as if she were living in St. Tropez or Cape Ferrat. Blonde in the Swedish style and as practical as any German, Irma never hid her contempt for the shortcomings of Bocas, both cultural and physical. Her husband Tony was Dutch. Tall and aristocratic in appearance, he sought to meet all Irma desired, except for her greatest wish, to return to Europe.

Irma was struggling with two heavy bags of fruit and vegetables. The house she and Tony owned was on the other side of town, close to Andino's dock.

"How are you getting those home?" I asked.

"Walk," she said.

"Hop in," I said, reaching for the bags.

As I drove the boat, I asked where Tony was and learned that he was investigating another property he thought they should purchase.

"I hope we don't buy it," she told me. "I don't want to spend any more time in Bocas."

I was listening to Irma and not concentrating. Again, I approached the landing too fast. I was still having trouble with the engine cutting out on me when I shifted into reverse. It happened again. The engine stalled.

I rushed forward, jumping onto the dock. To lessen the impact of the boat hitting the dock head, I reached down to fend off the boat with my hand.

Until that moment, I had no idea of the weight of a moving boat. I learned the hard way. The fiberglass bow mashed my fingers against the concrete.

I tied up the boat and attempted to hide my injury. As I reached out to take Irma's shopping bags, blood dripped from my crushed fingers.

"What happened?" asked Irma.

"Oh, it's nothing," I said, attempting to sound casual.

"But your poor hand is bleeding. Here, let me see it."

"No, really, it is nothing," I protested.

"But it is terrible. Poor man. We must take you to hospital."

Irma took off her shirt and wrapped it around the bleeding mess. Together we walked to the street where she stopped a passing car. Two minutes later we were at the emergency room door.

"What has happened this time?" asked the nurse, recognizing me from my previous visit.

"A small injury," I told her.

With the episode certain to get sensational news status in the Buena Vista, I was no longer resisting. I was ready for the full attention of the doctors and nurses.

"We will x-ray you first, and then I'll stitch you up," the nurse told me.

I felt disappointed. Surely this warranted the doctor.

Irma, her top half now draped in a borrowed men's shirt that did nothing for her figure, was restless.

"Well, Malcolm, thank you for the ride in your boat. Certainly, it was interesting. I am going to leave you now that you are in good hands." I felt deserted.

It was the middle finger of my right hand that took most of the blow. To my disbelief the x-ray failed to show a break. The nurse did a beautiful stitching job and one hour later and poorer by twelve dollars, I was on my way back home, though not by boat. It was three weeks before I could pull-start the engine.

There were other boating incidents. Six weeks after the Irma incident, Pat and I were leaving the home of Marilyn and Jerry after a well-lubricated dinner when I continued walking past the end of their dock.

A few weeks later, I was coming upwind and against the tide when I jumped to my dock with the bowline. The wind and the tide were stronger than I thought and pushed the boat away from me, pulling the line from my hands. Seeing my boat drifting downwind, I dove into the water and swam after it. Unfortunately, my cell phone was still in my pocket, an expensive experience.

My fame was spreading. I was bringing comfort to other men who were assured that whatever mistake they might make, they could not surpass the incompetence of Senor Malcolm. The only one who came anywhere near my total of mishaps was Jerry.

Jerry had instigated The Bocas Underwater Dock Inspection Society, whose unwritten by-laws dictated that whoever suffered the most total immersions from a dock would be chairman. For three years I held this distinctive post. Eventually my disaster rate decreased and the margin between Jerry and me slimmed down until one day Jerry admitted to a series of immersions that took him into the lead.

6

The Gringo Watering Hole

Pat was spared agonies from injuries. Her only trips to the hospital involved medical examinations for visas and to check on sick friends.

In the studio built to her specifications by Peter, she painted most days while listening to books on tape. She took breaks to play cards with Joan and whoever else could be persuaded to join them, and she made curtains for the windows.

Most nights we would eat out.

"With only two of us, it is almost cheaper to eat out and not have food going to waste," we would assure ourselves.

When we felt we were being extravagant, we would switch to having a meal at Don Chicho's, the restaurant owned by Virginia's family.

In the early days, the ex-pat community was united in an extended family. There were no more than thirty of us, and we all thought we knew each other well. We had our differences of opinion, approvals and disapprovals but nothing more serious than is to be found in most extended families enjoying congenial unity.

We were infused with the spirit of pioneers, and we stood shoulder to shoulder, a community of fellow souls, who had found their way to these islands from diverse countries of Caucasian cultures.

The Buena Vista was our tribal gathering post. Jim and Summayah provided California-style food, the latest gossip and a reliable verbal postal service.

"Hey Jim, when Dave and Linda come in, tell them to hold on. We'll be back for lunch, and save us a couple of servings of the taco."

"Will do!" Jim would respond. "They should be here in the next half hour. Wednesday is their shopping day. By the way, I hear you're looking for an outboard engine. Jody has one for sale."

Every excuse for a tribal get-together was fully exploited: each national holiday back home and then Halloween, Valentine's Day, Mother's Day, and Father's

Day interspersed with birthdays and the occasional marriage. If Hallmark had a card for the occasion, we had a celebration to match.

The wearing of costumes was not restricted to Halloween. The more outlandish the dress, the greater is the chance of your photo appearing on the Buena Vista clipboard, our equivalent of the big city society page.

Large bodied men, with coconut boobs and grass skirts, danced with pirates of indeterminable sex and Sixties flower girls, grown soft of body and broad of hip.

With identities supposedly veiled behind homemade masks, we shook off inhibitions and uncorked some long-bottled fantasies. We were bent on proving to ourselves and to those back home our wisdom in waving good-bye and investing in this utopia.

We were a bag of oddballs but united. We might have remained so had not *International Living*, an overseas property investment newsletter, placed Panama at the top of its list of the 100 best retirement paradises.

Suddenly, sleepy Bocas gained world attention. Travel editors of *The New York Times*, the *LA Times* and travel magazines dispatched writers to investigate. The planes filled with tourists and property seekers. The tempo at the Buena Vista shifted up several gears. An Argentinean television company flooded the town with film crew and ran a *Survivor* program on the Zapatia Islands. Chilean, British, Russian, French and Italian *Survivor* followed. The charms of Bocas were featured on TV screens in distant lands.

On special nights there were more people wanting to celebrate at the Buena Vista than Jim and Summayah could seat at one time. We were forced to choose between two sittings. Those opting for the first were expected to be finished and give up their tables two hours later. The second sitting had the advantage of no time limit but risked having only a limited choice of menu.

Our tribal traditions were being broken down by the influx of new faces. No longer dining as a family, we started to break into sub-tribes. Friendships changed, new faces eased out old, sending them to seek other alliances. Rivalries emerged. Invitations to parties, once broadcast to all via the Buena Vista verbal exchange, became selective.

"Hasta luego! See you tonight at Ted and Sally's."

"Oh, are they having something?"

"Oh dear! Maybe I shouldn't have said. It's Ted's birthday. You were there last year, weren't you? I thought they would be sure to ask you this year. Maybe they just forgot?"

The victims of the exclusions spent the evenings wondering what went wrong.

"I told you, dear, you shouldn't have hidden the rum that night when Marcos and the others were bent on staying until the last bottle was empty," he would say.

"That's not the reason. It was because you left to watch basketball the night they wouldn't go home," she would respond.

Sooner or later the excluded would be told of an overheard conversation.

"They're stupid old farts who don't know their ass from their elbows when it comes to having fun. They're in bed asleep by nine o'clock. We took them off the party list."

They in turn would respond with, "Well, we didn't want to go anyway. All they do is drink and make asses of themselves."

With more than one hundred Gringos, we no longer knew everyone's name, let alone how many husbands or wives each of us have had. It was no longer a matter of great interest when a new face appeared and was trying to get the attention of Cheto behind the Buena Vista's bar.

At the Buena Vista those who have property for sale were the most courteous to the new white faces, often treating them to a couple of rounds of drinks and inviting them to sit at their table.

The conversation might have gone like this:

"Down here for vacation?" the property man asked, addressing what appeared to be a husband and wife team.

"Sort of,' they responded in unison.

"Oh, what else are you doing?"

This question appeared to be no more than casual interest but in reality was the first, all important, opening play.

"Well, we thought we would look at property. Hal's due to retire in two years," said the wife.

You did not have to hear the conversation to know what was happening. When the property man moved closer to the new face, you knew the scent was strong. He was looking for the opening that would allow him to claim this lamb for his own.

"How did you come to choose Bocas?" asked the property man.

"The Internet," said the husband.

"Oh, did you see my listing of properties on the net?"

"We only saw The Blue Lagoon Properties," said the wife, causing the property man to wince.

"Are there other properties?" asked the husband, bringing the smile back to the property man's face.

"Well, yes, my partner and I have several properties to sell. Our website is Bocas Bargains. I am Bunty Bunker and my partner is Luigi Lachioni. But forget that, I would not want to step on the toes of Porky Francis and The Blue Lagoon."

"Well, maybe we could see your properties if we don't find what we are looking for with Mr. Francis," said the wife tentatively.

"Porky Francis has several properties to show you on some of the smaller islands," the property man paused to signal Cheto to refill the visitors' glasses.

"Salute!" The property man raised his glass to the visitors.

"Salute!" responded the visitors, clinking glasses with the property man and thinking how fortunate they were to get into conversation with this person.

"To continue," said the property man looking thoughtful, "Old Porky has some sweet little islands and, if it is peace and quiet you want, he is the right man for you."

"Good," said the visitors, feeling fortunate.

"Being on one of those islands, you will have all the seclusion you want. Why, you could be dead for a week and no one but your lady wife would know."

"Well, we don't have to be quite so far out, and we will have a cell phone," said the man, placing his hand reassuringly on his wife's knee.

"Cell phones don't like thunderstorms," said the property man. Then, feeling that it was time to bring in reinforcements and swing these folks in the direction of Bocas Bargains, said, "You going to eat? The best food in town is right here. My wife Suzie has a table over there. Let's join her."

"Thank you, but we don't want to barge in on you," again the couple spoke in harmony.

"Nonsense," said the property man, placing his hand on the lady's shoulder. "We are all family in Bocas. We are here to help each other."

"Not for me, one of those small islands," said Suzie

"Why?" asked the visitors.

"I like to have electricity and fresh water, and I hate sand flies. They breed like mad in the mangroves," Suzie confided.

"The properties looked so attractive in the photos," said the wife.

"Yes, they are attractive, but did you notice the mangroves?" asked the property man. "They are the dark green bushes all along the shore. They surround the islands, and you are not allowed to touch them. They are the breeding ground for barracudas and other fish."

"Do you have a card?" asked the man. "Your advice is most interesting. We'll definitely consult you before making any decision."

The property men do not always get their own way.

A family arrived, parents and three hungry-looking teenage children. The first to encounter them after their plane landed was a property man who just happened to be there at the time. From the look of uncertainty on the faces of the two parents, it was obvious that here were some first timers. The property man was quick to offer assistance, finding a taxi and helping with the luggage.

"First time in Panama?" asked the property man, as they rode in the taxi to the hotel.

"Yes, we're in Panama for a month, looking at properties," they told him.

Mark, the owner of extensive properties scattered around the lagoons and on the main island, could hardly believe his good fortune. For a week he herded this family as a shepherd herds his flock, ever conscious of the marauding intentions of other property men.

"Coming to the party tonight, Mark?" he would be asked.

"No, sorry, I can't. I have these clients come to town to see me and I owe it to them to stick with them."

"Bring them along with you?" suggested one of the other property men.

"Well, they're bushed. We've been out at Tiburon Point all day. They just want to grab a bite to eat and then hit the sack. We have another busy day ahead of us tomorrow."

"Well, let them eat on their own for once and you come and join us."

"No, they wouldn't like that. They came all this way to make a point of seeing me and I can't let them down."

After Mark had gone, we all agreed he had known them quite a long time if you added up the daily total of eighteen hours and multiplied it by the last seven days. That is more time than some of us get to spend in a year with our siblings.

At the start of the second week, Mark was looking depressed. Driving the family from island to island in search of the ideal beach property at the ideal price was proving costly in gas, to say nothing of the wasted time spent while the children had just a "quick swim."

In addition, the family seemed content to let him continue his habit from day one of paying for their meals, a not inconsiderable expense, given the appetite of three active teenagers. Only the frequent reference to the selling of the ranch back home kept Mark assured that in the end a substantial sale would materialize.

Towards the end of the second week, I spotted Mark walking down the main street. He did not have his brood with him, nor did he walk with his usual cocky gait. Furthermore, he was forgetting to greet everyone with his customary, "Hey, wapi, Que Passo? Hey, sexy, what's happening?"

"Where are your friends?" I asked.

"They have gone to David. They needed a break from the heat. They're going up to Bouquete to do some bird watching."

A week later I asked Mark when his friends were coming back, and he told me they had decided they preferred the Bouquete because there are more birds to be seen at the higher altitude.

"Have you told the property men in Bouquete about their little game?" I asked. "When they have finished touring Chiriqui Province, they will decide that after all it's Condor they want to live with and move on to Peru."

The behavior of last month's new and most junior employee towards this month's arrival has always interested me. With only four weeks on the job, the previously timid new girl or boy has changed overnight. This person now pretends an intimate knowledge of the operation of the office, both business and social.

"Oh, he's harmless, really," and, "Oh, we don't take any notice of that," are remarks bandied about with bravado.

When coming back to Bocas after a long absence, my face is an off-white with a touch of jaundice. After twenty minutes of exposure to the tropical sun it starts turning Campari red. To those who do not know me, I appear to be one of today's new crop of tourists. I cannot resist turning this into fun when the opportunity arises.

"Arrived today?" a man I have never seen before asks.

"Yes. How did you guess?" I ask.

"I can always spot a new boy. How long are you staying, may I ask?"

I say, "I am not sure."

There is a measure of truth in this because, if I were to have a stroke tonight and not die immediately, tomorrow I would be on my way to the clinic in David. I have the same superstition as Virginia's mom, Joanne, who follows every agreement to a future commitment with, "God willing."

"Well, this is the place to be, I tell you," continues my helpful friend. "If you can grab yourself a little piece of this paradise, you will have done yourself a good turn."

"You live here then?" I ask.

"Yep. We live here year round and love it. Great folks down here. My wife and I are here in the BV most days. Sometimes twice a day, lunch and dinner. Moved to Bocas a month ago. Sold up everything back home. I'm here 'til they bury me out there in the lagoon. Wisest choice I ever made. When you get the chance, you should do the same. We've got a great little community here."

I listen for a while, genuinely interested in hearing the man's impressions and the advice he is imparting based on his few weeks of experience. I am careful not to tell a lie or to play the game for too long. I do not want to offend his sensibilities to the point where I make an enemy. There are enough problems for Gringos in Bocas without fighting amongst us.

Where once we wished each other success, rivalries now made us less generous. We began judging our own success against the success of others. The competition became particularly fierce between those selling properties. Rumors became rife.

"He knew there would be problems with that land. All he cared about was to get the deal done."

"That is typical. No ethics whatsoever."

Almost all of the property men were selling their own properties alongside those of their clients.

"Well, yes, I will show that piece, but just because it is listed with me. I have to be honest and warn you the middle of Isla Carenero is sinking into the sea and the sand flies there are the worst in the area. I really couldn't recommend it to you over this piece of ours."

Virginia had cautioned us from the start not to criticize a Bocatoranian behind his back.

"It is best if you don't say nothing about nobody, Senor Malcolm. Not even to his worst enemy. You give someone something to tell and he tell everybody, even the person you talk about and he do it before the sun go down."

The same is now true within the Gringo community. "Let no one be willing to speak ill of the absent." We hear the two thousand year wisdom of Latin Poet, Sextus Propertus and today's advice of Virginia, yet cannot resist the temptation to gossip. Maybe it is the rum. We cannot blame it on the altitude as we once did in Kenya days. Gossip in the ex-pat community is as endemic as the drink at sundown.

The spoken words, usually embellished by third and fourth parties for greater effect, are passed along until someone takes it on himself to repeat the final version to the subjects of the ridicule.

Gringo social evolution is a micro image of universal social history played on fast forward. The shifting sands bring like together, forming new tribes that unite with their own internal loyalties.

As in any society there are those who become tribeless and stand on the fringes, unable to match the social requirements of any one fellowship. I fall into this category and Pat also, though to a lesser extent.

Since our arrival an increasing number of yachtsmen from North America and Europe have sheltered their yachts in either of the two Bocas marinas. Bocas has four advantages over most Caribbean ports of shelter. It is out of the hurricane belt, it has an airport within ten minutes reach of both marinas, the mooring prices are very reasonable and the security is good.

The boat people, as we who live on land call them, as a whole keep their distance from the local Gringos. Some park their boats and hasten off to their other lives. Others spend much of the year leisurely sailing the lagoons, exploring other parts of Panama and living relatively cheaply.

There are a few young retirees who sold their computer company stock options at the height of NASDAQ. Well loaded with cash and in satellite communication with the stock markets of the world, they spend some of their gains in the purchase of land and take long cruises when restless.

The Gringo community has provided jobs for many and helped to raise the standard of living. Along with this benefit there is the adverse situation of the rising prices caused by the influx of tourists. Some Bocatoranians are looking to sell their Bocas property and move to Almirante on the mainland, where the cost of living is considerably lower.

With minimum taxation of the foreign investor, there are some who repay this benefit by supporting local institutions such as the schools, the hospital, the old folks' home, the library, and the Bomberos with their newly founded boys and girls club.

7

Don Chicho's and the Vasquez Family

Virginia's family, the Vasquez's, owns Don Chicho's Restaurant. It is named after her father, although it is her mother, Joanne, who brought it into being.

Unlike the Buena Vista that carries the distinction of being the haunt of the Gringos, Don Chicho's Restaurant is generic to Bocas, catering to all ethnic groups. It provides substantial helpings of typical Panamanian food at prices that leave you wondering if there can be any profit for the Vasquez family at the end of the day.

Customers walk past a glass covered food counter, making choices that typically include chicken, fried, stewed or baked; fried fish; octopus; pork; beef; rice; chow mien; kidney beans; green beans; yucca and salad. For breakfast there are eggs, bacon, ham, a form of porridge called crema, toast, pasties, empanadas and carimonolas. The last is a delicious ball of fried yucca with spice meat in the center.

Where you go to pay Joanne, there are glass counters containing a variety of freshly made cakes and pastries. The choice of beverages includes coffee, sodas, beer, natural fruit juices, including mango, tamarind, papaya, and melon, and maize, a drink made of corn and milk.

"Buenos dias, Mr. Malcolm. What you up to today?" Joanne invariably greets me. She sits smiling from behind her cash desk.

Joanne, Virginia's mother, has been my "sister" since my introduction to the "family" of the Methodist Church. One of Joanne's great-grandfathers, Roberto Fernandez, was born on San Andreas Island, 120 miles off the coast of Nicaragua. He was a seaman sailing out of Philadelphia when he jumped ship in Old Bank and married her great-grandmother, Leticia Watson.

Joanne's father, Aubry Elisha Bent, worked on a wooden boat that ran from Colon, at the Caribbean end of the Panama Canal, along the coast to Bocas.

42

"Everything come to Bocas by boat in those days. There was no road like there is now," Joanne told me.

"In Old Bank my father met my mother, Melencia, and took her off to Colon. I was born in Colon. "My mother, she work for white people. At that time there plenty soldiers in Colon. I was the eldest. All the others was born in Old Bank. Julia and Earl came by my father, Victor, Frances and Julio by the next man, and Sandra by the last man.

"I went to the Salvation Army School. It was run by colored people from Jamaica. We had an ABC book and a doll book. It was not a deep Christian school." She continued, "I wanted to go to the Spanish School, but for that you had to have blood test and a certificate from the doctor saying you do not have worms. Both my mother and my grandmother worked and could not take time off. To go to the doctor took a lot of time.

"We lived in my grandmother's house on the top of the hill. Not many people lived in Old Bank in those days. Not like now. My mother baked bread and journey cakes and we children had to sell them every day after school."

"I hear people call them johnnycakes. Are they journey cakes, or johnnycakes?" I asked, breaking the theme to settle the matter of the correct name of these scone-like buns made of corn meal and often flavored with coconut.

"They journey cakes because you take them with you when you make journey," Joanne explained before continuing.

"When I was eleven I did get to go to Spanish School, but I find I did not like it because they was always after you to become a Catholic and take Communion. I did not want to change from Methodist.

"My grandmother arrange for me go each day to an older lady, Miss Melissa Rose, to get a little English. The parents of Miss Rose send her to the States when she was young and she learn to speak English real good. She charge fifty to seventy-five cents a week and I go from eleven till two when it was lunch break from the Spanish School."

"What did you do for fun in those days?" I asked Joanne.

"We work all week at school and selling bread and journey cakes. At weekend we have church activities, choir practice, concerts, and we bathe in the sea. When we older we like to dance."

"I hear you were a very good dancer," I said.

"We had to have permission to dance and we had to be home by nine. The boys played the mouth organ, steel drums, a bell and the maracas.

"School only go to third book in English. Then I go to stay the week with my other grandmother and aunt in Bocas and attend the public school.

"My grandmother so poor, she work for a Chinaman. In the evening she come home with his family's clothes for to wash and iron. I helped her. We ironed with coals. I ironed the little children's clothes; she ironed the sheets and big clothes.

"I worked very hard to buy my way because I knew this grandmother no love me as much as her other grans because I was not with her from the start. One day I hear her say to my aunt, 'Joanne, when she come here, she no bring anything. She live here everyday and don't bring nothing.'

"After that I leave and go back to Old Bank and then come every day to school by cayucu. In those days we no had motors. We paddle all the way and be at school by seven-thirty and then at four paddle back. In all weather we come.

"When I grow up, my mother tell me, 'Never look at policemen. Policemen not good persons. They fool young girls and then six months later leave the girls with babies coming.'

"In everything you have good and bad. I got to know Vasquez who was sent to be policeman in Old Bank. I married Vasquez when I twenty-two and he thirty. He has always been a good man to me and never give me trouble with other women.

"As is the way with the policemen, Vasquez was always being moved from one part of the province to another. When my first child Victor was born, I had no place to live but God came and opened a door for me. An older lady, Miss Ester, had a granddaughter die in childbirth. She let us live in half her house and she would hold Victor like she was holding her grandson.

"My aunt and I started a business buying plantains and bananas from the Indians and reselling them in the market. We began to make breakfast of coffee and bread for the Indians who were hungry coming in from the bush. One day my aunt saw me preparing soup.

"'What are you doing there?' she asked. 'I making soup,' I say.

"She says to me, 'Bring it tomorrow to the market.' I did and we sell it all and make four dollars. With the money we make, we bought four pounds of rice, some meat and lentils and made more soup."

This was the start of Joanne's restaurant business that led to her eventually opening Don Chicho's in the prime position on the main street, opposite the front of the Palazio, the seat of the provincial government.

Don Chicho's has become a part of Bocas culture. Indians, Afro-Antilleans, the mestizos, the foreigners and the passing tourists share tables. The meals cost between seventy-five cents for a plate of beans and rice to six dollars for lobster.

Joanne has achieved business success while bringing up five children, all of whom attended college. The children own businesses that include Virginia's service administering to the needs of Gringo property owners, an Internet cafe, the local cable television service and a metal workshop.

Joanne and her younger daughter Jacqueline are lay preachers in our church. Julio, the youngest son, is an executive at the Chiquita Banana headquarters in Cincinnati, Ohio, with responsibility for Latin America and the Caribbean.

"Joanne, she have too many employees," my friend Tony the Chinaman often tells me.

"They are her extended family," I would say.

"Ella atirais la casa por la ventana," Tony would respond.

"What does that mean?"

"She throw the house through the window. It mean free-for-all. When you have a party and invite everyone."

Joanne has seventeen full-time staff and five others who work shorter hours. Additionally, two ladies bake cakes and pastries and make patties for the restaurant. Three of her staff live in her home, two since they were babies. Against this measure of worthy achievement, I am not fit to be her brother. However, she tolerates me, even if she berates me frequently for my various failings.

Joanne introduced me to the Church soon after I arrived. Most Sundays I sit next to her in the front right pew, she on the aisle and me one in. Sometimes, I am the only white-skinned person in the congregation that totals thirty-five for the 7.30 a.m. service on a dry day. If it is raining hard, then there may only be four of us at the start, while others wait to see if the rain will let up.

When the minister appointed to take the service fails to show, Miss Joanne takes over. Her sermons preach the benevolence that is exemplified by her own life. When she is without her collection envelope, I sneak a look at how much she is giving and feel ashamed of my own contribution.

Pat is Catholic and her church is on the other side of the main street. It is five times the size of ours and has a much bigger congregation. The thirty-five of us out-sing the two hundred of them. Pat claims she hears my raspy, off-key voice when she is praying.

"Remember what your kindergarten teacher told you, 'Open and shut your mouth but do not make a sound,'" she reminds me.

Joanne is a few years my junior, but her maternal instincts give her the rights of an older sister. Her unconditional love is something I treasure deeply.

In 1986, Virginia, Joanne's oldest daughter, was awarded a Sam Walton scholarship to Harding University in Searcy, Arkansas. At that time she spoke very little English.

I will never tire of hearing her tell of her experiences among the students of this expensive Church of Christ University.

"Hey, Virginia. What's up?" she recalled being asked by students.

Virginia heard the question and looked to see what was above her.

"I don't see nothing up," she said, wondering if she was losing her eyesight.

"Because I am black, they thought I was a black girl from Arkansas trying to be funny.

Later they asked, 'Where you from?' I told them, 'I am from Panama.'

"'Oh, that's in the middle of Africa, that's nice,' said one of the girls.

"'Yes, it is in the middle of Africa,' I said.

"My roommate, she had a boyfriend. She always speak of him as 'The Faggot,' and I think Faggot is his name. One time I see Faggot at the University Post Office. He is with his friends and I call out, 'What's up, Faggot?' and he don't look at me. He just keep going.

"I say again, 'What's up, Faggot?' and he still keep going.

"I followed him to the student center. 'Hey, Faggot! Hey, Faggot!' I called out louder than ever. He stopped and go very red.

"He says to me, 'Don't call me that!'

"'But, Faggot, that is your name. Cindy always call you faggot,' I said.

"When I got back my room I tell Cindy, 'I saw Faggot in the dinning hall and I call out to him, 'What is up Faggot?' and he tell me that not his name.

"'Oh no, Virginia! Tell me you didn't! Please, please tell me you didn't!' she cried.

"That was the end of the relationship between Faggot and Cindy.

"One afternoon I read my program and read 'swimming'. I put on my swim costume and go to the swimming pool. There is no person there I know and I ask where is my class and they tell me room thirty. I walk into the room and everyone is fully dressed doing science. If I weren't so black, I would have been bright red."

Virginia attended Harding for four years. When she had heard that she had been awarded the scholarship, she thought it was for Harvard University and all of Bocas soon knew that was where she was bound. It was several months before she discovered her mistake. She never did tell the folks back home.

During the four years, she only saw her family once. After two years, the Walton Scholarship Administrator took her to Panama to serve as his translator and she was able to take time off for a quick visit to her family.

"I used to do real well at the end of school year. I get televisions, refrigerators, carpets, couches the other girls throw out. They have plenty money and instead of taking home, they dump everything."

Virginia loves to appear at our house in a dress that we have not seen before.

"Come, Miss Pat, guess what I pay for this."

"Well, it looks like a hundred-dollar-dress but knowing you, you paid twenty dollars."

"Oh, Miss Pat! You are so wrong. I pay two dollars."

It is the same with costume jewelry. Virginia has the knack for finding the bargain and possesses the elegance to make the bargain look sensational.

Pat painted a large oil on canvas of a beautiful black girl holding a baby. Virginia was the model and we named the painting "The Tropical Madonna." Virginia is not married and does not have a baby, but she is the caregiver to the young and old alike and shares her mother's generous nature.

Pat and I were Virginia's first "clients." We have known her since the day she met us at the airport at the start of our second visit. At that time, she was Peter's girlfriend of four years standing.

Virginia and Peter made a handsome couple. Peter, six-foot-four, blue-eyed and blessed with good looks comparable to Clark Gable, and Virginia, five-foot-ten, with a figure that turns any dress into a fashion piece, were the foremost interracial couple in Bocas. There was constant speculation as to when they would marry. They made a perfect match; Peter, the land developer, and Virginia, his confidant with access to those who might sell land, made a good team.

In agreeing to allow me to pay her on a monthly basis for the help she was giving us, Virginia unwittingly started a business. Six years later her company, Bocas Property Administration, handled pay and social security for eighty employees of twenty-two Gringo enterprises, ranging in size from my two-employee farm to a land development whose owners anticipate building more than two hundred housing units.

Besides attending to her own business, Virginia has continued to teach in our English program four mornings a week.

There are many advantages to having Virginia and her team of four secretaries help you with your interaction with the local government, businesses and services.

To be one of Virginia's clients removes the possibility of unpaid bills during absences from Bocas and errors in social security payments for employees, both potential pitfalls that can lead to complicated rectification.

A great time saver is you no longer have to stand in line to withdraw money from the bank. One of Virginia's staff visits the bank each banking day and will make deposits and withdrawals for you. Other advantages include access to Virginia's encyclopedic knowledge of where to shop for the best bargains on any of a vast number of possible needs, access to electricians, plumbers, roof repairmen, and casual labor and the organization of medical evacuation.

Ray Kennedy, who lives with his wife Lois on Isla Carenero, threw his hip out. Virginia had been dining with the Kennedy's. The hip throw happened when Ray, after refusing to let Virginia call for a water taxi, pulled his outboard motor to get it started. Having already cast off into the dark, Ray was immobilized and lying in agony on the floor of his cayuco.

Virginia paddled the boat back to Ray's dock, called the Bomberos, and stayed with Ray all night as he was taken first to the Bocas hospital, then to the hospital in Almirante on the mainland, and eventually to Changuinola, where the hip was put back in place.

Twice more this happened, and each time Virginia stayed comforting Ray and seeing that he got the immediate attention of doctors.

I cannot imagine Pat and my having survived the rigors that were to face me in the coming years had Virginia not been on our side. With each setback that came my way, Virginia was there to say, "Don't worry, Mr. Malcolm. We will make it."

While Pat is practical, I have been destined to learn only through making errors. But for Virginia, I would most likely have thrown in the towel and settled down to old age in a quiet Virginia backwater.

8

A Foothold in Town

Pat had no desire to drive the boat, and so it fell to me to do the shopping. The only store on Isla Carenero carried little more than eggs, tinned milk, and sugar.

Docking the boat in town continued to be stressful. I decided my nautical ineptitude was yet another manifestation of my natural inabilities, along with shortcomings in mathematics, spelling and singing in tune.

In my young army days, I had applied to become an army pilot. Along with forty-nine other officers, I went to be tested for pilot suitability. The selection was to last five days. Halfway through the first morning of math calculations and rapid response to image patterns, another officer and I were told to pack our bags and return to our units. I had flunked every preliminary test.

Docking was further complicated by a shortage of places to tie up to. I had been using the dock at Andino's supermarket, justifying this by making a purchase before setting off on other errands. With the Gringo community expanding and each family bringing an additional boat to town, the hunt for a place to tie up was increasingly tense.

Andino had not complained, but I knew the time would come when he would restrict the dock's use. I decided that the solution was to buy a waterfront lot in town and build my own dock. I wandered town with Dwayne, an old timer Gringo married to Albina Christie who runs the Aeroperlas office at the airport.

For two days we looked at the few available lots. Each had a disadvantage, but I knew that there was no time to waste. Soon, all available waterfront lots would be gone. Dwayne and I walked the waterfront several times on both days.

There was one lot I wanted to buy more than any that were on offer. It was next to Casa Luck, a general store that was popular with the Indians because its owners, Tony and Silvia Chen, have an extensive selection of cotton dress material.

"This would be ideal for me," I told Dwayne as we stood looking from the street at the empty lot. Beyond it was the sea and in the distance our house on Isla Carenero.

"This is the closest spot to our house," I told Dwayne.

"Not a hope," said Dwayne. "Everyone has been after Tony to sell this, but he never will."

The next day when Dwayne and I met again, he told me, "Tony wants to meet you. I think he might sell to you."

I met with Tony. Tony is Chinese. He looks like Buddha. He sits on a bar stool behind a counter at the front end of his store from where he can survey all that passes in the street. He is five years older than me, but his hair is black. He had been watching Dwayne and me pass by.

"You want to buy next door?" Tony asked me.

"Yes, I am interested," I told him.

"You no build a disco on the lot?"

"No, I like a quiet life. For now, I want to build only a dock. Maybe one day a house but never a disco."

"I think you okay. I speak to my wife. She in Colon. I see what she say."

A few days later, Tony called for me.

"Silvia say okay. She sell you the lot. There no need for a lawyer. The papers are okay. I no like lawyers. They no good."

Tony gave me the papers. They showed that Silvia Chen had purchased the lot from Estevan Thomas in 1963. I had Virginia call a friend in Panama City who went to the title registry office and confirmed the lot was owned by Silvia and was fully titled.

My son Hugo was visiting from London. Hugo's wife is a lawyer and, when I told him I was completing the deal directly with the owner without a lawyer, he filled with disbelief.

"Dad, you cannot do this! You are crazy! You must get a lawyer."

I did not get a lawyer. There are times when you must obey your instinct, and my instinct told me two things: that Tony and Silvia were above board and that if I did get a lawyer they would lose face and might cancel the deal. I went ahead and bought the property.

Tony and I soon became close friends.

"You like a beer?" Tony asked. He was already shuffling towards the back of the store, his sandals scraping on the concrete floor.

Lowering his rear onto an upright chair, he opened the beer cooler and passed me a bottle of Panama. After ten hours of watching the world from the entrance to his store, Buddha was in need of conversation. I sat on a low-slung wooden chair of the type found on steamships in the days of the *Titanic*.

Looking up at Tony, I could no longer see his chair. His Buddha body had engulfed it. He appeared to be suspended in air.

"When I had a bar in Colon City, many Americans knew me," Tony said, knowing well that I have heard the story several times before.

Storytelling was an evening ritual and when, after a few weeks, Tony's repertoire was completed, we would start again at the beginning. Like a favorite CD of classic songs, I never tire of Tony's reminiscences.

"When did you have the bar?" I asked as if I did not know.

"During the war and more time after. Colon was in the Canal Zone," he continued. "The Americans, they trust me." He was leading up to one of his favorite lines.

I fed him the lead, "How do you know they trust you, Tony?"

"Because they made me inspector of the whore houses," he chuckled at the memory.

"No, Tony," I said in mock surprise. "How many houses?"

"More than two hundred. I had to inspect them. I never did mess with the whores, but I had plenty opportunity. They come from all over for the American GI's. They come from Columbia. They come from Dominica. They come from all over because the American, he have money."

Tony and Silvia left the Canal Zone twenty-five years ago when his brother-in-law, who owned Casa Luck, died unexpectedly. They came to help out and stayed.

In addition to the rolls of gaily-colored cotton materials that fill the shelves down one side of their store, they sell bottled water, soft drinks, beer and a variety of household necessities from Alka-Seltzer to toilet brushes.

Their business survives on their Indian customers who come to them confident that they will be treated with respect. Both Tony and Silvia show great patience as the Guaymi ladies take their time choosing dress material.

"Where you from back in the States?" Tony likes to ask me whenever a new Gringo face is in his shop.

"Norfolk, Virginia," I say.

"No fuck,' says Tony, knowing well that being Chinese he does not have to attempt to pronounce the "r."

Behind Tony's guise of ritual humor and storytelling lies an astute mind. If ever I were to write a spy novel, Tony would be one of my secret agents. From his daytime post in the entrance to his store, he observes all that passes, both on the side street and the main street beyond.

Tony sees, remembers, assesses the implications and makes his deductions. When Tony gives me advice, I listen because his wisdom is based on fact and astute analysis.

Tony has another source of knowledge. Being a member of the Chinese Association, he is privilege to their exchange of information. The Chinese own most of the best properties in town and contribute stability to the community. Being both Bocatoranians and Panamanians, their loyalty to town and country goes unquestioned.

Virginia, Joanne, Tony and Silvia are Pat's and my first line of support in our daily lives. We refer to them for advice frequently, trusting them implicitly.

When I received news the mayor wanted to see me in his office at ten one morning, I stopped by Don Chicho's which faces the mayor's office. Joanne was as usual at her cash desk.

"Why do you think the mayor wants to see me?" I asked her.

"Maybe he wants you loan him some money, Mr. Malc. I hear he have been asking people for money. You no give him any. It is not his place to be asking Gringos for money."

"Well, I have done my bit already," I told her. "I bought the air conditioner for his office."

"I did hear you did and that was stupid I did say," said Joanne.

"Well, Joanne, if you had sat through a meeting in that office you would understand. Besides, it did not look good for Bocas to have a mayor's office that had no air-conditioning."

"Well, you no give him nothing today he can take home and don't you give him no money. You never will get it back. You go in there and ask him lend you money and see what happen."

Joanne had given me a good idea.

Sharply at ten, I reported to the outer office of the mayor. Someone knocked on the mayor's door and without delay ushered me inside.

The mayor arose from his desk all smiles and offered me his hand. I crossed the space of his office with alacrity, grabbed the extended hand and said, "Good morning, Mr. Mayor. I am so pleased to have this chance to speak with you. I need to ask your help. I need to borrow two hundred dollars."

The mayor was speechless. He stood with hunched shoulders, arms lowered and palms turned towards me. His gesture indicated he had nothing to say, let alone lend me.

"Well, another time, Mr. Mayor," I said and showed myself out.

"You win that one, Mr. Malc," said Joanne. "Maybe now he leave you alone."

9

A Lost Deposit and a Found Farm

With the friendship of our support team, our confidence about life in Bocas was on the rise, and I stepped up my search for the right piece of land for a farm.

A corner of Isla Solarte caught my attention. It was close to the Indian village from which I had bought the black soil and the chicken dirt. It was waterfront and included a small beach of soft sand and a bluff ideal for a house. It was just ten minutes by water from Bocas town.

"You be careful of anything on Solarte," Tony warned. "Plenty problems 'cause no one know who have right to what."

I hired a local lawyer to investigate, and he assured me there was no problem and that the land had clear title, belonging to a Gringo currently in the States.

Both Pat and I were excited. When back in Virginia, I contacted the owner, agreed on a price and paid a deposit.

Two days later a third party called me from California.

"If you buy that land, I will stop you from using it." The Gringo sounded aggressive and desperate. "I employ three lawyers, and I will have all of them work against you. I will make sure you are prevented from building on the land for at least ten years. I will see to it you never have electricity."

I was glad Pat was on the extension. She would never have believed this tirade if she had not heard it for herself.

"The only way I would let you buy that land is if you deeded it to the Indian Village on your death."

"My instinct for self preservation would not allow me to do that," I said. "I would be dead within a week."

"What are you implying?" The temper at the other end was reaching hurricane force.

"Forget it," I said calmly. "I came to Bocas for a tranquil life, not to war with anyone. If the land is that important to you, you buy it."

When I had told my four sons that I was searching for land on which to build a survival farm they made no comment. They had witnessed the results of my alarmist actions before.

In the early seventies, I had owned a small art gallery in Bury Street, in St. James, the center of the London art trade. Alarmed by reports of pending industrial anarchy as Communists infiltrated union committees, I left my gallery in the charge of my assistant and joined "Better Britain." The late Colonel David Sterling had established Better Britain to provide support to the moderate union leaders who were being challenged by an organized and well-financed cadre of young Communists. I became David's "chief of staff" of a staff of four.

David was a man of great imagination and initiative who, as a young officer in the army opposing Rommel in North Africa, had formed the Long Range Desert Group. With his small band of selected volunteers he had snuck around Rommel's south flank and inflicted destruction on his supply depots and desert air bases.

When David sounded the clarion call to action on behalf of the moderate union members, the liberal press ridiculed him. When they found his number two was also a retired military man, they could hardly believe their luck. We became fodder for their journalist appetites without a chance to respond. My sons at school read of their father's exploits in the daily press.

Convinced of the possibility of a major disruption of life in Britain, I purchased large quantities of emergency food supplies in the form of one thousand cans of cods' roe, a similar quantity of canned rice pudding and three thousand, three hundred pounds of Western Australian honey. I envisioned our family trading these non-perishable staples for other food and necessities.

The cods' roe and the rice pudding I stored in the attic of the family's home in the countryside south of London. I was no longer living at home, but nevertheless my ex-wife was understanding and let me have access to what was now her house for the purpose of saving them all from starvation.

The rice pudding and the cods' roe provided no problem. The honey proved otherwise. When I was completing the purchase deal with a London food broker, I neglected to inquire as to the nature of the packaging of the honey. I assumed the honey would be delivered in one-pound jars. The rice and the roe had come in one-pound cans.

The family attic being full, I persuaded Sally, the owner of the house where I was now ensconced, to allow me to use a section of her basement as a storeroom.

I was still thinking about starting to clear a space in the basement when an eighteen-wheeler appeared at the front gate, disturbing the peace of the neighborhood and provoking the interest of other home owners. Fortunately, Sally was at her yoga class.

"You for the honey?" asked the driver.

"Yes," I said. "But I thought the honey was still on its way from Australia and was not due until the end of the month."

"Well, mate, you thought wrong. It is here. All fifty drums of it."

"What drums?" I asked. "It is supposed to be in one pound jars."

"Well, mate, it isn't. It's in f…heavy drums. Who you got to help?"

"No one," I said.

He looked me up and down. "You used to carrying heavy weights, mate?"

"Well, I don't do it every day," I said.

"Well, you are today," he said. "I'm not helping you. It's against rules. I will move the drums to the tailgate. After that you are on your own. You will have to stack them on the sidewalk. I don't have time to hang around while you carry them into the house."

The drums were yellow. In black lettering was written, "Wild Australian Honey. 66 lbs. net weight." The drums had thin wire handles. I could just manage to walk carrying a drum in each hand. My route took me up the front steps, along a passageway the length of the townhouse and then down the basement stairway. I could not decide which was the most painful, going up the front four steps or down the fifteen basement steps.

My shoulders ached from muscles pulled down by the weight and, in spite of wrapping the thin wire handles with face towels, my fingers felt as though they would be crippled for life.

Sally returned home before I was halfway through.

"What, may I ask, do you think you are doing?"

She did not wait for an explanation. "I am going to meditate in my room. Please do not disturb me."

In selecting the land for my farm, I had four requirements. The land must be accessible by boat. I did not intend to buy a car or a truck. The land must be volcanic and therefore fertile. The land must have an ample source of fresh water. Lastly, the land must be exposed to the prevailing wind.

I let my needs be known in town and soon had many offers of land. At the best of times, land purchase in Bocas is tricky. There are two types of possession, titled land and right of possession land. Most of the land on the islands is owned by right of possession, the right having been granted in the first instance to Panamanians, who have lived and worked the land for a number of years. The right exists for as long as the owner lives on the land and continues to improve it. The current owner can sell rights of possession to the next owner.

"Mister Malcolm, me mom she have finca for sale."

"Where is it?" I asked.

"It's Bastimentos side. It very good finca. Very cheap 'cause we need money now for hospital for me mom."

"How many hectares?" I asked, a hectare being approximately two and a half acres.

"We no know. Maybe one hundred."

"Has it been surveyed?"

"No, we no have money for survey. You get survey."

"You don't have any papers to the land then?"

"No, you help get the papers. We live there so many years. We live and work there. No problem; it our land."

The same piece of land could be offered to you three times in a week, each time by a different person claiming ownership. Many foreigners have bought bargains only later to find the seller had no right to the land. Of course, by then the money paid had long disappeared and there is no practical recourse available to the buyer.

Even if the documents appear correct there is a need to research beyond them. In the past, rights of possession have been issued without true verification of the land's history. Later on, maybe a few years later, after the land has been improved and buildings erected, a more valid owner appears. Then it becomes necessary to either purchase the land a second time or enter into litigation that may take years to resolve.

Faced with this conundrum, I did not expect to resolve my search quickly. However, luck turned my way.

When I backed out of making the purchase on Isla Solarte to avoid ten years of contention, I lost my deposit. The seller was active in wheeling and dealing in Bocas properties and a shrewd businessman whose generosity did not extend to returning deposits, whatever the circumstances. He did, however, have a conscience and a few days later tipped me off about a small farm on the mainland in Laguna Tierra Oscura. The name means Dark Lands Lagoon, although technically it is not a lagoon but a bay formed by the mainland and the south side of Isla Cristobal. A feeling in my gut told me that justice was about to be settled and I hastened to visit it.

I climbed the low bluff from the dock and stood looking back down the three and a half mile length of the bay. I was reminded of a Scottish loch. Somber in the shadow of the surrounding hills, Tierra Oscura is cool and tranquil. I felt the breeze and breathed its clean air. My heart was racing. The land in Tierra Oscura is volcanic. All that remained was to find a water source.

I walked up the gentle slope, pushing through scrub and long grass, passing banana plants, orange and lime trees, and tall pejibaye palms with fruit hanging in clusters beneath their short spiny leaves. There was a single breadfruit tree, a massive mango, whose fruit looked to be more accessible to parrots than man, a water apple tree and a large overgrown area through which poked the spiky leaves of pineapple.

Felipe, the Indian owner, had grown tired of farming and given up on the chore of keeping nature at bay. He no longer lived on the farm, preferring his second home on the other side of the lagoon. A twenty-year veteran of the banana company, he spoke excellent English and had an air of confidence that led me to believe he was of above average potential.

"What sources of water are there?" I asked. I had already seen what appeared to be a spring near the edge of the lagoon.

"Plenty of water, Jefe. There is a river on this side." I noticed he was addressing me as boss and wondered if he was expecting me to employ him.

We made our way to the river that turned out to be small creek forming the boundary with the next-door farm.

"Plenty camerone, Jefe." Felipe used his machete to spear piece of bamboo lying on the creek bed and deftly flicked it on to the bank. Out fell a shrimp the length of my outstretched fingers.

"Very good to eat when smoked," Felipe told me.

By now I was excited. The farm appeared to meet all my needs. It was small, only some ten acres, but the soil around this lagoon is considered among the best in the area. My excitement was further raised by the topography. Most of the land bordering the water in Tierra Oscura is either low lying and swampy or rises steeply, making farming difficult. This land sloped gently down to the lagoon. I knew drainage would be no problem.

I walked to the top end of the property, hacking my way through the scrub, hoping that any snake nearby would slither quickly out of my path. Felipe started to follow until I asked him to leave me on my own.

The property line on the other side was marked by flora de paz (Flowers of Peace, so named because they often grace cemeteries) with distinctive ocher colored leaves. Here, tall trees supported by waist high buttresses reached high into the sky forming a canopy. Beneath the canopy there was much less light and scrub was less dense. I was able to follow the flora de paz back to the edge of the lagoon.

My decision was made. If Felipe did indeed own this farm, I would buy it; and, if he did want to work for me, I would make him the manager.

10

Overheated

Not long after Silvia and Tony sold me the land for the town dock, Tony called in the middle of a hot, dry morning.

"Malcolm. You come here now. You come quick." His need sounded urgent.

"What has happened Tony?"

"They dump rock in the street. You need to move it or it go in the night."

"What rock, Tony?"

"The rock you need for fill the land. The rock you tell me get for you."

"But I only asked you to do that an hour ago. Has it really arrived already?"

"Yes, rock man good friend of mine. What I ask, he do quick."

I had asked for the rock in anticipation that one day we would build a house on the site. In fifteen years' time we might be less enthused about living on Isla Carenero and having to make the crossing to town in all kinds of weather.

A house on our lot would put us within three hundred yards of the bank, the city hall, Don Chicho's, and our two churches. Until our dying days, we could make the necessary journeys without risk to life or limb.

I foresaw the price of rock increasing with the rising demand for construction activity created by the influx of Gringos. Now was the time to prepare the ground.

Armed with a shovel, I arrived to find the rock covering the sidewalk and stretching halfway across the road, hampering traffic. Taking up my shovel, I started to clear the center of the road, throwing rock and heavy clay to the top of the pile.

"What you doing, Mr. Malcolm?" I looked up and through sweat filled eyes saw Small, alias Herman, alias Tim, towering above me.

Small is a powerful, athletic black man worthy of the centerfold of *Playgirl*. A month previous he had built a sea defense of huge rocks along our waterfront on Isla Carenero, picking up rocks five times larger than any I could manage.

60

"Give me that shovel. I do this for you. Where you want the dirt? In the yard?"

"Yes," I said. "I need to get this off the road and sidewalk before tonight."

"No problem, I do it."

"I will help you. I will borrow a shovel from Senor Tony," I said.

I worked alongside Small. My contribution to our joint effort was minuscule compared to what my companion was achieving, and it rapidly exhausted my limited bank of energy. Stupidly, I believed that having committed myself, I could not slack off or take more rests than Small.

Every half hour I slipped into Casa Luck and bought two sodas from Tony.

"You take it easy," Tony said when he caught me wiping sweat from my face with the bottom of my mud-stained shirt. "That is young man's work. You old man like me."

"Tony, it is good for me. I need the exercise," I told him.

It was late in the afternoon when we finished, with Small going solo for the last twenty shovelfuls. We adjourned to Tony's for a final soda and to attend to the matter of pay.

Small left to go home. I stayed to ask Tony's help.

"Tony, I need some of your magic medicine. My back is aching. I dread to think what it will be like in the morning."

Tony handed me a bottle of clear liquid in which a stick floated. "Here, you take it. Have Pat put on your back after you take bath. You keep the bottle."

"What do I owe you for it, Tony?"

"Nuffin. You buy plenty sodas, I give you present."

I was gingerly lowering myself into the boat when Small reappeared.

"Mr. Malcolm, I need you help me. I need you lend me twenty dollars. I go home and my wife she awful sick. I need to take her to Changuinola."

"Oh, I am so sorry. What is wrong?" I asked. "Can you not take her to the emergency room here?"

"She has to go to Changuinola when she sick," he said in an impatient manner, and I realized he was stressed. "I need money for the water taxi and the bus and to stay in the hotel overnight."

I hurriedly handed over twenty dollars.

"Good luck!" I said. "Let me know how she gets on."

I arrived back home to find Pat understandably upset. I had been away for six hours, leaving her trapped on the island.

"Where have you been all this time?" she greeted me.

"Moving a ton of earth off the road."

"What were you doing wearing that shirt? That's the one I gave you."

"I am sorry," I said. "I had to get over there fast."

"Won't you ever learn to use your work shirts? Take it off and give it to me."

I took Pat out to dinner that night at Le Pecado (The Sin) while the shirt soaked in Clorox. Pat's hands smelled like the pump room of a public bath, and I felt doubly guilty and worried about the chemical entering her bloodstream. I thought of telling her once again that the skin is the largest human organ and readily absorbs any toxins that come its way. I decided it was not the occasion to do so.

We were given a table on the balcony, from which we could watch the evening strollers on Calle Rev. Ephraim Alphone.

"Isn't that Small down there?" asked Pat.

"It can't be," I said. "He is in Changuinola with his wife."

"It is him," Pat said in triumph, realizing that I have been duped and not for the first time.

Small was strolling with a girl attached to his arm. He was wearing a Hawaiian style shirt and black jeans. The girl's white blouse contrasted with her black skin. Buttoned low and with the tails tied high beneath her breasts, it was little more than a bra. Her pants were low slung on her hips, and the two of them looked as though they belonged on Rodeo Drive. I was too fascinated to be annoyed.

"Small. He have no wife," Virginia laughed when Pat told her.

"Really, Mister Malcolm. Can I have twenty dollars to take my mom to hospital in Changuinola? You must check with me before you give anything to anyone."

The next morning I awoke with a headache and was unable to stay standing up. I had sunstroke, and for the next three days I stayed on a mattress on the floor of Pat's air-conditioned studio. I listened to her books on tape but could not follow the stories because I kept falling asleep.

"You should never, never drink sodas when you are in the hot sun and working," Arlene, a retired pharmacist, told me.

"Sodas are the very worst thing to drink in those circumstances. You were lucky not to have done permanent damage. Drink only water when expending energy."

That Christmas, Small appeared at our front door with a sad look on his face.

"Small, if you are here to borrow money, I will lend you twenty dollars but only when you have first repaid the twenty you already owe me."

Small smiled, wished Pat and me a happy Christmas and went to call on the folks next door.

11

Julia's Party

Joanne's two sisters, Julia and Sandra are in the choir. They sit in the choir pews in front of Joanne and me. When Mass in the Catholic church is over, Pat comes and joins us. She is usually in time to hear the sermon.

The minister was twenty minutes into the sermon, and my concentration was wandering. I was watching Julia, who was staring at the minister with what appeared to be rapt attention. Her black hair had copper streaks and was neatly arranged in waves, testifying to her skill with rollers.

The choir wore maroon robes that hung tent-like, hiding their Sunday clothes. I had mixed feelings about the robes. Before they were introduced, I could admire the figures of the younger ladies. "After all," I told myself, "there has to be some temptation in order to test my will to resist." On the other hand, the uniformity of the robes added to the effect when the choir swayed side to side to a rousing hymn tune.

I saw Julia steel a glance at her watch and then readjust her concentration. Her sister Sandra is the choir mistress. She was surreptitiously shifting through her music folder in preparation for the choir's weekly performance. She eyed her guitar, eager to be playing the first number. It was time for the minister to conclude. The choir was becoming restless.

The sermon over and the notices read, Sandra came forward and adjusted her music on a stand that Pat had decorated with a floral design.

"Go fish, go fish, go fish on the other side," Sandra led the choir in a favorite song and the choir swayed joyfully. Once again, I regretted losing the name of the evangelist from Roanoke, Virginia, who wrote this song. I wished he could be here to see his work performed with such enthusiasm.

The service over, Pat and I walked up the street to Don Chicho's for our usual Sunday breakfast of dos huevos fritos con tocino (two fried eggs with bacon). Julia joined us at our table.

"What the minister think he do taking so long today I do not know. And me so much to do."

"I thought you were listening to every word," I said.

"No, for sure I no listen to every word. I have to think on my party."

The coming Tuesday was Julia's birthday, and Pat and I were invited.

We walked to Julia's house. We heard the music from two blocks away. The evening was rain free and the party outside beneath palm trees. Already, many people were sitting on metal folding chairs around a large circle of gray concrete.

The music came from a borrowed disco that was being played by one of Julia's sons. Bob Marley was singing "Lively Up Yourself," and the volume was at maximum. Conversation was an effort and, being partially deaf, my reception is intermittent. I wondered what would have happened if it were raining. Julia's home is above the grocery shop she and her husband own and is no more than four small rooms.

Julia, her full body resplendent in white shirt and tight black pants, is dancing with a fellow who drives one of the town's taxis. We made our way to the drinks table, carrying the bottle of Caballito Gin that Julia suggested be our gift. It appeared that everyone had come bearing Caballito Gin. On the concrete beside the table was a cooler filled with bottles of Coke and cartons of milk. I mixed Pat a gin and coke and took a gin and milk for myself.

Tony arrived on his own by taxi, Silvia being in Colon with her sisters. He shuffled up to the drinks table acknowledging greetings. Tony was the only Chinese guest and Pat and I the only Gringos. Everyone else was of African heritage. Armed with his first gin and milk, Tony sat on the other side of Pat.

We watched the dancers. Most were close to our age. They were dancing salsa, moving to the fast beat with effortless grace. They held their upper bodies erect and motionless, moving only their arms and lower body from the hips down.

They appeared to expend no energy, and I recalled how the women of Kenya moved with ease even when carrying heavy loads on their heads. Their gracefulness I attributed to their African genes.

These people first heard salsa and reggae when they were still in the womb. They have danced to its beat since they took their first steps, and they have courted each other to its rhythm. Dance is an integral part of their lives and comes as naturally as breathing.

To dance like these people is the dream of many a Gringo, but few ever achieve it; and, I know that I never could. I have seen tourists make inelegant exhibitions of themselves when Las Brisas Hotel has sponsored the Bastimentos "Beachboys Band" on the hotel verandah.

The Bocatoranians and Gringos come to listen to the band. At the start everyone is standing around drinking beer and being sociable. The dancing will follow later.

Tourists staying at the hotel attend and often become itchy to get the dancing underway. Usually a tourist couple starts swaying where they are standing and then progress to taking small steps. When the locals see this, they make space and turn their attention respectfully to the dancers, who then soon move to the center of the dancing space.

In the belief that they are showing the locals a trick or two, the couple often becomes ever more energetic with swirls and twirls of aerobic caliber, all danced to Latin tempo. Being naturally polite, the Bocatoranians applaud the couple when they eventually take their bows and vacate the floor.

"You no dance?" Tony asked Pat. "Why you no make your husband dance with you?"

"No, he doesn't want to dance with me," Pat said. "He likes to dance with the young chicas with the tight bodies and cute little butts."

"Tony, I cannot dance like these people dance," I told him. "I would look stupid."

"You don't have to dance," Tony agreed, handing me his empty plastic glass, a signal for a refill.

A quartet arrived; a guitar, a sax, a drum and a mouth organ. Their music replaced the disco and the dancing continued.

"Who is that dancing with Julia?" I asked Tony.

"He's her brother. I don't know his name. He's all right. He is a good man. He lives in Old Bank. He do nobody no harm."

I remembered seeing the man before. I had taken visitors over to Isla Bastimentos one Sunday after church and we had set out to walk the concrete pathway that runs the length of the town of Old Bank.

Wooden houses with balconies overlook the path and from one came loud music, so loud that we could hear it long before seeing the house. An old man was dancing on the balcony with a younger woman. We had passed by wondering if this was the continuation of Saturday's party. When we returned an hour later they were still dancing. I had remembered him because his face had shown his absolute joy of dancing.

Pat and I were wondering when the food was going to arrive. We had been there for two hours, and the gin was beginning to get to me when Julia grabbed my arm and pulled me to my feet.

I found myself in the center of the circle. Everyone was clapping.

"Go on, Senor Malc," someone called.

I have seen the photographs of that dance. Julia and I are bumping each other with our backsides, our arms high in the air. The scene is totally lacking in grace. True to their good manners though, Julia and I had been given a raucous applause.

Pat, Tony and I left the party after my exhibition. There was word that the food would soon arrive, but we had heard that more than an hour ago and by then I needed some solids to counter the Caballito.

That day was a Tuesday. The party eventually ended at 7 a.m. on Friday.

PART II
The Challenges

12

The Farm Begins

I named the farm Finca Tranquilla, Tranquil Farm. The name speaks of how I wished life at the farm to one day become, but first there was a great deal of work to do.

"Jefe, the finca needs plenty work." Felipe was envisioning an army of men under his command. "I need plenty time to clear the jungle."

We were sitting in his wooden house on the other side of the lagoon. He had given me the seat of honor, an armchair of Victorian era, probably discarded from the home of a banana company executive. I suspected its springs had given out before it came into Felipe's possession.

I would have rather been sitting on the wooden crate occupied by Felipe. The crate had height advantage. I leaned back to establish the relaxed, in control posture of a boss. The back creaked ominously, and I quickly sat upright and shifted my weight to the front edge of the chair.

"When did you let the jungle take over the farm?" I needed to put Felipe on the defensive.

"Not long, Jefe. It not my fault I no keep the farm clean. I have plenty problem with them." Felipe gestured with his head to Dilma, his wife; Berta, his daughter; and Ricardo, Berta's husband.

Dilma was at the charcoal fire that smoldered in an extension to the one-room house. She had a gentle face with a sloping forehead and a friendly smile. She was considerably overweight from a diet predominantly consisting of plantains, yucca and dachin. Ricardo, Berta and a child stood in the shadows looking on. Dilma and Berta did not speak English. Ricardo did, but Felipe appeared not to mind him hearing where the blame was being placed.

"He drinks plenty and no work. He goes to Changuinola and he no come back for days, and when he does he's drunk," Felipe told me in a confidential manner, establishing a separation between the two of us and his son-in-law.

"How will we get the farm cleaned up?" I asked.

"I will need six men for a week," Felipe told me.

"That makes seven of you. Not counting Sunday, that means forty-two man-days. It's too much. I will have to talk with Senor Dave."

At the mention of Dave Cerutti's name, a troubled look clouded Felipe's face. Dave Cerutti and his wife Linda live at the far end of the next-door lagoon. They were then the only Gringos living permanently in either of the lagoons. Tobe, a West Indian, assists Dave in the management of his finca. Tobe has a reputation for being a shrewd manager.

"Jefe, how about three men then," Felipe offered.

"Two and you."

Felipe smiled, "Jefe, you are a hard man. How you expect me to supervise the men and work?"

"Easy. You work alongside them."

"Who do the other things that need be done?"

"What other things?"

"Fishing. How I feed my family if I no fish? You no want we go hungry?"

"Felipe, I am paying you to work eight hours a day. You fish in the evening or send Ricardo or Berta to fish."

We settled on two extra men for a week.

"Jefe, I need three machetes and a box of files to sharpen the machetes."

"Fine!" I said. "I will buy them at the Cooprativa and bring them in the morning."

"Jefe, I need money for gas."

"Why?"

Again the patient smile that was intended to make me realize how little I know about farming.

"Jefe, I have to go look for the two men."

I parted with ten dollars for gas, telling Felipe to be sure to get me a receipt.

"Jefe, I need boots. You bring me boots tomorrow?"

Felipe explained to me that it is customary for Jefes to provide boots for their fulltime workers. While I am considering this, he signaled to Dilma and she came forward with a smoked fish.

"Jefe, you eat. Dilma, she make very good smoke fish especially for you."

I picked the fish up with my fingers. It was hot to hold. I carefully bit into its side. Felipe was right, it was delicious. I signaled my appreciation to Dilma. Her fat face assumed a modest smile.

"What size boots?" I asked.

"Seven," said Felipe with a look of triumph.

"Jefe, you please bring us rice and tins of tuna when you come tomorrow. We short of food till you pay me. I then repay you."

"Why tuna? There are plenty of fish in the lagoon."

"Berta prefer tuna," Felipe said and then asked, "You like Dilma's fish?"

"Yes, it is excellent."

"I give you two fish to take. One for you and one for your lady."

"Thank you," I said.

"Jefe, you lend me ten dollars now and I repay you?"

I handed over ten dollars and decided it was high time to leave. As I headed the boat out of the lagoon, I looked back to Felipe's house. The four of them were standing on their little dock watching me. I waved and they waved backed.

"What are they saying?" I wondered.

I had an uneasy feeling they were celebrating the dawn of a new era, one in which they will be well looked after. I thought, provided Felipe does a good job of taking care of the farm, it will be worth it. Then, I realized I forgot to ask for a receipt for the ten dollars cash advance.

13

The Funeral

A bell was tolling. I tried not to hear it. It was the middle of the night, and I did not want to wake.

I had heard it before, half a century ago in the approach to the harbor of Hong Kong. I was half awake but trying to cling to sleep. I remembered the fog had been so dense we could not see from one side of the liner to other. We were creeping along, our engines barely audible. The bell had sounded again, closer this time. A deep melancholy cry, made menacing by its obscurity.

I heard Pat's voice, "I wonder who died?"

I lost my grip on sleep and was pulled from the ship's rail.

"What are you talking about?" I asked, and then hearing the bell again, I added, "What time is it?"

"Almost three."

"It must be a Catholic," I said. "We did not have anyone due to die."

Tony opens his shop precisely at 8 a.m., and soon after I visited him, curious to hear who had died.

"Amando, the undertaker," the Chinaman told me. "It's no problem. He make his own coffin before he die."

"When?" I asked Tony.

"He die this morning. You no hear the bell?"

"No, Tony, I meant when did he make his coffin."

"I don't know, sometime before he die. Maybe last week, maybe before. His funeral Sunday after Catholic Church finish. He alright man," Tony added. "He leave no debt."

Neither Pat nor I knew Amando, and we did not attend his funeral.

The next week the bell tolled again. Senor Lancelot Adolfo Samms Navaro, a much-loved Methodist had died at age 94. His funeral was delayed eight days so the Reverend G. Santiago Samms, Adolfo's son, could leave his parish in Detroit,

Michigan, and travel here to conduct the service. Our own minister, the Reverend Theophilus Lewis, assisted him.

We sat wedged buttock to buttock. Ushers kept adding one more to the end of our pew, and we pressed ever tighter. Joanne and I were in the fourth row. The rows in front of us were occupied by Adolfo's surviving relatives who included eleven of his twelve children, thirty-five grandchildren, and numerous great-grandchildren.

The six fans hanging from the tin roof could not handle the heat rising from so many bodies. I had forgotten my handkerchief, and Joanne offered me the face towel she carries in her purse. We shared the towel to mop our foreheads. I looked around. The sides and the back of the church were packed with standing men, women and children. No air could pass through the windows. I was thankful the walls were made of concrete and the risk of fire was minimal. Escape would have been impossible.

I read in the service sheet that Adolfo, who was a carpenter, "was the second of ten children." One brother and two sisters were alive, and four sisters and two brothers were deceased. I point this fact out to Joanne.

"He was a good, clean-living man, and the Lord gave him a good, long life," Joanne told me.

We sang, "What a Friend We Have in Jesus," "Amazing Grace," and "How Great Thou Art." We alternated singing in English and Spanish, verse by verse. Between singing, relatives and close friends came forward to tell what Adolfo had been to them.

The service over, we slowly exited to the street. Members of the Bomberos band were formed up in front of a four-wheeled wooden cart. The Bomberos in their red and white uniforms contrasted with the predominantly black dress of the mourners.

With Adolfo's coffin safely transferred to the cart, we set off on the mile-long walk to the cemetery, the two ministers leading the procession, followed by the Bomberos, the cart carrying the coffin pulled by six of Adolfo's male descendants, Adolfo's family and then the rest of us. The last group was those who, with a mind to the return to town, were pushing their bicycles. The procession filled the whole street and stretched back a quarter of a mile.

The beat of the base drum set the pace. We moved off so slowly that we trod on the heels of the people in front as others behind pushed forward.

"Lo siento, lo siento," we keep apologizing. The midday sun beat down on us. The wise had umbrellas and carried bottled water. In keeping with the Bocatoranian's tradition of sharing, I was offered both shade and water.

By the halfway mark, the tempo had picked up. The band members no longer able to restrain their natural love of rhythm and movement, the music became more joyous and we soon were swinging into the cemetery and passing down the lines of white painted tombstones and mausoleums.

After the interment, a repast was held at the family residence.

For many of the Caribbean Bocatoranians, a second post funeral gathering takes place on the ninth night after the passing. It was on the ninth day after his death that Jesus appeared to his disciples, and many Afro-Antilleans pay respect to the significance with a gathering that they call The Nine Night. What happens that night varies according to the dictates of the bereaved family. Some Nine Nights are reverent and respectful, with prayers and the singing of the deceased's favorite hymns. Others celebrate the deceased's parting with liberal quantities of alcohol, loud games of dominos and draughts, and much good humor.

It is claimed by some champions of the latter that, given a sufficiency of Caballito, the deceased appears to his friends sometime before the new dawn. Those attending The Nine Night are often of the opinion that they are excused from going to work the next day.

I remembered my Uncle Alistair's cremation at a church in North London. The music was canned, and the minister officiating spoke meaninglessly about a person he had never seen alive. We were herded in and out of the chapel like sheep being put through the dip.

I decided to alter my will. My funeral will be in Bocas. As to The Nine Night, I hope that my survivors will compromise and start quietly for the sake of the likes of Joanne and then, after she has retired, bring out the gin.

14

Tony in Hospital

"Torijos put me in jail ten times," Tony said, sitting on the side of his hospital bed, his swollen feet resting on the floor.

"That was before he became dictator. He was head of police in Colon. He was a gentleman. He never beat me up."

"What did you do to cause him to put you in jail?" I asked.

"I the leader of a gang of fifty. We not criminals. We political." Tony was looking serious as he remembered those years when as a thirty-year-old living in Colon City, he was labeled a Communist.

"The rich landowners pay the women one dollar a day to break coconut husks to make oil. One dollar a day not enough to live on. We go to the farms and burn the buildings."

"But that was criminal, Tony!" I protested.

"Not if they no prove it," said Tony.

"They take me to jail but they have no witness. The judge say, 'Take it easy, Tony,' then after a few days, they let me go. One time I in jail on December 24. I worried because my family have nothing for Christmas, but the judge, he let me go."

"Tony, your life must have been in danger," I said.

"Maybe, but maybe no. I had big shot friends in Panama City. In Colon, police make it so no one give me job. I go to Panama City and speak to my big shot friends. They go Colon and say, 'How come you make it hard on Tony?' The police say, 'We did not know Tony your friend.' Then I get work.

"Later, when Torijos President, he come to Bocas. Everyone want to speak with him, but he no have time. Then when he pass by my shop, he see me sweeping the street and he say, 'Hello, Tony!' He remember me. We were good friends. He a gentleman, not like Noriega."

Two mornings ago, Tony fell to the floor and could not get back on his feet. Silvia rushed him to the emergency room. His blood pressure was dangerously high, and his feet were swollen like pumpkins.

It was still high. Silvia was sitting in the wheelchair used to move Tony to the bathroom, while Pat and I were on the empty bed beside him.

The room had long been in need of renovation. The floor tiles were cracked and the walls, once yellow, had aged with grime. A pane was missing from the jalousied windows, giving the nighttime mosquitoes easy access. There were none of the luxuries of a North American hospital; no phone, no television, no radio, no button to push in an emergency.

"Tony, how is the food?" I asked.

"The food is shit," said Tony. "I no eat."

"We'll bring you food," said Pat. "What would you like?"

"They no let you bring food from outside," Silvia said. "Tony on diet. Too much fluid in his body."

"When you come next, bring more toilet paper. I had to give the old man some." Tony was referring to the man who had been his neighbor 'til this morning. The hospital does not provide toilet paper, soap, pillows or mosquito repellent.

The sound of a man singing came from the end of the passage. We heard nurses reprimanding the singer. The commotion approached. A drunk supported by a nurse on either side was maneuvered into the room. He was still in full song. The nurses lowered him onto the furthest of the three beds.

Looking around, the drunk spied Tony.

"Hey, Chino, look at me," he was waving at Tony.

Tony ignored him.

"What happen, Chino? Why you no speak to me? You don't like me?"

"Who is he?" I asked Tony.

"He no good," said Tony. "He no problem."

The visiting hour was coming to an end. We were loath to leave Tony there, but Silvia assured us he would be all right.

"I'll be okay," said Tony. "The nurses take good care of me. They are very kind. When I fall this morning, ten of them pick me up."

Tony chuckled at the happy thought. It might well take ten nurses to lift Tony off the floor. I knew what it was like trying to lift his bulk. When we had returned from a ride in my boat, Tony got out of the boat by crawling on his hands and knees. Getting him back onto his feet was a considerable challenge for two strong men.

15

First Night at the Farm

Felipe's first months managing the farm went well. Once the initial clearing of the scrub was completed, he kept the farm clean with occasional help from Ricardo.

At that stage, calling the property a farm was a misnomer because, apart from a couple of sacks of cacao beans, a few bunches of bananas and the produce of eight orange trees, we had nothing to sell. It was clear that it would take a few years to get the farm to the point of being self-sufficient.

Having returned to Bocas ahead of Pat, I decided that it was time for me to spend a night or two sleeping at the farm. There was a two-roomed native house. It had a palm frond roof and a porch.

"I am going to spend the night in a hammock on your porch," I told Felipe.

"I stay with you tonight," Felipe announced.

"You don't stay here every night?" I asked, surprised.

"No, Jefe. I spend night with my family."

"Then who stays on the farm at night?"

"I do," Felipe said, without showing any recognition of his inconsistency.

I gave up for the moment. It could wait until evening when we would be sitting on the porch.

It gets dark quickly in Laguna Tierra Oscura. No sooner was it fully dark then the still of the night was shattered by a croaking as loud as the roar of a lion.

"What the hell is that?" I jumped up from the crate I was sitting on and peered into the darkness.

Felipe's answer was drowned by croaking from all around. That first croak had been the signal for every toad in the neighborhood to join in. The combined croaking shut out all other night noises.

I had with me a battery lamp, one of those you charge up at home and it lasts for about four hours. I turned on the lamp, and five minutes later the glass was thick with insects. I turned it off and in the dark attempted to arrange my mosquito net over the hammock. I groped to find matches, lit a propane gas cooker and opened a tin of soup. I knew Felipe was watching me.

"Like some soup, Felipe?" I asked, hoping he would say no.

"If Jefe pleases, I have soup."

I poured the soup into two mugs trying to ensure equal parts by measuring with a finger.

I had some ginger snaps but not enough to share. I opened the packet as quietly as possible under cover of talking to Felipe.

"The breeze is gone. It is hotter than I had expected." I could feel rivers of sweat running down my chest and forming a damp band at my waist.

"Hot night, no rain for sure, Jefe."

I dunked a ginger snap in my soup, put it in my mouth and mashed it with my tongue before swallowing quietly.

Felipe got up and went to the steps that lead down from the porch.

"Where are you going?" I asked.

"I be back, Jefe."

In the darkness, I heard him start the motor of his cayucu and head in the direction of his house and Dilma.

I found the hammock less than comfortable, and I wondered if my back would survive the night. The air under the mosquito net felt close to boiling. I discarded the net and lit an insect repellant coil.

I looked at my watch. It was barely past eight o'clock. There was nothing to do but listen to the croaking toads and wait for Felipe to return. I strained to hear the sound of his engine over the croaking but instead heard other noises.

I thought I heard voices, and I feared unwanted visitors. I had no gun and no dog and would be utterly at the mercy of robbers. I was the only foreigner and white man on the lagoon. The nearest neighbors would never hear my cry.

The hour to nine o'clock was incredibly long. I consoled myself with an assurance that Felipe would be back. When still he did not show, I began to wonder if he, too, feared night visitors and had abandoned me. Then, my imagination took a turn for the worse, and I started thinking that he could have set me up to be robbed by others.

With this thought in mind, I moved a table and some wooden crates to block the entrance and transferred my hammock to the far end of the porch, where I would be out of machete reach. I lay in the hammock clutching my own machete.

I decided that if robbers came, I would tell them to take whatever they wanted. I would be generous and ingratiating and offer no resistance. What chance would I have wielding my machete against men of such strength, armed with machetes honed to a razor's edge? I also decided that if I lived through the night I would not stay at the finca again until I had dogs, a gun and a trusted friend who would not desert me as soon as supper was over.

It was half past ten when the croaking stopped. I know, because all evening long I was checking my watch, counting down the hours 'til dawn. It stopped as suddenly as it began. One moment it was there, and the next there was total silence.

Is there something or somebody out there that caused the toads to give up? I wondered. I slid out of my hammock and stared into the darkness. Nothing moved. There was not a sound. I coughed to see if perhaps deafness had suddenly befallen me. My cough rang out into the night and I imagined watching eyes.

Then I felt ashamed. Is this the way of a man who is seeking enlightenment? Would the Dali Lama have behaved like this? I thought again about fear and examined its futility. Given the situation and my inability to escape, the feeling of fear contributed nothing to whatever might be my fate. I started to relax.

With nerves steadied, I felt better able to cope with the remaining hours of darkness. I half slept, but still each sound, real or imagined, quickened my heartbeat. I told myself the grunts and bumps were the noises of anteaters, raccoons and other night hunters, but I was never quite sure.

At the first light of dawn, I removed my defenses and stretched out, not in the hammock but on the cardboard Felipe had spread on the floor for his own bed. It was there that Felipe found me when, promptly at seven, he arrived to start the day's work.

"You sleep good, Jefe?"

"Of course, but where were you?"

"I had problem, Jefe."

"What problem?"

"Problem gone away, Jefe. No matter now. Plenty work to do, Jefe. You like I start now, or we have breakfast?"

"You start now," I said emphatically.

I boiled water to shave and make coffee and after shaving put my washing things into my pack. There was no way I was going to stay another night.

16

Felipe Goes Astray

Berta was pregnant, very much so from the look of it. She was fifteen years old. It is not unusual for Indian girls to be having babies by then. Without electricity, there is no television; and, without television, what else is there to do to relieve the boredom of twelve hours of tropical night?

I used to down-cry television as being another of the capitalist curses foisted on the third world, along with Coca-Cola and McDonald's.

Our second Christmas in Panama, I paid to have Ramon's house connected to the electric supply. I had decided to do this after watching the children huddle over a kerosene lamp, doing their homework and breathing in fumes.

I thought having electric light would benefit their health and make studying less of a hassle. How mistaken I was! One week later, Ramon had acquired a television set and their single-roomed house became completely dominated by the visions and sounds of another world, one that was often portrayed as extremely violent. The environment for homework deteriorated.

Now, I am close to advocating electricity and television for every family instead of providing free condoms that are seldom used in the heat of the moment.

In Berta's case, she had a husband. The term husband does not necessarily mean that there has been a wedding or any other form of contractual arrangement. A couple is recognized as man and wife when they become exclusive to each other and live in the same household. Husbands come and go with little ceremony, often dodging paying child maintenance. This is a reason why the extended family is of vital importance.

"When will the baby arrive?" I asked Berta.

Without looking up, she had raised and lowered her shoulders. I took it she did not know.

"Next week," said Dilma, and again Berta shrugged as if in disagreement with her mother.

Six weeks later, Berta was still lying in the hammock, bigger than ever and breathing heavily. I wondered how many babies might be inside her.

"She go to doctor in Changuinola tomorrow," announced Felipe. "Last time she saw doctor, doctor say if baby no come soon, he cut her open."

"Who will take her?" I asked.

"Ricardo and Dilma take her. I stay here for finca."

I was relieved. Each time I had seen Berta these past few weeks, I had feared being incorporated into a birthing team.

With Berta safely in Changuinola, along with her husband and her mother, and with Felipe looking after the farm, Pat and I returned to the States for two months. Through Virginia I heard that Berta's child had been born dead and that because of complications associated with the birth the three of them had delayed returning to the lagoon.

I was approaching the finca by boat on my first day back, when I saw three figures waving from the dock in front of Felipe's house. I waved back and continued on my way but, when I looked again, the waving had become frantic and I changed course.

As I neared the house, Dilma and Berta turned away and entered the house. Ricardo remained on the dock, waiting to help me tie up the boat.

"Everything okay?" I asked.

Ricardo did not reply.

"I am sorry about the baby. Is Berta okay now?"

"Berta okay. Dilma not," Ricardo informed me.

Inside the house, Dilma was seated across a hammock, legs either side, feet on the floor. She was crying.

"What happened?" I asked.

"Felipe very bad man," Berta was shouting.

There was a long silence while we all listened to Dilma sobbing loudly. Berta took on the expression of an angered voodoo doll, her face tormented with hate. Ricardo kept his face turned to the floor.

"What has Felipe done?" I asked.

"He said we not go to farm. He never want to see us there again," said Berta "Why?"

"You ask him why," said Berta.

I could get no further words out of her. Dilma notched up the sobbing a couple of decibels, and Ricardo continued his non-participation stance.

"I am going to speak to Felipe," I announced and left to find him.

The farm was deserted and "dirty" as Virginia would say, meaning that the grass was overgrown and the scrub trees were already beginning to reappear. It was not long before Felipe arrived, paddling his canoe from the direction of another Indian home.

"Buenos dias, Jefe," Felipe said, all smiles as if he was certain I was pleased with his work of the past two months. "I saw you come and I come immediately."

"Felipe, what is going on?" I asked. "Why have you told Dilma and the others they cannot come to the finca?"

"That their decision, Jefe. Not mine."

"What do you mean?"

"Dilma say she no come to finca, and Berta and Ricardo say if Dilma no come, they no come."

"I don't understand. And why is the farm such a mess?"

"I do my best, Jefe. Ooh, I do my best. Plenty, plenty rain, Jefe. Never been such rain. All day rain."

"But the rain does not stop you from cleaning the finca. That is no excuse."

"Only me here, Jefe. Ricardo not work here any more. Rain make grass grow plenty fast. You hard man, Jefe. If you no like my work, you tell me go."

"Oh, yes," I said, "and you will be off to the labor department in Changuinola claiming I fired you without warning when your family is sick and you only are here to work. I would have to take you back and pay a fine."

"I no do that, Jefe. You like father to me."

"Oh, yes, I know all that stuff and Dilma also thinks the same way. I want to get to the bottom of this. I am going back to speak with Dilma and the others."

"Okay, Jefe. I tell you they make trouble."

Felipe helped me untie my boat and watched as I set off back across the lagoon.

"Felipe says it is Dilma who says she will not go to the finca."

Berta translated for her mother, and Dilma let out a wail. This time Ricardo spoke up, "Felipe, he have new woman," he said angrily. "Dilma says she no go to finca until new woman is gone."

"But how can he do this? This is his family."

No one chose to answer, and so I left to return to the finca and Felipe.

"Jefe, I had problem." The two of us were sitting face to face, either side of the picnic-style table on the knoll in front of the little house.

"Tell me all, Felipe," I said in the same consoling voice I would use were he one of my sons. "You can tell me what happened."

"Jefe, Dilma, Berta and Ricardo, they all left me and go to Changuinola. I all alone on finca here for you, Jefe. They no come back. They stay in Changuinola many days, many nights." He stopped, uncertain whether he had to explain further.

"Yes, go on. What happened?"

"One night come woman to see me. What could I to do, Jefe? In night she come all alone, Jefe."

"What did you do, Felipe?"

"I look after woman, Jefe."

"Well, that does not mean you have to desert your family. They are your responsibility."

"New woman my responsibility now," said Felipe.

I had to call a time out. I needed to consider the facts and the options open to me. What right did I have to tell Felipe to whom he should give his attentions? What was in the best interests of the farm? How would the other three survive if they did not have access to the farm and its products? Who would employ Ricardo? Who would provide for the still recovering Berta?

"Felipe, this is my decision," I said. "You will please tell your new lady she is not to come to the farm. Because you are no longer living on the farm, Ricardo and Berta can live in the house. You will still be responsible for the maintenance of the farm, and Ricardo will work under you."

"Whatever you say. You the Jefe," Felipe replied.

17

The Plane Crash

Before I tell you about the plane accident, I need to make you aware that no account of a happening in Bocas is ever limited to the truth. Bocatoranians of all origins delight in storytelling; and, if there is a bone of truth, it is soon fleshed out into a matter of great interest, worthy of being told over and over until it becomes part of the folklore. Such is the account of the plane crash.

I am telling the story just as it was told to me the day after the event. I have no doubt it is exaggerated. I am a friend and admirer of the Bomberos whose contribution to Bocas is much more than putting out fires.

A plane belonging to one of the two airlines that serves Bocas was coming in to land on a clear, sunny morning on which nothing should have gone wrong. Among the passengers was a man with a broken leg. He was nervous about anything happening to further hurt his leg; and, out of respect for his concern, he was seated in the front row where no one would have to climb over his outstretched limb.

On the plane was an architect from England, a man of considerable enterprise and a born leader.

As the pilot put the wheels of the plane on the tarmac, he saw a figure on the runway taking pictures of the landing. He swerved to avoid hitting the photographer and in so doing took the plane off the tarmac and into the banana plants that flanked the runway. The plane came to a sudden halt amid the bananas.

There were a few moments of inaction within the plane while the passengers took stock of this unusual happening. It was the architect who then took command. Going to the front of the plane, he opened the door to the cockpit. Inside, the pilot and co-pilot were writing reports on the accident.

"Hadn't we better get the passengers off before the plane catches fire?" is what I am told the architect said.

The pilots agreed this was a good idea but, being more concerned about who would be blamed, continued to complete their reports.

The architect decided it was up to him to organize the evacuation and led the way by opening the escape hatch and walking out onto the wing. From there he jumped to the ground and sank knee deep into the mud. As the other passengers followed, he directed them to continue down the wing until they were able to land on firm ground. Everyone exited except the two pilots and the passenger with the broken leg, who was left still sitting in the front seat.

Meanwhile, there was a high level of activity at the Bomberos station. The news of the plane crash exceeded in importance any emergency call since the earthquake of 1991. All present at the station rushed to the fire truck, impatient to be in action, but first the driver had to find his keys. After some moments, everyone dismounted and went to join the search.

As the story goes, the driver found his keys, climbed back into the seat and sped out of the station and onto Avenida Luis Russell, the road heading for the airport, unaware that the other firemen were still searching the station. He arrived at the airport with the truck, but no companions. He was reversing the truck, ready to go back to the station, when the rest of the crew arrived by taxis.

Positioned close to the plane, the firemen rolled out the hose and held the nozzle pointed at their target. The signal was given for the water to flow.

Nothing happened. No water came gushing out. The firemen put down the hose and everyone went back to the truck to see what was wrong. It was then the water came full force out of the nozzle whirling the hose around and spraying in all directions.

At what point the man with the broken leg and the pilots left the plane has never been made clear to me.

It was the Bomberos who evacuated Ray Kennedy from Isla Carenero on each occasion when he threw his hip out. Ray has told how their skill and gentleness in moving him in and out of their evacuation launch was far superior to his experiences of ambulance service in the States.

The Bomberos are currently in the process of organizing a club for the teenagers of Bocas, a much-needed asset in this town that has no permanent social facility for the young.

18

Enlarging the Farm

"If I were you, I would buy it," advised Pat, who was talking about a supposed fifteen acres adjoining the finca. I had heard that day it was for sale.

"I don't need any more land. I have enough already, and more land means more workers."

"You'll regret it if you don't. You don't know who you'll get as neighbors, and the boundary is very close to where you will build a house."

"I haven't decided where I will build a house," I said, not liking being told what to do with my project.

Pat and I are both strong willed, and neither of us will allow the other to become the dominant partner. This is why we have separate ownership of property and separate bank accounts.

Until my costs in Panama dictated I sell my cottage in Peary, the fishing hamlet on the Chesapeake Bay, we were a source of continual interest to the other hundred residents. What was until then my waterman's cottage, was on the east side of a spit of land and looked out to the Bay. Pat's cottage and studio were three hundred yards away, facing westwards onto a broad tidal creek.

Our neighbors, not realizing that we slept together in one or other of the cottages, usually Pat's, found our separated living most peculiar and anticipated a divorce. Pat was the frequent beneficiary of fresh fish and vegetables, gifts from interested watermen. Nothing ever came my way, but since we not only slept together but also ate together, that did not trouble me.

"It's up to you. It's your farm. If it were mine, I would buy the extra land."

I waited a day and then bought the land. I had it surveyed after agreeing to the purchase. The survey showed eight and not fifteen acres.

"I bought that extra land," I told Pat.

"I told you to," she reminded me.

"Well, I did it because I suddenly saw a use for it. I am going to plant hardwood trees and do my own bit to redress the loss of forest. Before this idea came to me, I did not see how I could make use of the extra land."

I walked the new finca with Felipe. Apart from some tall balsa and a few hundred cacao with their pods of chocolate beans, there were no trees of merit. With the scrub cleared, there would be space for planting hardwood seedlings.

"Felipe, I have to leave tomorrow for the United States. I want you to hire two men for a week and get all the scrub cut out," I told him.

"Jefe, you have good holiday. You no worry; I run the farm for you good."

"When I come back, we will buy seedling trees. How many trees do you think we can plant on this new land?"

"Three hundred," said Felipe quickly.

"I think many more. We will start with three hundred and then see where we go from there."

"Jefe, you bring back a watch for me?"

"Maybe, Felipe. If I do, I will not give it to you until I see what you have achieved in my absence."

On my return to the farm a month later, Felipe, Ricardo and I debated whether to plant only teak trees or a mix on the new acreage.

Clearing land and planting rows of teak trees could be highly profitable. In Panama's humid climate with its high rainfall and strong sun, teak grows rapidly. Some claim you can harvest the trees ten years after planting the seedlings. There are others who question the quality of teak grown on the Bocas side of the mountain.

"Not a good idea, Jefe," said Felipe.

Ricardo nodded in agreement.

Felipe explained, "Teak tree not from Panama. It come from other country. Plant only teak trees and disease come and trees be sick. Better you plant mix: six teak, six cedro, six criolo, six roble and then same again. That way if teak disease come it no spread far."

I had respect for Indian advice. Their knowledge carries the experience of their forefathers, who lived in harmony with nature. Their survival was dependent on understanding Nature's ways and her cures.

"The teak tree very hard on land. Take too much from land. After, land no good for other plants," Ricardo added.

"I have heard it said that the trees are not liked by birds," I said. "They do not provide food for birds, and their leaves do not provide protection from hawks."

"That is right, Jefe. We no want many teak trees," concluded Felipe.

We jointly decided to purchase a mix of hardwood seedlings and plant them in scattered groupings of different types. This would not make the money a successful, disease-free teak plantation would make, but at my age that is not so important. More important was to avoid the disappointment of ten years later seeing rows of diseased trees.

This decision meant we did not need to cut the existing lumber and instead could plant our seedlings in the areas between. The whole effect would be more attractive than regimented lines of the same size teak.

"Ricardo go with you, Jefe, to Changuinola for buy trees. I stay here and make holes for planting," Felipe directed.

Ricardo was decked out in his best: floral shirt, pressed blue pants, and leather formal shoes shined to perfection. I was in my working clothes: khaki shirt and pants, washed but not pressed, and farm boots whose shine left a lot to be desired.

It took us thirty minutes to reach Almirante by boat. Over the last mile, I turned back the throttle to reduce our wake. On either side there were low, wooden buildings barely a foot above sea level. Old men and children leaned out of glassless windows to wave. Very young-looking girls paddled wooden canoes with still younger children peering over the rails. Faces were wreathed in smiles.

To the right, the buildings formed a continuous frontage. There were several that housed small businesses repairing boats or selling gasoline, fish, or dry and tin foods and basic household needs.

On the left were the recently constructed shacks of squatters who had cleared spaces amongst the mangroves and built on stilts. Their homes were connected to firm land by flimsy looking walkways.

Discarded plastic bottles of many colors; soggy, rotting clothing; old sneakers; and beer cans littered the water's edge or floated, drifting with the tide and pushed here and there by the wake of the water taxis. It was the debris of every developing country in a time when money is better spent on medical services and education rather than the niceties of the surroundings.

I brought the boat to a halt alongside one of the stores and, leaving Ricardo to do the mooring, paid my respects to the owner, a happy, gracious lady not much younger than me.

"How everything down Dark Lands then?" she asked.

"Fine," I said.

"When did you last visit your finca?" I asked her.

She had told me that her family had a finca in the lagoon, but I had never been able to get from her exactly where.

The word family is used in its most extended sense in Bocas, where siblings often have different fathers and every one seems to be a cousin.

The greeting "Que pasa, primo?" (How goes it, cousin?) is used liberally and not restricted to blood relatives. If you like someone sufficiently to warrant inclusion as family, you use the title primo or prima, according to their sex. Virginia is "prima" to Pat and me.

"No, me no go. Me plenty business attend here," she answered my question.

I wondered about this, because I had never noticed any transactions in her store other than children spending my shoeshine money on candies or a soda. However, she seemed content to pass her days, watching the comings and goings of the water traffic and chatting with those who have an hour or two to pass.

"Where you now go, then?" she asked.

"To Changuinola to buy some trees."

"Oh, that is nice."

"Okay if I leave the boat with you for a few hours?"

"Sure, I look after boat for you. Put the gas tank under de counter."

Ricardo found us a pick-up taxi and sat in the front. The taxi driver was curious as to why this smartly dressed Indian and this scruffy old Gringo were traveling together. He kept turning to look at Ricardo as he drove the roller coaster road through the foothills that separate Almirante from Changuinola.

I tried not to be concerned about the driver and told myself he probably made this journey several times a week and the chances of his having an accident this day were slim. Nevertheless, I was thankful to be in the back.

We stopped three times to pick up extra passengers and soon were filled to capacity. A young Indian girl was sitting next to me, nursing her baby. She might have been twelve years old. She was proud of her child and kept looking up to make sure I was still watching. She had an innocent, trusting smile, and I was afraid she was going to ask me to become a godfather.

I turned my attention to the other side and studied the passing countryside of lush, green vegetation that will be there as long as Panama keeps its forests. I thought of Africa and the young mothers who cradle starving children in their own emaciated arms. I remembered standing on the equator in Kenya more than forty years ago and lamenting the demise of its equatorial forests and the subsequent parching of the land.

Ricardo was enjoying his status up front. I was glad, believing that this would enhance his enthusiasm for the finca and the advantages it brings him.

Before reaching the outskirts of Changuinola, we crossed the iron bridge that carries the road and rail traffic high across the Changuinola River. It is single line only, with the rail tracks down the middle and on either side, unsecured planks of heavy lumber for the wheels of the cars and trucks. For much of the way, there were low guardrails on the outside but in places there were none. The first time you cross, it is scary if you have my form of imagination, but by now I was immune, well almost, to apprehension when crossing.

At the tree farm, I continued to let Ricardo take the lead. We had a general look at all that was available before discussing the quantities to purchase of each species. After these decisions were agreed, I left it to Ricardo to select the individual trees, examining each as to its condition. The seedlings cost thirty cents each, and I gave Ricardo the money to complete the deal.

Back in Almirante with three hundred little trees in six cartons, each seedling in its black plastic wrap, I handed Ricardo the money to pay the driver, telling him what tip to give. While he attended to this, I loaded the boat under the watchful eyes of the storekeeper.

"Before we leave, we are going to get some lunch. What can we bring you?" I asked.

"Fried chicken would do me well, thank you," she said.

Ricardo and I sat on the terrace of a small restaurant beside a dusty road. A low wall separated us from the traffic. We both ordered sancocho, the typical Panamanian lunchtime meal of chicken broth, meat scraps, yucca and dachen.

"What will you have to drink?" I asked Ricardo, remembering Felipe telling me that he had given up alcohol.

"Beer," said Ricardo.

We ate in silence, neither of us knowing the other's language well enough to make conversation easy.

Before we had finished the sancocho, Ricardo had signaled for more beer. He reached for his leather wallet, making it clear he had the money to pay and that he was treating his Gringo companion. I declined, but watched with concern as he dispatched the second beer without seeming to taste it. I settled our bill, which came to a total of three dollars, including paying for the chicken take out.

"We need to get going fast," I told Ricardo.

We delivered the chicken and bought from the lady a Coca-Cola and some crackers for Berta. I had my shoes cleaned, and the shoeshine boy bought a Coke.

Back at the farm, we placed the trees in the shade and gave them a good watering. Felipe watched, promising that when the sun was low he would start planting.

It was five days before I returned to the farm. I was met by Felipe.

"All trees planted," he said with pride.

I walked with him to the front of the tree area, and he pointed out the first of the seedlings. They looked happy in neatly dug circles, each with a stake to mark its presence.

"Great! Good job, Felipe!"

He smiled, "I always do good job for you, Jefe."

"I will inspect the others later and also look to see where we will plant the next three hundred. Where is Ricardo?"

"Ricardo no here, Jefe."

"Where is he?" I asked, fearing the worst and imagining him drunk and incapable of work.

"I don't know, Jefe. I not responsible for Ricardo."

I found Ricardo in his house with Berta and Dilma. They all looked sullen and angry.

"What is happening now?" I asked.

"Felipe all time shouting at Dilma," Berta told me. "He said bad things all time. He shout at Ricardo, too. We frightened to leave Dilma alone."

"Felipe very bad man. Him crazy." Ricardo was speaking clearly, and I could tell he had not been drinking.

A feeling of depression overcame me, and I wondered if those Gringos who say there is no such thing as a good Indian worker are right. I suspected Ricardo was not free of his drinking addiction, and Felipe was unable to stop tormenting Dilma.

I felt responsible for the family as a whole and in particular Dilma and Berta, who were the least able to cope on their own. At the same time I had to keep the farm running. I was wondering why I ever landed myself with these problems.

"I want you, Ricardo, to sit down at the table with me and Felipe," I told him. "Go and find Felipe and ask him to come to the table."

I was uncertain as to what to do. On the evidence of today, Felipe had done a good job planting the trees with care, while Ricardo had stayed in the house on the pretext of protecting Dilma.

Once again, I felt like judge and jury.

"Felipe, you did a very good job planting all those trees." I started off with a compliment before pitching in with the tough stuff.

There was a shout of outrage from Ricardo who got up from the table and stormed off. Felipe gave me confidential look as if saying, "There you are, you see what I have to deal with."

I called Ricardo back and he reluctantly returned.

"Why did you leave?" I asked.

"I plant every tree. He no plant one tree. He with other woman all day. He never here. I do all work." The sentences came rapidly and with intense feeling.

I turned to Felipe.

"No, Jefe! I plant most trees," he said.

"No," said Ricardo.

I turned to Felipe and said, "You are to come with me now and show me exactly where you planted each tree."

I turned back to Ricardo and told him he was to follow us.

"Now, Jefe, or tomorrow?" asked Felipe.

"Now, immediately," I said.

Felipe was suddenly heavy-footed. It took only a few minutes for me to know which of them was telling the truth. Once we had walked beyond the first trees, Felipe wandered desperately looking for sticks marking the seedlings.

I turned to Ricardo. "You show him where the seedlings are."

Ricardo without hesitation led us to each planting.

I gave orders to Ricardo to see that Felipe left the finca the next morning. I told Felipe never set foot on the land again. Ricardo became the farm manager.

19

The Need for a Townhouse

I was late returning that evening. In the rapidly failing light, I had not seen Pat standing in the rancho at the end of our dock. I was securing the boat when she spoke, taking me by surprise.

"What have you been doing all this time?"

"I will tell you over dinner," I said, throwing her a line to secure the boat. "Just let me take a shower and change and then we will go to town."

"Too late!" she said. "I got tired of waiting. I've already eaten. Yours is in the kitchen. You'd better eat first before it gets cold."

Pat followed me into the house.

"Ready for a scotch and ginger ale?" I asked.

"I've had one. Besides, I'm working tonight," and so saying, she went to her studio and closed the door.

I did not go to the farm the next day. Instead, Pat and I talked about why I needed to be at the farm so often and why my visits there last for most of the day.

"I'm tired of being left alone on this island with no one to talk to," she said. "If you are going to keep going to your stupid farm, you have to find me a house in town so I can meet people."

"Well, what about our building a house alongside Tony and Silvia? We own the lot, and we should do more with it than just use it for parking the boat."

"It's up to you, and it's your property; but, I tell you, if you don't do something and do it quickly, I'm not coming back." Pat ended the discussion by going to her studio.

After lunch, I talked to Tony.

"You build house next door. I think good. You my friend. You quiet man. You no make too much noise."

That night I drew a plan for the new house. The lot was narrow and long, ten meters frontage and twenty in depth; but, because I own the concession rights to the waterfront, we could use the land between the end of the titled lot and the dock. This added another twenty feet.

"We will construct the house in two parts," I said. "One half will front onto the street and the other over the water with an overhead terrace stretching out above the dock. Between the two parts we can have that enclosed garden we have always longed for."

Pat took my drawing and made alterations.

"There is no point in having large windows down the sides when all you are going to see are the neighbors' houses right up against you," Pat said.

Pat rubbed out my windows and replaced them with tall narrow ones, separated by large spaces of solid wall.

"I agree!" I said. "That is much more interesting and more elegant. Also, it creates superb hanging spaces for your paintings."

I imagined masterpieces in oil that portray scenes generic to Bocas.

"When you have painted sufficient to fill the walls," I said, "I will get you an exhibition in Panama City and the world will wake up to the new P. Buckley Moss."

"We'll see, but first let's get this house built," said Pat.

"We should aim to make the house termite proof. The war against them can never be won, and I am tired of worrying about them," I said.

"Well, build in steel and block, and tile the floors," Pat said.

"I want to use only Bocas labor. This will be an important house, and I want Bocatoranians to build it and feel pride in it."

The contractor with the most clout in town was Mr. Victor Thomas. A member of a well-known Bocas family, his older brother Tito owned the Bahia Hotel and had been governor of the province at the age of twenty-eight. Victor had the looks of a film star from the subcontinent of India, perfectly proportioned features, medium height and the figure of young man. He was always well dressed in long trousers and a quality shirt, left open to display an impressive collection of gold chains and medallions.

Shortly after taking me on as a client, Victor was elected Representante, making him second only to the Governor in the Bocas political hierarchy, a post that carries considerable power. Victor was already building the Bishop's Palace, a substantial compound of impressive buildings funded from Madrid by the Spanish Catholic Church. I reached an agreement with him for the construction of the foundations of our house and, depending on the success of that phase, I would consider his continuing from there upwards.

20

Taken by Surprise

Back in the States for meetings and public appearances by Pat, I was troubled by the lack of news of progress on the new house. The foundations should have been completed according to Victor's projections. I set off for Bocas a couple weeks ahead of Pat.

The flight from Panama City to Bocas always seems to take longer than the flight in the other direction. When leaving Bocas, I fall asleep soon after the islands of the archipelago are lost to sight. When headed for Bocas, I am too excited for sleep.

A moment after accepting a paper cup of coffee from the flight attendant, the small plane fell twenty feet, leaving my coffee momentarily suspended in midair. Then the coffee fell, and I felt it scorch my thighs. I looked down and watched a brown stain spread across the lower half of my shirt and across the lap of my shorts. It gave the appearance of my having had an accident. I prayed I would pass through Bocas' little airport unnoticed.

We were approaching the first of the islands. I watched waves roll relentlessly onto the coral reefs, shooting plumes of white skyward. Beyond the reefs the waves reformed, smaller and less powerful, and headed for the white sands that separate the turquoise blue of the sea from the lush green of the jungle.

The plane banked in preparation for its landing, and I mopped at my shorts with my handkerchief. Everything smelled of coffee. If I had been traveling with Pat, I would have been wearing trousers and a proper shirt and most likely would not have accepted the drink.

The pilot lined the plane up with Avenida Luis Russell. He flew down the street a few feet above the green tin roofs of the wooden houses and put his wheels gently down on the tarmac. We sped down the runway, banana trees and waving children to either side. The engines roared in reverse with a sound so intense that it could be heard all over town, and we came to halt before turning to go back to the terminal.

A sign stretches across the front of the small white building announcing Bocas International Airport, a reminder of the days when there were scheduled flights from Bocas, Panama, to San Jose, Costa Rica.

As the flight attendant opened the door and lowered the steps, I saw the Bomberos band hurrying into place either side of the terminal door. I was elated. The band, formed from members of the town's fire department, signified the presence of a VIP, no doubt the minister of tourism or some other high-ranking government official, for whom such welcomes were normal.

I remained in my seat signaling the other passengers to leave ahead of me. When the band had started and everyone's attention was taken, I planned to exit quickly and make my escape via back streets to the dock and home. After changing my clothes, I would return for my baggage.

From my window I could see the Bomberos at the ready with lips to the wind instruments and cymbals and drum sticks poised. They were dressed in their best uniform: black caps with shiny peaks above equally black, happy faces; red shirts; and immaculate, white trousers tucked into the tops of highly polished black boots. These are the men and women who wait to save us from the fire that might sweep through our largely wooden town.

Most of the Bomberos are volunteers and have other jobs. I spotted my friend Vaya who works in construction. In his massive hands, his saxophone looked minuscule, like a child's toy.

I thought the VIP must have missed the plane, because the last person was on the ladder and still no sound.

"You must leave now, Senor," said the flight attendant.

I got up from my seat and went to the door holding my computer in front of me to cover as much of the brown stain as possible.

As I put my foot onto the first step of the ladder, the band burst into a triumphant musical salute worthy of a state visit. When I reached the tarmac, I looked up and saw Virginia, jumping up and down, waving the national flag and shouting, "Welcome home, Senor Malcolm!" A moment later she was taking my computer from me and positioning me at the head of the Bomberos, ready to march down the street to the center of town. The mayor took his place on one side of me. On the other side stood District Representative Victor Thomas, my building contractor.

Proceeding toward the Palazzo, I distractedly waved to those watching, too full of embarrassment to do justice to the occasion. I cursed myself for accepting the cup of coffee and for dressing so inappropriately.

This formal greeting had been staged by Virginia on the excuse that it was a "thank you" for my work with the English program.

In Bocas, the salutation "buenos dias" is often followed by "mucha lluvia," meaning "plenty rain." With more than one hundred inches of rainfall a year, this ancillary greeting is habitual during the rainy season. Even if the sun is shining on a particular day, it is still acceptable to add "mucha lluvia," because you would be referring to the previous day and the lingering presence of mud.

Standing in the street looking at our building site, Victor Thomas could see I was disappointed. I had been away for two months and had expected to find the foundations dug. Instead, I was looking at half a dozen bomb-like craters filled with water.

"Mucha lluvia," said Victor.

"Rain every day," said Tony. "They no do good in rain. Next month better."

There is a perpetual optimism in Bocas that transcends the climatic pattern.

"By the time you next come, the foundations will be completed and we will be ready to pour the first floor," Victor assured me.

The optimism in Bocas is not limited to weather. It is the same with the availability of materials. Other than wood and landfill, building materials come from the mainland, carried from Almirante in The Palanga, a vintage car ferry reportedly stolen from Latvia by Russians and towed to Panama.

With other construction projects competing for cement, rebar, salt-free river sand and a host of smaller building needs, the logistics of having the right quantities present when needed would challenge the most capable of army quartermasters.

At the time, logistics were further complicated by the absence of secure warehousing. With building lots ten by twenty meters, there is not the space on-site to construct a storage shed. Materials left in the street were liable to be "borrowed" during the night, never to reappear.

"Building here is cheap compared to the States," prospective land purchasers are assured by eager sellers of land. "The minimum wage for construction workers is only one dollar fifty an hour."

If the property owner has construction experience, does not have to take periods of absence, and is unusually patient, the dream house can be built without suffering moments of despair and anguish. In my case, I am the least qualified to be playing this game. Construction dumb and often absent, it was inevitable that our house took twice as long and cost twice as much as predicted.

A cheap source of labor is only one factor in costing a house. If materials are expensive after paying road and ferry costs and labor less skilled and without the latest tools, the difference narrows.

I believe many Gringos, whatever their experience, end up paying at least thirty percent more than a Panamanian would pay for equivalent work.

"Hey, take it easy, man. This Gringo has plenty money. No need get job done quick."

When this was overheard and reported to me, my first feeling was one of anger. Later, I considered the viewpoint of the other side. Uncertain of future employment, the wish to have the current job spin out is natural. Against not having a wage to take home to the family, I can understand the temptation to go slow.

That night, Peter repaid recent hospitality by treating me to a meal at a local restaurant. I chose a fish that I thought would be red snapper but, in fact, may well have been barracuda. It was tough and not that pleasant, but I did not want to appear an ungracious guest and ate it all.

With Pat still to arrive, I was alone. As I lay in bed, I was aware of a tingling in my face. It was not painful, just small prickly sensations. When I went to shave in the morning and looked in the mirror I saw a blowfish looking back at me.

My face was so puffed up my eyes were barely visible. My lips were pouted into folds of purple flesh. For a moment I thought what I saw was an illusion. Then I came to and hurriedly called Virginia.

"Something very strange has happened," I announced.

"What now, Senor Malcolm?" Virginia sounded resigned to sorting out my latest drama.

"It's my face. It is huge."

"What did you do to yourself, Senor Malcolm?"

"Nothing! It just happened in the night."

"You had better let me see it."

"Virg," I said. "Could we meet somewhere private? I don't want everyone seeing me like this."

"Wow, Senor Malcolm! This sounds serious. I'll meet you at the super's dock."

Virginia was waiting for me when I arrived at the dock. There were others standing around, but they were too polite to comment and looked away pretending they hadn't noticed my clown face. Virginia hurried me into a taxi.

I expected high drama when I walked into the hospital. I was anticipating being flown over the mountains to the modern clinic in David. Instead, the young girl behind the desk showed little interest and told me to sit on the bench and wait my turn. I sat next to a mother whose baby obviously had a fever. I tried not to breathe.

I thought of claiming frequent visitor status and demanding to be given priority. After all, this was my third visit to the emergency room and that should count for something.

"When did this happen?" the girl asked half an hour later.

"During the night," I told her.

"What did you eat for supper?"

"Fish."

The girl was taking notes. She was not in any hurry and allowed herself to be interrupted several times by people asking unimportant questions. I thought how back in the States my dire condition would have caused doctors to be summoned immediately to my bedside.

I was rehearsing my Spanish on the subject of Patient's Rights when the girl said, "Go into that room and take down your pants."

I did as I was told and stood in my underpants, expecting the doctor to now appear. For ten minutes I stood rehearsing a new script describing the fish and how I normally had a very different face. I was about to pull my pants up and take charge of the situation when the girl entered the room with a huge needle at the ready.

"Bend over the table," she ordered. I did as I was told, feeling like a naughty boy about to get a beating. She took hold of the top of my underpants and pulled it down to expose a chunk of my buttock. She thrust the needle into my exposed flesh. I bit my tongue as she pushed the contents of the syringe into me.

"There. You will be fine in six hours," she said. "If not, come back and see me."

"There is no need for me to see a doctor, then?" I questioned.

"I am the doctor," she said.

With my shorts still at my knees, I shook her hand, thanking her profusely. Six hours later, my face was back to normal.

21

Don't Kill the Cow Too Quick

"Kill the cow too quick," Tony commented, as we passed Genio Chow's casino, the newest addition to the town's entertainment.

The casino occupied one half of what was Genio's general store before he decided to lease half the space to Ruben Chau to use for a marine store and fill the other part with slot machines and electronic games.

"Bocas people no like slot machines," said Tony.

"They like dominos," I said.

"No dominos, do-mi-no," Tony corrected me. "Domino like bingo. You no say bingos."

"Bocas people like cards, domino and bingo," he explained. "Slot machine too quick. One pull and twenty-five cents gone quick. Kill the cow too quick." His Chinese diction made the word "quick" sound like it had two syllables, with emphasis on the last one.

"Bocas people also like lotto," I noted.

Two Bocatoranians are licensed to sell national lotto tickets. They travel the streets with special wooden display boards that fold together when the rain comes. There are five drawings a week. Each is televised, and Tony's Silvia seldom fails to watch.

Silvia has won prizes on a number of occasions. I once won three dollars, but that had been the extent of my luck. I wondered if Silvia wins because the Chinese are naturally better at selecting numbers or because she perhaps buys more tickets than she lets on.

We were making our way to Kunha's Chinese restaurant for chop suey. Tony was walking with a stick, and we were making faster progress than before his stroke. Pat and Silvia were somewhere behind us. Silvia had kept us waiting as she put the finishing touches to her appearance. When Tony became impatient, the two of us went on ahead.

We exchanged greetings with others walking in the opposite direction or sitting on the concrete benches on the edge of the park. With momentum up, Tony kept going, while I broke ranks for a brief word when necessary and then hastened to catch up.

As we entered the restaurant, Tony stopped by the door to the kitchen and called out, "Hey, Kunha!"

He kept calling, "Hey, Kunha!" until the owner heard him, left off from cooking and came to shake his hand.

Until his stroke, Tony always ordered fried fish and fried potatoes and drank a few beers with his meal. Now, Silvia restricts him to chop suey and a single beer.

"The old man going die soon," Tony said.

We were discussing Rolando Sun, whom Tony was befriending. Rolando could be found on most evenings sitting in the shadows at the back of Casa Luck smoking a cigarette and drinking a soda. He was matchstick thin and my age, though Tony said he looked much older.

"He no eat much food. He have pension, but only twenty-nine dollars every fifteen days."

"Why so little?" I asked.

"'Cause bank take rest," said Tony. "He borrow eleven thousand dollars from bank for repair his house. His family take most of it and house never get repaired. Now soon fall down. I give him fifty cents this morning. He go and buy cigarettes, no food."

On the walk back we stopped at Don Chicho's for desert. Silvia let me order Tony a Jell-O and a cake for her. Pat and I had chocolate ice cream.

"Mr. Malcolm, you are a mess," said Joanne. "You have your money all over the place." She was looking at the untidy collection of dollar bills I had pulled from my pocket.

"I have been at the farm all day, Joanne. I have not had time to get organized."

"And how is the farm then, Mr. Malc? You sell all you grow?" Joanne asked.

"Yes, thanks to you buying all the plantain."

Joanne had at first said she did not want any plantain but, when I told her there were others eager for them, she asked me to wait while she checked in the back. She returned and paid me for all that I had.

As we walked the last part of the journey home, Tony said the previous president, Ballabares, warned the President Mireya Moscoso he might seek to oust her.

"Mireya tell him he no threat. She can travel to United States. He cannot. United States no give him visa. We have saying, 'No tevista porque tu no va.' Do not get dressed because you not going."

22

Pig Wrestling

If the farm was to be self-supporting in a time of world disaster, it needed to have a source of protein in addition to its chickens and the fish caught in the lagoon. I decided we needed to buy some pigs.

Ricardo and I, along with another Indian hired for the day, set off to buy pigs from a pig breeder located a few miles outside of Almirante.

We took a taxi to the farm, where I let Ricardo select a young boar and two sows from the pen that contained pigs weighing between fifty-five and sixty-five pounds. Again, he was enjoying his responsibility, taking it seriously and unhurriedly, making a choice and then, upon consideration, changing to an alternative.

The selected pigs were caught amidst ear shattering squeals and placed head first into white grain sacks. Each was then weighed on a hanging scale. I paid for them by the pound and we placed the sacks in the back of the taxi and returned to the boat.

We were on our way to the finca and passing the dock where the ocean-going banana ships load their cargos for the European markets when I realized it was 11:30. This is the hour at which it is customary to stop work and take the midday meal.

I steered the boat beneath the bow of a banana ship and found a ramp from which Ricardo and the other Indian could jump ashore. I told Ricardo to find a restaurant and order three meals and three bottles of water and come back with them as soon as possible. I expected them to be away for ten minutes or fifteen at the most.

It was a very hot day. I had forgotten my hat. I got some protection from the sun by holding my folder with the receipt for the pigs above my head. In front of me on the floor of the boat were the three sacks each containing a pig. The pigs were understandably agitated by their strange circumstance. They were casting about, trying to stand and falling over in increasing confusion.

The minutes passed and all the while the pigs and I became more uncomfortable with the heat. I kept looking toward the spot where Ricardo and his friend had disappeared.

There was a sudden increased commotion, and looking down I saw that one of the pigs had forced its snout through its sack and was turning its mouth sideways. To my horror it was chewing the sack apart with surprising ease.

Before I could think what to do, the pig had its shoulders and front legs free of the sack and was propelling itself toward the bow of the boat. It clearly had the intention of diving into the oil slicked black water of the harbor.

I lunged at the creature in a rugby tackle, throwing my arms around its shoulders. It broke free with ease and I was left holding the sack. The pig, now completely free, was attempting to climb on to the foredeck to dive and swim for shore.

In desperation, I launched myself once more, this time grabbing for its protruding ears. Having never done this to a pig before, I was unprepared for what happened next.

The pig let out a terrifying screech that would have made me let go, had it not been for the other effect. To my delight, the pig meekly rolled over on its side and gave up the fight. Holding one ear with my left hand, I took the bow mooring line in my right and bound it around the creature's two hind legs. With control reestablished, I sat down in the stern, keeping the line in hand ready to forestall any further attempt at escape.

If I had grown up with pigs, I would have known you cannot bind together a pig's hind legs because they have virtually no knuckle. With rapid, piston-like movements, the pig worked a leg free. I moved with speed and before the second leg was clear, I had pulled the line tight around it and it was back in control.

I reviewed damage to my hands. The skin across my knuckles had been scraped off during the wrestling match, and pig grime showed on the exposed flesh. I panicked until I remembered the little bottle of essential oil of lavender I always carry with me. Still holding tight to the mooring line with its captive pig, I applied the oil liberally to the wounds, ignoring the stinging pain.

The smell of pig was everywhere, stronger it seemed than it had been at the pig farm. I smelled my hands and then my shirt and I realized it was coming from me. I wondered if the pig smelled me on him and was equally put out.

I became aware of voices and looking up I saw several stevedores and seamen watching from the bow of the banana boat far above. They were calling to me, but I could not catch what was being said. Obviously, the advent of an aged, gray-haired Gringo pig wrestling in the bottom of a boat in the midday sun was a novel form of lunchtime entertainment.

The shouting took on increased urgency and was becoming mixed with laughter. I looked up again. Hands were pointing behind me. I looked back and there was a second pig half way out of its sack, following precisely the procedure adopted by pig number one. No wonder pigs are considered intelligent.

Battle recommenced, with the spectators above divided between those cheering on the Gringo and those calling for the pig. This time, however, I knew the form. Subdued by the ears, the pig allowed me to tie one of its hind legs with the stern mooring line. I now sat with a line in either hand, reining in on either pig when it showed the least inclination to make a break.

I looked at number three's sack. There was little movement, but what there was caused a new concern. The sacking that lay over the side of the pig's torso was rising and falling in rapid motion. I imagined the pig suffocating. I looked again at the other two pigs. Both had begun to froth at the mouth, white spume bubbling out. I looked up at the audience, hopeful for advice.

"Agua, agua," the spectators called in chorus.

I took hold of the bailing bucket and scooped up filthy harbor water, throwing it over all three pigs.

"Mas agua, mas agua," the chorus continued.

I kept throwing water over the animals until Ricardo and his friend appeared carrying a Styrofoam box and a bottle of water.

Neither Ricardo nor the Indian showed the least surprise. I looked at my watch. It was 12:30, the time when work begins again. Ricardo offered me the box containing my lunch.

"Keep it for Berta," I said. "Just give me the water."

As I steered out under the big ship's bow, a cheer of "Ole! Ole!" rang out from the stevedores. I stood and turning to look up, raised both arms above my head in the salute of a victorious toreador. Unguided, the boat swung off course and I lost balance, nearly falling overboard. The spectators, delighted by this unexpected finale, acknowledged it with raucous laughter.

Within five minutes of reaching the finca, the pigs were grunting with pleasure as they explored their new home and the delights of being able to rout out goodies in an open-air pen.

I looked at the two I had wrestled with and felt a special bond. I could not countenance the thought of ever slaughtering them. Perhaps I am not cut out to be a farmer.

23

The Cost of Construction

"We thought you were about to get back," said Dave. "There has been a sudden burst of activity at your house."

"You mean there hasn't been activity all the time?"

"You're joking," said Dave.

We were talking with Dave and Linda at Albrook, the domestic airport, in Panama City. We were waiting to be called to pass through security.

During the days when Dave was captain of a luxury catamaran, the two of them lived here in an apartment between the infrequent visits of the yacht's owner and family. Linda is the all-time expert on where to buy what you cannot find in Bocas.

"You are crazy if you think they are going to do much while you are away," said Dave.

"Did you like living in Panama City?" Pat asked before I could get upset at the prospect of disappointment.

"It was great," said Linda. "Panama City has so much going on and then there is the Embassy and things happening there and lots of cultural events."

"It was alright," said Dave. "But I got bored."

Dave is a man of action whose past careers have given scope to his construction skills, his creative talent and his knack for improvisation. In 1995, he sailed the catamaran to Bocas and into Laguna Bocatorrito. A year later, he bade farewell to the cat and its owner and started building a house on the hillside at the southern end of the lagoon, a house with one of the world's finest views.

At that time Dave and Linda were the only Gringos living in Buena Esperanza. From the start, his neighbor, Ramelio Green, otherwise known as Tobe, had been his right-hand man.

Tobe is an African Panamanian who has lived all his life at Buena Esperanza. He farms about thirty head of cattle besides helping out his new neighbors. Dave is San Diego born and bred. A strong man, with a ponytail left over from his

106

hippy days, his eyes are always smiling. Tobe and Dave have similar humors and rib each other with mutual respect.

Linda is still the city girl at heart. She dresses elegantly and keeps a spotless house, not an easy achievement in the tropics. Linda was the founder of the Bocas Garden Club and its first president. The club, more than any other Bocas institution, has brought together Gringos and Panamanians in sharing their mutual interest in all manner of subjects relating to plants and their uses. The club has further benefited the community by donating and planting flowers and shrubs in the central park and building a trash collection center on its edge.

At one time Dave and Linda's house had a palm frond roof that became home to a colony of bats. Dave strung a net between the roof and their bedroom to catch the bat poop but it was not one hundred percent successful. Dave replaced the fronds with a fiber sheeting and the bats departed.

When changing the roof, Dave fell twenty-five feet to the ground and cut open an artery in his arm. By the time Tobe got him to town, he was faint from loss of blood and unable to stand.

At the beginning, living isolated, dependent on generators for electricity and the rain for water was hard on Linda. Gradually, she adapted. Their finca, Green Acres, has become a local attraction for its beauty, variety of plants and trees and Linda's recipes cooking with homegrown chocolate.

I sat on the right side of the plane so as to get an aerial view of the house as we came to land at Bocas. I was expecting to see at least the framework for the roof completed. Victor's prediction had been that the house would be closed in by now.

The house had grown to be the largest single-family building project in town. It was not my wish for it to be so. It had just happened this way. Now, with the house costing so much, I was stuck with it. Nobody was going to walk up and take it off my hands for anything like what I had spent.

Victor saw me looking dejectedly at the dismal amount of work achieved in the past two months.

"When it rains we cannot use the welding machine," he offered as the reason.

"The rain will stop soon," he continued. "Once we have the roof on, the rain will not matter and we will soon be finished."

"How much more is the house going to cost me?" I asked.

"Not too much more," was Victor's answer. "The finishing will be easy."

The Gringo community felt sorry for me. They saw how I was caught in a deadly hold. I had spent heavily on the foundations and first floor of a large and complicated house made of non-traditional materials with a labor force that lacked experience and up-to-date equipment. Added to this, they knew I was being ripped off from all sides whenever I was not there to protect myself.

"Want a bag of cement at a discount price? Go and see Malcolm's night watcheeman."

"Oh, yer?"

"Yer, and if you want rebar, zinc or whatever, you can get as much as you want for a case of beer."

This was not a good time. The house was draining my resources and taxing my nerves. The farm was an unending source of problems. I started to question why I was here. I could have been sitting back in Virginia, tending the garden that was now sadly neglected and working from our business headquarters, instead of via the Internet from a sweaty office on the edge of a jungle.

The days were up and down. Each morning as I headed over to the construction site, I feared what Victor would tell me.

"The sawmill did not have the wood ready."

"The Cooprativa has run out of rebar."

"They sent the wrong size T bars."

"I need money by Friday to pay the workers."

I thanked God for my stalwart three, Tony, Virginia and Joanne. They provided both sympathy and encouragement.

"God is testing you, Mr. Malcolm," Joanne told me.

Don Chicho's was closed for the night, and we were sitting on a sofa in her back room watching her favorite late night game show. Joanne is very perceptive and instinctively knows my moods.

"Him is giving you a bit of what He gave Job."

"Well, I wish He would decide He has tested me enough and let me out of this mouth of the whale, or should I say the mouth of the bull."

"Him will in His own good time. When He is ready. Meantime, I keep praying for you."

Tony has the patience of his Chinese heritage. He and Silvia had endured two years of construction in what was previously their front yard—unending dust penetrating their bedrooms and living room, the din of hammering, the screech of saws, the pulse of salsa music from the workers' radios, the presence of others ten feet away from dawn to dusk.

"I am sorry, Tony," I said.

"It no matter. One day will be finished."

I imagined he and Silvia ruing the day they sold me the lot.

"You my good friend. You like brother. We no mind 'cause you and Pat good people. We like you."

Virginia was forever optimistic, "It will all be over by Christmas."

"Which Christmas?"

"This one of course, Senor Malcolm! Why you always think the worst?"

"Virg, Christmas is only four months away. Be realistic."

"Okay, a little longer perhaps."

I was lying on the small sofa in her office, legs over one end and head and shoulders propped against the other. Virginia was at her computer answering e-mail from other clients.

"You like a Samson?" she asked.

Without waiting for an answer, she went to her little kitchen and poured me a glass of this traditional drink that tastes like prune juice and has an alcoholic content of sixteen and a half percent. It is her customary treatment for my bouts of depression.

"There, take this and you will feel better."

"How much money do we have in the account?" I asked.

"Wait, I tell you."

Virginia keeps immaculate records. Without her I would have been in an irretrievable mess. Filing is yet another of my incapabilities. Both Pat and I would be unable to operate in today's world of endless documentation and form filing, if it were not for Virginia and Tricia Miles, our guardian angel back in Mathews, Virginia. Neither of us is capable of reading the instructions on how to connect a VCR to a television, let alone complete a health insurance claim.

In no time Virginia had the answer. The news was not good.

"Virg, we have got to make some savings somewhere. The money is running out fast," I said.

"I will not take my fees until the time is better," she offered.

"That is very kind of you, Virg, but one, I would not allow that and two, the problem is larger than what you cost me. I am going to have to look for a loan."

"I wish I had money to lend you," she said. "I have just fifty-seven dollars in my account."

My three friends and Pat's equanimity were just keeping the balance tilted away from my throwing in the towel.

24

Bianca Joins the Family

Strange men had menaced Berta.

"They threw rocks at her when she washing in the creek," Ricardo told me. "We need gun."

This was the second time Ricardo had asked for a gun. The first time had been to kill the hawks that were eating the little chickens.

Ricardo and I went to Changuinola with the intention of purchasing a gun, but first I visited my attorney to check on the law relating to firearms.

"You are not to have a gun," he was adamant. "You have a gun on the finca and someone gets shot and you will be in trouble whether you fired the gun or your man fired the gun. Instead you have a big dog."

I was relieved. I did not fancy entrusting a gun to Ricardo, given his possible addiction to alcohol. On our way back to Almirante, we visited a kennel and bought a rottweiler bitch puppy of three months that already had the name Bianca. She is the dearest dog to those she knows and terrifying to those she does not. Bianca and Berta became close friends, and there has been no more mention of anyone troubling Berta.

25

Virginia and Peter Part

Pat and I arrived at Don Chicho's one evening to find Joanne missing from behind the cash desk. Shortly after, Pat was told Joanne wanted to speak to her upstairs in her sitting room. Pat went aloft while I was left wondering what Joanne wanted to share with Pat and not with me.

Soon Pat returned.

"Peter has told Joanne that his relationship with Virginia is over," Pat said.

For the past couple of weeks, Pat and I had seen this coming.

"Peter was my first and only boyfriend," Virginia told us months later when at last she was able to talk about the subject.

"My mom was very strict when I was young, and I had to live by her rules. Then I went to college in Arkansas, and when I come back all the boys I liked were taken."

Besides this problem, there were few local boys who had been to university and most of those had attended school in either Panama City or San Jose, Costa Rica. Virginia, with four years of exposure to North American culture and its easy access to knowledge, was a challenge most macho Bocatoranian men would hesitate to take on.

When Peter came to town seeking to buy land at prices that had changed little over the past thirty years, he was the topic of much interest. His height, good looks, charm and knowledge of the language earned him many friends. At that time, being short of money, he mostly ate at Don Chicho's, where Virginia, helping out her mom, often served him.

Virginia and Peter became a team, with Virginia introducing Peter to landowners and bringing with her the credibility of her family's name. Peter acquired prime properties with a shrewd eye to both the short and long term, building houses to sell on Carenero and acquiring a portfolio of properties for investment. I was the third person to purchase a house from him.

We had often entertained Peter and Virginia to dinner on their own. On other occasions we had included them in larger parties. Virginia was very attentive to Peter and his every need, and in turn he showed love and affection for her. They were a constant topic of Gringo and local conversation as everyone waited to see if and when the marriage of these two local stars of different colors and backgrounds would come about.

Peter had been in New Zealand for his annual Christmas visit to his parents. Meanwhile, Virginia had increased the number of her Gringo clients to seven and rented an office on the top floor of a house facing the park. Her time, when not teaching in school, was fully occupied. Every Sunday she would run Don Chicho's while Joanne spent the day reading the Bible and attending the two Methodist Church services.

Peter returned from New Zealand and had an unexpected windfall. An aunt left him money in her will. The Gringo bush telegraph picked up the news and spread it with the usual remarkable efficiency. Even allowing for the customary exaggeration, the sum was, by Bocas standards, very considerable.

Putting the newfound money to immediate use, Peter acquired more land. He started to build a house for himself, a mammoth wooden palace on the seaward side of Isla Carenero, with a view that lays claim to being the finest in the region. He did not consult Virginia in the plans; and, when we found this out, those of us who cared for her well being started to worry.

Peter's older sister arrived in Bocas from Miami with a boyfriend, and Pat and I joined a small dinner party for them in a local restaurant on the far side of town. It was a strange evening in which Virginia, Pat and I might just as well not have been present. We were sitting at one end of the table, excluded from the conversation. If we had gotten up and walked out, I doubt the others would have noticed.

A few days later, Peter called Joanne, explaining that Virginia was not worldly enough for him and that the cultural differences between them were unbridgeable.

26

The Storm

I was conscious of the distant thunder. More than ever, I wanted the storm to pass to the north. When I had crossed the bay before the end of the day's work to meet with Victor, he told me that tomorrow would be the long-awaited pouring of the upper concrete floor.

"If it is not raining in the morning, we begin pouring at seven. If it is, we will wait until the rain stops," Victor told me.

We had been standing in the street between stacks of cement bags, piles of rock and two cement mixers, one of which I had purchased new in desperation when Victor's disappeared for days. The house was months past the intended completion date and many thousands of dollars over budget. I had already sold my fisherman's cottage in Virginia to keep the money coming. We were barely at the halfway point.

If someone had walked up to me then and offered to buy the building for what it had cost me to date, I would have kissed him or her, however hairy, and made a deal on a promise. I was spending money like an owner of a luxury yacht with a crew of six but without the fun.

I lay in bed worrying, going back over all the things I should have done to avoid getting in this mess. Bill Speakman, our accountant, had telephoned me the previous day to ask how the house was progressing.

"You should have let me handle it, and I would have made sure you had a fixed price and time penalties," Bill said. Besides being our accountant, Bill likes to try to be our father. He had never been in favor of my "Panama Follies," as he called them. Part of the problem was that he could not achieve a rigid control of all that I was doing.

"Bill, things work differently down here," I tried to explain.

"Why don't you come down and see for yourself? There is only one contractor capable of building this house. In his other role, he is the leading political honcho. I do not want to be suing the town's top guy; and, anyhow, he would never agree to work under threat of a time limitation when it rains more days than not."

"What has rain got to do with it?" Bill had said. "What are tarpaulins for?"

Bill is always asking me questions like that. It is very unfair, because I know nothing about construction and Bill knows everything. He spends his evenings reading *Means Estimating Tables* and memorizing the national building codes.

"Bill, just get on the plane and hop down here, but get your shots first."

There was no reply to this suggestion. Bill neither appreciates snakes nor the manner in which I handle a boat. Instead, he switched to discussing a change in our business accounting procedures, another subject my brain finds difficult to follow.

Pat was awake.

"What's on your mind?" she asked.

I wondered how she knew I was also awake. Maybe she heard my mind racing in its agitation.

"I was worried the bad weather was heading this way," I said. "We cannot pour the floor if it is raining in the morning, and we need a complete day of pouring so the whole floor can be done in one setting."

"Oh, don't worry," she said. "If you don't pour today, you will tomorrow."

"Yeah, fine!" I said. "But I will be paying for forty men to do nothing all day."

I went on to explain that the pouring of the floor was a formidable task. In preparation, a wooden scaffolding of ascending steps had been erected and rose twenty feet from street level at the front of the house. Victor had recruited a team of forty from around town and from Isla Bastimentos. They were to form a human chain to pass buckets from the cement mixers up the steps of the scaffolding and across the zinc under-flooring to the point of pouring and then, via a second chain, return the empty buckets to the mixers.

A violent shockwave hit the house, shuddering the timbers. In the same instant, a blinding white light flooded every corner and a thunderclap as loud as an exploding eighteen-inch shell split our eardrums. We jumped out of bed and ran to the window. All was silent as if the commotion of a moment past was a dream, but a smell of singed wood and fur told us otherwise.

Then the rain started. First a few heavy drops evenly spaced and then quickly more. Within a minute a deluge of water came streaming down so that from the window we looked out as if from behind a waterfall.

It was a beautiful storm, full of fury: the pounding of the rain on the tin roof, the lightning's illumination of the palm trees and the water of the bay, the drum rolls of the thunder, the sudden cooling of the air. We watched nature's sonne luminaire late night special and, before the magic passed, returned to bed and made love.

At the first signs of dawn, I was up and headed over to the building. The sky was clear and the storm far off over the Caribbean.

The scene at the front of the house was like a Hollywood set with filming about to begin. The army of actors was assembled and waiting, the props in position and the two cement mixer operators at the ready. All we needed was the director.

"Where is Mr. Thomas?" I asked, showing impatience.

"He come soon, Mr. Malcolm," said a chorus of voices.

I realized I had made a mistake. I had expected Victor to be present exactly on time for this important event, and when he was not I had broken the number one rule in Panama, "Do not get impatient over matters of time." Seven o'clock in the morning is only an approximation, seldom to arrive before and usually a little after.

Victor arrived and gave the command to proceed.

We all turned our attention to the cement mixers. Neither would start.

It was an hour before my mixer fired and the bucket brigade rolled into action. A mechanic continued to work on the second machine, and we all waited in suspense. An improvised part was fashioned and miraculously it did the job. We reached our full potential around nine a.m. and by nightfall the complete floor was poured. We celebrated with two cases of beer purchased from Tony.

27

The Scream

There was nothing remarkable about the funeral of Lucille McFarlane until the scream. Virginia and I were sitting in the third pew on the right hand side. Across the aisle, family members took the first five pews. Between the family and us was the coffin.

The coffin had a window that was uncovered to afford mourners and those who were just curious a last look at Miss Lucille.

"That is a very fine coffin," I whispered to Virginia. "The wood is beautiful."

"You don't want one that good, Senor Malcolm." Virginia's voice had left me unsure as to whether this was a statement or question.

"To have it buried in the sand? Never. No thrifty Scot would waste the money. You can bury me in a cardboard box and spend the savings on the party."

I had read the written eulogy, "Miss Mack, or Aunty Luz, is mother of twelve children of which the three oldies die, and leave nine children, fifty-nine grandchildren, fifty-four great-great grans, and eight great-great-great grans."

Virginia took the printed sheet from me and looked at the photograph.

"That no look like Miss Luz. I will have a good photograph of you when your turn comes."

I found Virginia's advance planning a shade disconcerting. She had turned the page and was reading the eulogy.

"We will include Pat's children, Senor Malcolm. You don't have enough family to look good. You only have four children and six grans."

Sandra, the youngest of Virginia's aunts and only a few years older than she, rose from the choir stall. She had waited until the church was almost full before taking a look through the coffin window. Sandra never hurries her walk when she knows eyes are on her. She posed beside the coffin, as if for photographers, and looking down, allowed herself a long moment of apparent contemplation.

Sandra runs the children's Sunday school that follows the morning service; and, during the long summer holidays, she is the leader of a two-week Bible study program, attended by more than sixty children. She is a generous Christian.

Sandra is also an entrepreneur, bicycling the town selling home baked pasties for fifteen cents and twenty-five cent chances on numbers she records in a well-worn notebook. She reminds me of Billy Joel's "Piano Man." If she had been given voice training and guitar lessons, she might have become a star. She still dreams of stardom, but with each year that passes her chances diminish and her audience remains the congregation of our church.

The service had been scheduled for 2 p.m., but the rain had been streaming down in monsoon-like cascades and the Reverend Theophilus Lewis delayed the start to allow the town's taxis to go the rounds one more time. Eventually, at 2.30 p.m., the coffin window was closed by one of Lucille's daughters and a purple shroud was placed over its length.

In spite of Virginia's amusement at my off key singing, I enjoyed the hymns. I decided to add "Abide with Me" to the hymn list in my laptop in a file under the title "My Funeral." Later, the choir, which included one daughter and one grand-daughter of Lucille, surpassed itself with "Swing Low, Sweet Chariot."

"When the time comes, I want them to sing 'Swing Low' for me," I whispered to Virginia.

"Sure, Senor Malcolm. I will tell them at tonight's party."

The Reverend Theophilus Lewis spoke eloquently and with feeling about the Christian example set by Miss Lucille; then, following prayers, he signaled the pallbearers forward and began to remove the shroud.

At that moment the scream erupted. A mixture of agony and rage, it could be heard far beyond the church. As unexpected as an assassin's bullet, it was over in an instant, leaving behind an eerie silence and our nerves jumping.

As if the scream had been the signal, a rising crescendo of sobs, cries and shuddering broke from the family, engulfing us in a confusion of sorrow. The level of emotion was unbearable and everywhere people were crying. The tears were not for the death of Lucille but for the breaking hearts of those who knew her best and loved her deepest.

Before the pallbearers reached the coffin, a granddaughter was there. Lifting the lid of the window, she clawed at the glass above Lucille's face.

"Mi abuela! Mi abuela!" ("My grandmother! My grandmother!") she screamed, pressing her lips to the glass.

The pallbearers rushed forward to wrestle the girl away, but other women of the family joined the melee and for a moment I thought the coffin would fall.

It was the husbands and brothers who restored order, restraining their wives, sisters and daughters and forcing them back into the pews. Meanwhile, the Reverend Lewis' voice could be heard by those of us at the front as he quickly concluded with the benediction.

We came out of the church into a gray drizzle and took our places in the procession for the walk to the cemetery. Everyone had an umbrella, and we needed to spread out to avoid tangling with each other. The coffin was placed on the town's wooden funeral cart, and the pallbearers took up positions either side of the long shaft that projected from its front, ready to haul the cart to the cemetery. A base drummer struck the solemn funeral beat and we set off up Avenue Norte, with the band playing "Nearer My God to Thee" in slow time.

I lost Virginia somewhere in the sea of umbrellas and found myself walking beside Lili, graceful as ever and full of innocent mischief.

"When I die, I hope I am in Hawaii," Lili told me.

"Why?" I asked.

"Because then they will take my body, put it on a raft and send it out to sea. I want my body to be useful and feed the fishes."

"Are you sure you are still allowed to do that?" I asked. "Is it environmentally acceptable?"

"It better be," said Lili in a manner that did not countenance further challenge. "Better than burning or filling up the ground."

I regretted discussing this subject. Before coming to Bocas, I had also wished that my body could be committed to the sea. Now, I wanted my body to be a part of the Bocas burial ritual. I had discussed this with Miss Joanne and Miss Elvia, the co-chairs of my funeral arrangements.

"I want you all to have a great fiesta after my burial," I had told them.

"The march through the town and the committal of a body to the ground is an essential prelude to the fiesta. It builds the atmosphere. A burn up is like a registry wedding. Not for me, I want all the trappings and then plenty of rum served at the wake."

I caught up with Virginia as we were entering the cemetery. The procession wove its way down paths, passing graves large and small, until we reached an open area close to the sea. Here, among the tall sand grasses, was the space the town had designated for Lucille.

We stood beneath umbrellas while the gravedigger tried to repair damage caused by the heavy rain. The trench walls had collapsed inwards, filling the grave with sand and water. He was throwing water out with a shovel, but other water kept seeping back and we realized the water table had risen.

Some enterprising members of Lucille's family produced four heavy squares of cement with a tiled surface on one side, borrowed from another gravesite. These were placed in the hole, ready to support the four corners of Lucille's coffin and keep it above the surface of the water.

The Reverend, eager to get the coffin into the ground before the walls shed more sand, proceeded with the graveside service.

When the ladies of the family saw that Miss Lucille was about to be put away forever, the wailing began again. Scuffles broke out as the men struggled to restrain those who still held tight to the coffin rails. Little children, not understanding why their mothers were crying and their fathers fighting, began to sob. A bugler played last post followed by reveille.

The coffin in place, the women recovered sufficiently to toss their bouquets of flowers onto its lid. The men helped shovel in the sand. Virginia and I headed back to town.

I spent the rest of the afternoon catching up on business via the Internet. Three hours later, I passed the McFarlane house. The fiesta was going strong, and there was much laughter and no sobs.

28

Advice from Down Under

There are many who said I had wasted my money, and that was true. However, if I had left my savings invested in the stock market, I would have been in the same position. In the meantime, I had fun or, at least at times, I thought I was having fun. At other times, however, I suffered excessive mental anguish.

"Everyone has a talent," Pat tells children in schools back home and I repeat in the classrooms of Bocas.

"You should do what you do best," we both say.

I was ignoring the dictum and seeking to prove myself invincible. I knew nothing about construction, and I was unable to contribute much to discussions with Victor.

"Mr. Malcolm, I think you best find an expert who know about this type work. He then can work with Mr. Thomas," Virginia advised.

I agreed and hired an engineering professor and an architect from Panama City to make periodic visits but, even with their help, progress was full of stops and starts. It became clear work slowed the morning after Pat and I had left Bocas and did not pick up again until Virginia reminded everyone we would be back the next week.

The habit of delaying until the last minute is universal. In Bocas, where rain is a major and unpredictable handicap, the outcome is likely to drive owners to the brink of despair.

"Mind if we take a look?" The accent was from down under. It sounded more Aussie than Kiwi. The man and his female companion had already taken off rucksacks and placed them on the rough concrete floor of the front room. The downstairs structural work was complete. The tile layer was due to start the next week.

Upstairs, Covetex walls, made of Styrofoam contained within wire mesh to which cement had been plastered, divided the front half of the house into Pat's studio with attached bathroom and guest bedroom on one side. Across a passage-way my office, a bodega and laundry room occupied a smaller area.

Work had just started on the upstairs back, where the apartment would con-sist of our bedroom suite and the upper floor kitchen separated by a tile counter from the dining-sitting area. Both the bedroom and the dining area led onto an eighteen-foot covered terrace that overlooked the bay. We expected to take our meals on the terrace, only retreating inside in the most severe of storms.

"You are welcome!" I told the visitors, who introduced themselves as Steve and Annie. They looked to be in their early forties.

"Going to be a hotel, is it?" Annie inquired.

"No! A house," I said. "One day it might well be a hotel. However, I have designed it so that it could be divided into four separate units, either apartments or a combination of offices, a restaurant, and an apartment. That will be after I am gone."

"You must have a big family," said Annie as we walked the corridor between the downstairs bedroom and the guest bathroom.

"Yes. One wife, ten children, numerous daughters-in-law and an assortment of grandchildren, with more to come."

"Surely they are not going to live here all at the same time?" Annie asked.

"I doubt it, but you never know what will happen these days; terrorism, clouds of pollution, droughts, plagues and all the rest of what is going on in the world. Peaceful Panama with its abundant rainfall and clean air could be the last refuge."

"Did you read Neville Shute's *On the Beach*? What you're describing sounds familiar."

"Something like that, only with a happier ending."

We stood in the grand hall. It is the space between what was originally to be separate buildings but which Pat and I had decided to enclose, thus joining the two ends of the house.

The grand hall is my name for this space. It reminds me of the grand halls in medieval castles. It is spacious in all directions, with the roof forty feet above the floor and a wide staircase rising to a gallery that runs around three sides and forms the link between the two upstairs sections. The space is smaller than a grand hall in even the most modest castle but, given the proportions of the house, it has the same feeling of spacious extravagance.

"May we take a look upstairs?" asked Steve.

"You are welcome to go anywhere at your own risk. We don't have the banis-ters in place, and it's a long way to fall."

"Is this going to be a bar?" asked Annie, still on the ground floor and pointing to a long concrete counter.

"No, that is separating the downstairs kitchen from the eating area."

"An upstairs and downstairs kitchen?" she queried.

"Remember, one day the house may be divided up. This quarter with its view of the sea would make an attractive restaurant. In the meantime, we will be using the kitchen when we entertain large numbers."

"Oh!" was Annie's sole comment, and I feared she thought me super rich and throwing Hollywood-style bashes.

"The first guests will be the congregation of the Methodist Church. The church is just across the way. When the house is finished, we will all have a celebration breakfast and the minister will bless the house."

We joined Steve upstairs and I explained the layout. The apartment with its one hundred eighty degree view of the bay impressed them.

"The house is lovely, and we would move in tomorrow if we had the chance," said Steve before adding, "but I think you have some problems that need to be put right before you go any further. I build houses back home, and I do know what I am talking about. You don't mind me telling you some things do you?"

"No, not at all," I said, hoping neither of them detected the rise of my stress level.

"Well!" he said. "It looks to me as though your contractor has used ordinary PVC for the hot water system. He should have either used copper piping or the new PVC that is special for hot water pipes, but I doubt it's available in Panama yet. We have only just got it back home."

"What should I do?" I asked.

"You need to have it replaced before you go any further. You will have to open some walls up, but at least you will be doing it before the plastering."

"Anything else?" I asked.

"The waste pipes for the toilets are the thinnest PVC, the type used for guttering. That needs to be changed, or you may well find you have unpleasant smells coming from the middle of your concrete walls."

"What else?" I asked. I was rapidly sliding into depression.

"I suggest you hire a knowledgeable inspector to watch over the work. He needs to go over what has been done to date. The faults should be rectified first, and then he should watch each subsequent procedure. That's what happens back home."

"I have one already," I told him.

"Then I would replace him."

I relayed the news to Victor.

"I always use PVC for hot water systems," Victor told me indignantly. "There is never a problem. The plans do not say copper or specify special PVC for the servicio. We can make the changes, but it is going to be expensive."

I knew the cost would be mine. I was leaving for the States in the morning, and I did not know what to do. If I authorized the changes, would they be done correctly? What would be the cost? Victor was telling me that he could not give me a quote until the work was done. He did not know how long it would take or the cost of the copper piping.

"Leave off closing in any more piping for now," I said. "Start the tiling downstairs and put up any walls upstairs that will not have hot water or drain pipes in them."

I was wishing the Australians would come by a windfall and call to purchase the house as is. As the plane took off from Bocas on the first leg of our journey home, I looked down on the long green roof with the feeling that it could well become the death of me.

29

A Time of Despair

I was in my office in Mathews when I received an urgent telephone call from Virginia.

"Senor Malcolm, Victor has given me a bill for forty thousand dollars. He says he need the money Friday to pay the workers. Can you send the money today?"

I broke into a sweat.

"Okay, I will do my best, but the earliest I can get the money to you is tomorrow. Meanwhile, tell Victor I need a contract for the completion of the house. I am going to have to obtain another loan, and the bank will want a detailed and firm quote."

It was the fall, the busiest time for our business, as collectors buy Pat's art for Christmas gifts to themselves and to others. We had shows to appear at and board meetings to attend. I had no option but to leave Virginia in the front line, fighting my battles over both the house and the farm, which she informed me was looking dirty.

I began wondering if the many who were thinking me crazy were right and that my obsession with Panama was doomed to disaster. I contemplated what I would do if someone offered to buy my properties at a price approaching what I had already invested. Although Pat refrained from mentioning this possibility, I knew that she would be in favor of our leaving.

For many couples, living in Bocas is more to the man's liking than to that of his spouse. When we came here it was to break the pattern of obsessive hard work. It was not either of our intentions to have the new life consume us. It was to be an escape used on a few occasions during the year. I was the one who had let this get out of hand and in doing so I had been inconsiderate of Pat's needs.

My selfishness troubled me. I have been accused several times in my life of only being interested in my own gratification. There was no question that the course I was steering was not ideal for Pat.

When I contemplated calling it quits, I came up against strong reasons for not doing so. Apart from failing in what might be the last major endeavor in my life, my being in Panama was assuming a new importance. Along the way, I had been writing vignettes describing my experiences, and the possibility of combining them into a book was emerging.

From my early twenties, I had a desire to write but never had the confidence to attempt more than a few articles on art and travel and a children's book that Pat illustrated and sold to her collectors.

When tempted to commit to the challenge of writing a book, I had always been dogged by a humility I suffered at age thirteen, when my junior school cheated on my behalf by helping me to rewrite an essay to obtain admission to the next school. The stigma of failure had endured throughout my life, convincing me that to write a book was way beyond my capability.

At my new school, another boy and I shared last place in every class. Both of us would have been asked to leave but for the other boy being an English baronet and therefore of the English aristocracy and I a star in the school rugby team. Before my seventeenth birthday, my father took me away, sending me to school where the ratio of teachers to students was one to three. In that environment, I began to learn and a year later earned a place at The Royal Military Academy at Sandhurst.

At the academy I was hopeless in French and not much better in science and economics. However, I excelled in military tactics, which balanced the books for me and allowed me to graduate with a respectable placing.

My failure with the French language had born in me the wish to one day conquer my linguistic shortcomings and be able to communicate in another language. With every year added to my age, the prospects of achieving this became less likely. Only when I had committed to Panama did they revive.

Without the experience of being unable to learn in the normal classroom, it is difficult for others to come close to understanding the humiliating effects of being learning different. Today, there is a better understanding of dyslexia and the world is kinder, but when Pat and I were young we were thought to be lazy and slow learners. In both our cases it left us short of confidence.

The prospect of both writing a book and being able to make myself understood in Spanish compelled me to press on in a final effort to achieve success. I knew I should not abandon ship at this time.

30

Confrontation

Victor was again asking for money, but still he had not given me a price for completing the house and, without that documentation, I could not get a further loan.

The situation was becoming desperate. The continued construction was dependent on my getting the money to Virginia by midday on Friday so the labor force could be paid. Victor appeared to have no reserve or, if he did, he was clearly not willing to bring it into use.

I decided the time had come to hire a lawyer to demand a contract for the final construction phase. Clearly, my asking Victor carried no weight. The problem was finding the right lawyer.

The local lawyers were unlikely to welcome the task of breaking a state of impasse with the head political figure in town. They were dependent on Victor for approval of their clients and their own construction plans.

Again, Virginia saved the day. She told me of Petra Soriano and, in my absence, hired her on my behalf.

Petra is not very tall. She comes up to my shoulder, and I am not tall. What Petra lacks in size, she makes up for in fight. She has the determination of a pit bull terrier and the same direct approach. She works independently from her office in Panama City.

I was not present when Petra and Victor met on the ground floor of the house. Pat and I were in the Shenandoah Valley of Virginia hosting an Open House for collectors of her paintings and prints.

I am told the meeting was fiery, with the diminutive Petra issuing demands for documentation from a surprised Victor. Victor decided he did not have to comply with her wishes and that the real reason for the confrontation was that I had been refused further funds. He withdrew his labor force.

In three days, Petra had worked out a contract with Rolando Robinson, a general contractor from Chiriqui Grande on the mainland. She and Rolando, together with an architect and an engineer, both from Panama City, were at the building inspecting the work to date.

The transition from Victor to Rolando caused hard feelings.

My building inspector sent me an e-mail message warning that if I endorsed the change recommended by Petra, I would put several local workers out of a job and that on my return I would face many unhappy people. I forwarded his message to Petra just in case I did have trouble awaiting me.

Victor claimed he had been cheated, but when I saw the reports of the architect and engineer, I learned the extent to which I had been scammed. If I had continued with Victor beyond this point, I would have soon been ruined.

The reports, substantiated by photographs, documented the substandard work and erroneous certification of the degree of completion of the electrical and plumbing.

Without the strength and resolution of the diminutive Petra and without the willingness of Rolando to step forward immediately, I would have had no alternative but to surrender the building. I had been forced into a position from which I could no longer keep the business with a Bocas contractor. I had a contract that stipulated that the house was to be completed within five and a half months and the price of the contract was fixed. I was once again in a position to borrow money.

Rolando brought his foreman Luis and other key workers from the mainland, finding them rooming accommodation. He hired those of Victor's team whom he believed to be have been giving value for their wages and who wanted to continue to work on the house.

Three weeks later, when the taxi from the airport brought Pat and me to the building site, the hustle and bustle of activity drove away the old fears. The relief was enormous, and for the first time I felt release from the nightmare.

Rolando's physical presence reminds me of Pooh Bear. He is not tall, but his shoulders reach forever and his body is compact. His head is large and, like Pooh's, his neck is hardly there at all. Unlike Pooh, he has the wisdom of Owl and the energy of Roo. Like Christopher Robin, Rolando is true to his word. He does not make a promise unless he knows he can come through. He tells you what his services will cost and that is it: no compromise, take it or leave it.

Rolando accepts that his quotations for a job usually turn out to be the most costly, with his rivals underbidding him by an appreciable margin.

"Mr. Malcolm, when I quote, my quote is genuine. If someone doesn't want to pay my price, he can go to the next man," Rolando said and then added, "Anyone can quote a lower price, but no one can complete the job properly for less than I quote. Quoting a price is worth nothing if you cannot finish the job without asking for more money. It will cost the owner more in the end, because the contractor does not have any money to pay, regardless of what the contract says."

Petra and Rolando rode out of the darkest mists of my life, turning despair into hope. Together, they threw me a lifeline. Both recognized that I had been swimming in a sea of ignorance and the waters had risen over my head. I grabbed the lifeline, weathered the storms of anger of those who felt cheated by the change of regime, and began again to sleep without waking in sweats of desperation.

The first task facing Rolando was to put right the errors of the past, cutting open walls and bringing the plumbing and electrical up to standard. He was present on the job many times a day, checking each detail as if this were his own house.

31

Tony Goes to the Clinic

"How much does Tony weigh?" I asked Silvia.

"Why you need know?"

"Because the boys at Aeroperlas need to know the weight of each passenger."

"Two hundred pounds," Silvia said, without looking up from her crocheting.

"I think he weighs more."

"Tell them two hundred pounds," said Silvia, making it clear that this was the end of the conversation.

I was buying tickets for all three of us to fly to Changuinola. The next day, Tony had a ten o'clock appointment with a heart specialist at La Clinica Santa Isobel.

Tony needed support when he walked. His feet were swollen and his movements unsteady. As his proxy brother, I assumed the duty of traveling with him.

At the Aeroperlas desk I was told, "We will not know until the morning if the plane is coming here before going to Changuinola. If it does not stop here, there is no way we can get you there."

The Aeroperlas staff was genuinely sorry. They knew the situation, but there was nothing they could do to help us.

"Can he go by water taxi to Almirante and then by bus to Changuinola?" one suggested.

I had thought of this prior to deciding we should go by plane.

Getting into a water taxi was an athletic feat for those over forty, on the portly side and less agile than in past years. The maneuver involved bending over and squeezing beneath the boat's canopy, while making a long step down into a narrow space between the seat rows. It was an undignified movement with the potential for landing in the lap of a passenger already below. It generated apprehension in the best of us.

Twenty minutes later you made the movement in reverse, stepping up onto the dock while again bent double. The first time I did this, I heard the sound of a rending seam and realized it came from the seat of my pants. That day I walked around Changuinola with a hand behind my back holding together the two sides of my seat. After failing to find a safety pin in four shops, someone directed me to a pharmacy.

The road between Almirante and Changuinola is scenic but mountainous and full of steep bends. If we had chosen to go that route, we would have hired a taxi, but for Tony to make the journey there and back in a day was out of the question.

"Why not speak to Captain Mathews?" someone suggested.

Captain Marvin Mathews had a Cessna 172.

"For ninety dollars I can take you, Senor Antonio and Silvia to Changuinola and back," said the Captain, who is Bocas born and bred.

"How long will you wait for us?" I asked.

"One hour free of charge and then after that ten dollars an hour."

"Done," I said. "We will be here at nine in the morning."

Getting Tony into the plane proved easier than expected. There were low, convenient steps and, with Marvin, I shoved from behind while Silva pulled from inside the cabin. We got Tony up, in and turned around. I took my place beside Marvin.

With the minimum of formality, we were airborne and flying west along the coast of the island. Below, I could see cayucus heading to market laden with plantains that, along with yucca, are a staple in the local food supply. Other cayucus appeared empty, their owners beneath the surface searching for lobsters.

I sneaked a look behind me. Tony and Silvia were looking straight ahead, focusing on Marvin and willing him to get safely back to land.

We crossed to the mainland and followed a canal dug by the banana company a century ago when its produce was shipped from Bocas. Today, the bananas are hauled in containers pulled by an old diesel train to Almirante where ships await to take them to European distribution centers.

When the canal linked up with the Changuinola River, Marvin abruptly reduced power. I felt Tony's hands clutching the back of my seat. I turned to give him a reassuring smile. Below was a green carpet of banana plants, their massive leaves waving in the breeze—like flying over the cornfields of Iowa, I was thinking, or snorkeling above a bed of lush sea grass.

Marvin executed a perfect landing, and we transferred Tony from the plane to a taxi. Five minutes later we were at the clinic.

While Silvia registered Tony with the receptionist, I read the notices pinned to the wall behind her desk.

"Parto sin Dolor, $485." I translated this as "Birth without pain."

"Parto Normal, $365." I contemplated birth with pain for the saving of $80 dollars. $80 was a big sum in this economy and supposed many had to make this their choice.

"Cesares, $715." and "Histerectoma, $915." I wondered what these operations would cost back in Virginia.

"Urgencios, 30%, additional."

"How long do you have to wait to avoid being an urgencio?" I asked the receptionist in Spanish, imagining a mother having to hold on to her emerging baby to avoid this seemingly unfair surcharge.

The receptionist pretended not to understand my question. I tried demonstrating, clutching my tummy and reeling as if in agony. She was not amused, and Silvia suggested I sit down.

It was five minutes to ten and the specialist had not yet arrived. I was back at the receptionist's desk. This time she understood me perfectly as I explained about the waiting plane and asked for assurance that Tony would be the first patient to see the doctor.

We maneuvered Tony into a wheelchair, ready to push him into the doctor's office. We were getting anxious. I stood by the door watching cars arrive. Each time a clean, new model pulled up, I was certain it contained the big man.

Time passed. I gave up standing by the door and returned to the receptionist to ask if she had any news as to the whereabouts of the doctor. As I approached, she picked up her phone and, turning her back on me, dialed a number and started a conversation. I suspected she was talking to her daughter.

I took a chair opposite a TV and watched Disney cartoons in Spanish.

"Well, at least I am learning something," I told myself, as I tried to catch words spoken in the high-pitched voices of animals.

I was having difficulty hearing and turned up the volume. Most of us old soldiers who fired rifles in the days before earplugs have poor hearing. I have spent thousands of dollars on hearing aides over the years, only to forget to take them out before walking into the shower. In Panama there is no point trying again. The humidity corrodes hearing aides within three months.

I noticed there is a lot of physical mayhem expended between these carton characters. Bullets, bombs and heavy weights dropped from cranes knocked victims down or squashed them wafer thin, but always they recovered, becoming the aggressors a moment later. Everyone survived to fight another day, unlike the violent Hollywood movies in which lives are destroyed in the most horrific of ways.

I wished that Panama would follow Ecuador's example and ban the showing of the more violent programs.

The receptionist was off the phone. With a disapproving look at me, she crossed to the TV and turned down the volume.

Another hour passed and still no doctor.

"Malcolm, you need drink?" Tony asked.

"Sure, Tony! What would you like?"

"Coffee," Tony said.

"No," said Silvia. "He no have coffee. He not allowed coffee."

I went to a nearby store and bought four fruit juices, one for each of us and one for the receptionist. We drank ours, but she pointedly kept hers intact. I took it as a personal slight.

"Silvia," I whispered. "You ask her what has happened."

"No, I don't think," said Silvia, strangely shy.

"Yes, you ask," Tony said in a loud voice. "Malcolm is right. We need know."

Silvia asked, and the receptionist said she would call the doctor's office in Panama City and make sure he was coming. There was no answer to her call, and we remembered it was Saturday.

Silvia and I changed seats. She was now watching the cartoons, and I was talking with Tony.

"Tony, I wish that other doctor had never told you to stop drinking. That has been the cause of your problem. In the old days when you and I walked down the street at midday, you got some exercise."

Precisely at twelve noon each day, Tony draws the steel doors across the front of his store and begins his two-hour break. Until the doctor decreed no more alcohol, Tony and I would set off for what we called our cup of coffee. Halfway down the street was a darkened bar without windows.

On the far side of the circular counter that surrounded the barman, Tony had his own seat. On the days when I was late, I would not be able to see him until my eyes had adjusted to the dark. Tony's drink was Cabello Rum with warm water and mine the same. We would be back at our respective homes within the half hour.

When Tony was denied this pleasure, he had no reason to walk any further than the length of his store. The only exception was our once-a-month sortie to the Chinese restaurant in the company of our wives.

"I never drink much," Tony said.

"Tony, I remember parties at our house in Carenero. Sometimes you drank a great deal."

"Only at parties. I never drunk."

"Do you remember how after a lunch party we nearly lost you in the sea?"

"No, I no remember," said Tony.

"Yes, you do! You were climbing out of the boat on your hands and knees, and we were behind you pushing. We nearly pushed you clear over the dock and into the sea on the other side. We had to grasp you by the waist of your pants to keep you from taking a dive. It was a close call. I thought we were going to be left with your pants in our hands and you at the bottom of the ocean."

"I remember!" Tony chuckled. "That was good time."

It was coming up to midday and still no doctor.

"Do you know a doctor in Panama City?" I asked Tony.

"I have good friend doctor in Panama. He was friend of me in Colon."

"Would he see you, Tony?" I asked.

"Of course, he see me. He no charge me. He longtime friend."

"Is he a heart doctor?"

"No, he doctor for old people."

"I think we should go to Panama City and see him. He will tell you which heart doctor to see."

"He a very good man. He was in trouble in Colon. He play politics, and Torijos crack down on him. He not allowed to work, but then he allowed to work again because he the only old person doctor."

"He was against the dictatorship?"

"Something like that. When he work again, other doctors no want to help him for fear they get trouble also."

"If you go to Panama City to see the doctor, is there somewhere you and Silvia can stay?"

"Yes, I have sister-in-law in Panama City. She have nice house near airport."

We left the clinic. The receptionist was happy to see us go. She smiled at Silva but did not look at me.

We flew back to Bocas, and Silvia telephoned her sister. The following Tuesday, Silvia bought tickets for the three of us to fly to Panama City. After much debate, I decided not to accompany them. Isla Carenero Elementary School was celebrating its anniversary and I was to crown the queen.

Silvia's sister had said she would meet them at the airport with a wheelchair and a taxi.

32

Animal Mismanagement

On Rolando's advice, I hired Javier, a man of almost my age, to visit the farm for three days and two nights each month. Supposedly an expert in animal husbandry, Javier was to improve the production of the farm.

Through Javier I acquired six goats, seven sheep and seven geese. Javier constructed corrals for the new livestock and improved our pigpen. With him came a boy called Ido. Ido was to work full-time every day looking after the animals and seeing that they were fed at the right times, kept clean, and had continual access to water and salt.

Ido had given up on schooling and, being slow by nature, had few prospects in life. I was glad to give him a future.

"You like animals?" I asked him in my improved Spanish.

He looked at me without expression, and I repeated the question. It appeared he considered the question needed no answer. I tried again with greater emphasis on the interrogative. Eventually he nodded.

Javier told me that Ido was a good boy and would work hard. I believed him. I considered the prospects of the farm much improved. It seemed simple. You bought your animals with one male to every five or so females. You provided food, some home grown and some purchased, and then, in due course, counted the number of babies in the litters and calculated how much you would earn selling pork or goat or whatever in so many months' time.

How naive I was!

One of the goats had twin kids. From the first day, Pat and I delighted in watching their frisky and adventurous behavior. A week later, I could find only one.

"Why only one?" I asked Ido.

He looked at me blankly and gave no response.

I found Ricardo and asked him what happened.

"Crocodile eat," he told me.

Crocodiles were a threat I had not anticipated. Ricardo pointed to the mouth of the creek where scrub trees joined the mangroves and told how the goats got free and wandered into the trees. There, one of the little ones, I was told, had been taken by a caiman.

One of the sows was ready to give birth, the first pigs to be born on the farm. I was excited. Pat and I had to leave Panama in a week, and I was hoping the babies would arrive before our departure. This did not happen and, when I next got back, the mother and all her babies were dead and buried.

"Ido, he make bad mistake," Javier told me. "He pick up mother wrong way." He showed how Ido had held the pig from behind, clasping his hands in front of the mother's belly. "Mother die and babies die."

Something was very wrong. Once again I had doubts about the future of the farm. Maybe I should have just hired men to keep the jungle down and not have dreamed of making the farm self-supporting.

33

Buying a Horse

I decided I needed to have a horse before I got much older. In ten years' time, I would find it hard going to get to the top end of the farm. Now was the time for a horse and me to make a bond. I had seen horses on a hillside in Laguna Bocatorrito and set off to investigate.

"What's her name?" I asked, stroking the neck of the three-year-old filly.

"Her name Lluvia, which mean rain," said the elderly Indian.

Eduardo Atencio was two years my elder. He had seven sons, four daughters and twenty-two grandchildren. Half his family lived on his right of possession finca. The farm bordered the northern shore of Laguna Bocatorrito, and from his house there was one of the prettiest views in the archipelago, looking down to where Dave and Linda Cerutti live on the southern shore. Eduardo believed the farm covered about five hundred acres. He had worked the land for fifty-three years, farming cattle and breeding horses.

"How much do you want for her?" I asked, examining the three-year-old filly, as if I knew what I was looking for.

"She mighty fine horse," mused Eduardo.

Eduardo was land rich but short of immediate cash. He was prepared to sell me one of his six horses, and we had reached the point where we both agreed the filly was the one most suited to me.

"She is gentle lady," Eduardo had told me. "We old men, you and me, we played marbles together. We not young like we can ride any horse. You ride big boy horse and you not the boss."

It was not the first time I had heard the reference to playing marbles together. It is the Bocas way of commenting that people are of the same age. I knew what Eduardo meant about being the boss.

It had been more than forty years since I rode. In Kenya I owned a stallion called Pronc. He was barely of medium height but a tank of a creature, whose one previous owner was an Afrikaner farmer of considerable weight. It was a matter of continual dispute as to which of us was in control.

"Well, tell me a price and maybe I buy her," I said casually.

"I can no tell you price. The horse belong my grandson BoBo. It is he horse. He need to say what he sell for."

"Where is Bobo?"

"That not he proper name. We call him BoBo, but he proper name is Gilberto. He come back later."

"How much you think he wants?"

"Maybe two hundred."

"Tell him I will give one hundred and fifty and I come back in the morning."

The next morning Eduardo was waiting for me.

Neither of us was in a hurry to recommence negotiations. Better we appeared relaxed and unconcerned.

"How come you speak such good English?" I asked the Indian.

"Lady taught me every day after Spanish School. Lady name Veronica Ansel. She black lady. Her grandfather preacher. She teach me ABC and all else."

"Your father paid Miss Ansel to teach you?"

"No, I no see my father 'til I twenty-three. My mother gave me to Miss Ansel when I was baby. Miss Ansel and me lived many places, Watering Key, Nancy Key and all around." Eduardo had used the English names for Cayo de Agua and Solarte.

"We very poor. We go wherever able to have food."

"How long have you been married to your wife Augustina?"

"Forty years. Before that I was vagabond."

"You mean you hunted the girls?"

"Yes! That what young man do. Tell they what they want to hear. They believe you. Then it is easy."

"You tell them you love them, but the word 'love' has a different meaning from what the girls want to believe?" I asked.

"Something like that," Eduardo said with a laugh.

"What did Bobo say about the price?" I slipped in, judging this to be the right moment.

"Bobo says he no sell for less than two hundred and fifty."

"Okay. No deal. I will look elsewhere." I turned to go back to my boat.

"I will see if Bobo agree to two hundred," offered Eduardo.

"Tell Bobo my last price is one hundred and seventy-five."

"Okay, you have deal. The horse yours for one hundred and seventy-five."

"But you haven't asked Bobo," I protested.

"No need! I know he agree one hundred and seventy-five."

A moment earlier I had thought I was doing fine with my negotiating. Now, I had a feeling Eduardo was the winner. I was glad Pat was not present to witness my ineptitude.

"I will be back tomorrow with my friend. Javier will examine the horse. If he says she is fine, I will pay you," I promised.

Old man Javier was impressed with the filly.

"Very pretty horse. She have no problems. What he want for horse?"

"How much you think she is worth?" I countered.

"One hundred and fifty. No more than one hundred and seventy-five."

I paid Eduardo our agreed price, and we made arrangements to use his large canoe to carry Lluvia to Tierra Oscura the following day.

Again, I justified my need for the horse.

Like the farmer of a mega acre sheep station in the outback of Australia, I needed to inspect my boundary fences at frequent intervals. I had to be sure squatters did not establish themselves on my land. Of course, with only twenty-one acres, Ricardo would get to know if anyone was living in the 'outer territory,' but it was the principle that mattered. Riding the boundary of my property was how I wished to perceive myself; moreover, horse riding is good for the body.

Over the years, Pat and I have supported various organizations that provide horseback riding for those who suffer from chronic muscular problems. We have witnessed the way in which the movement of a horse is transmitted to the body of its rider and how muscles that do not function in other situations come to life. The same transmittal of movement will benefit my aging body and help to keep its muscles exercised and strong.

This was how I explained it to Pat, when I broke the news that I had purchased Lluvia.

I liked the name Lluvia. It is a soft, feminine sound and, besides, rain is essential to life. Since becoming a novice farmer, I had experienced the importance of rain at first hand, witnessing my corn struggle to survive and then, after a day of tropical downpour, regain its verdant vitality. Too much rain was not a problem for my farm because the land sloped into the lagoon. Lluvia was a perfect name for Finca Tranquilla's filly.

"You want ride Lluvia to the creek?" asked Eduardo.

We were standing in front of his house on the top of a steep knoll. Paco, the young boy who had raised Lluvia from a foal, had galloped the filly to us, displaying the bravado of one born to the saddle. Now, we were to take her to the creek and from its steep bank maneuver her into the canoe.

I hesitated, but Paco was nodding his head enthusiastically. I did not want to disappoint either him or the large audience of mothers and children assembled to say farewell to the filly.

"Sure," I said, moving to stand on the upside of the steep slope to make mounting easier.

Given my portly figure and the lack of spring in my legs, I was conscious that the spectacle of my struggling up into the saddle would be far from elegant.

Putting my foot in the leather stirrup, I had a distinct feeling I was making a mistake, but it was too late to back out. I took hold of the pommel of the western style saddle with my left hand and, after making a few tentative warm up flexes of my knees, launched myself upwards, heaving on the saddle.

The saddle slipped towards me, giving way to my poundage. For a moment I thought I was not going to make it, but I managed get my leg over and center the saddle on Lluvia's back. I sought the other stirrup with my right foot, and, as I did so, Lluvia reared up, thrashing the air with her forelegs. I dug my knees in and leaned forward and Lluvia came down but began side stepping down the steep slope. I became unbalanced and the saddle slipped again and this time I went with it, falling on the downhill side and rolling over twice before coming to a halt on my hands and knees.

All but one person showed considerable concern as this old man gingerly got to his feet and stretched his limbs to assess the damage. Paco was the exception.

Paco's face was wreathed in smiles. I had paid heavily for failing to check the tightness of the girth. Paco had played an ace in an attempt to prevent Lluvia from being taken from his charge. It did not work. Nothing now could stop me from winning Lluvia's love.

Moving Lluvia by cayucu to the finca was a lesson in the use of log canoes for animal transportation. On the bank above the creek, Eduardo and three of his sons hobbled a fore and back leg of Lluvia and then forced the filly on her side with her back to the creek and the canoe. Next, they hobbled her other two legs and tied all four together. Paco cradled Lluvia's head and talked soothing words to her, and she remained surprisingly calm.

The large cayucu, made from the trunk of a single, massive tree, was secured tight against the bank. In it had been laid a bed of palm fronds and banana leaves.

The four men eased Lluvia slowly down the steep slope and backwards onto the bed of leaves. There she lay with her legs tied in a bunch above her. She raised her head once to look about but then settled back to await whatever her fate might be.

The weight of Lluvia put the cayucu deep in the water and, when we reached Finca Tranquilla, it grounded when the sea was still knee deep. With five of us on one side, we tipped the cayucu halfway over; and, while Paco held Lluvia's head above water, we pulled the filly feet first from the canoe. As soon as her legs were untied, she stood and followed Paco ashore. Before she reached the top of the bluff, she had her head down grazing in her new pasture.

34

More Changes at the Farm

When riding Lluvia a week later, I noticed the chivo (male goat) was limping.

"What happened to him?" I asked Ido. Again, the blank stare.

There were only two of the four turkey chicks, and I was told that hawks had taken the other two. Next, four geese were missing, and this time Bianca stood accused.

The pigs were not putting on weight. They looked anemic and nervous.

I sat down at the table with Javier, Ricardo and Berta.

"We are a disaster," I told them. "We are incapable of looking after animals. I am going to give up farming and sell the finca."

"It is Ido," Berta announced.

"What do you mean?" I asked.

"Ido, he hurt the animals."

"How do you know?"

"I see him this morning when I was washing clothes at the creek. He threw rocks at the sheep."

I called for Ido, and we all walked to the sheep pen. As we approached, the sheep moved away, and I saw that the ram was dragging a rear leg.

"Did you do this?" I asked Ido.

He stared me straight in the eyes but said nothing.

"Let me talk to him," said Javier.

"You talk to him and then bring him to the table." I turned to go back to the house, beckoning Ricardo and Berta to follow.

Javier joined the three of us. Ido was not with him. He was packing his bags.

"Ido goes today," Javier announced. "He is loco."

The pigs were still a great disappointment. Although they were being given plenty to eat, they were not gaining weight. Javier said he did not understand why.

I called in another consultant, Amando, a handsome Panamanian married to Cindy, a Canadian girl from Vancouver. Amando is a graduate of El Instituto Agropecuario, Jesus Nazarent de Atalaya. A moment's look and he knew what was wrong.

"They are filthy, Mr. Malcolm. It is no wonder they are sick. Pigs are clean animals. They cannot live like this. They are eating dirt along with their food. The only water you have for them is from the creek. That is brackish water with salt. You need to have plenty of fresh, clean water."

To prove his point about the water in the creek, Amando made me taste it. I agreed.

Javier attended the farm as consultant for the last time, and Amando, Rolando and I designed a new pig house with concrete floors and four separate pens. It had proper feeding troughs and fresh running water.

A month later, I found no sign of Berta at the farm.

"Where is Berta?" I asked Ricardo.

"With her mother."

"Where is her mother?"

"In Changuinola." He was not looking at me. I sensed something was wrong.

"Are you living alone on the finca?"

"Yes."

"Is Berta or Dilma sick?"

I got no answer.

"When are they coming back?"

He shrugged his shoulders.

We had lost another pig. I had thought it looked poorly last week, but Ricardo had said it was fine. Now, there was a freshly dug grave.

"Did you make Ricardo dig out the grave?" I was asked when I lamented my loss that evening in the Buena Vista.

"No, I didn't like to show mistrust," I said.

"Well, there are three possibilities," said a local expert on all matters.

"Either the pig is under the earth," he took a long pause for effect, "or nothing is under the earth and your pig is in someone's tummy," there was a titter of laughter from the audience, "or, wait, wait for this…" we waited in suspense, "or, it's Berta who is under there." This time there was loud laughter.

"My advice to you, my friend, is to get your little old self down there and stand over Ricardo as he digs out the hole. You might be in for a surprise."

I didn't sleep well that night. I had had the same thoughts, but I had sidelined them because the consequence of the third choice was too much to contemplate.

The second was not that much better, given that Ricardo was my one hope remaining for working the farm.

"What's wrong, Mr. Malcolm?" asked Virginia. "You look like you did not sleep. You been in trouble with Miss Pat?"

I told her of my concern.

"Well, you waste your time in worry. You should have asked me. I know where Berta is."

"Where is she?"

"She is living in Changuinola."

"For Heaven's sake, why didn't you tell me?"

"'Cause I didn't know 'til yesterday, and I didn't see you since then."

Bianca was about to pup. Any day she would produce her first litter. I wished there was a woman on the finca to keep an eye on her while Ricardo was working. Bianca was bought to protect Berta. Now, when it was Bianca who needed caring for, Berta was missing.

"Ricardo, you do not want to have a woman with you on the finca?" I asked the next time I saw him.

"No," said Ricardo. "Better no woman."

"Too much trouble?"

"Yes," he acknowledged. This time he smiled.

He was working well and taking a pride in his responsibilities. I invited him to lunch with me at a restaurant in Bocatorrito. He changed clothes and once again was the better dressed of the two of us.

Cipriano, the owner of the only restaurant in either lagoon, was a retired policeman. He and Santa Flores, his wife, and son Herman catered to tourists visiting the lagoon to watch the dolphins. All three of them were masters at preparing fish dinners. Their restaurant was over the water, a quarter of a mile from the finca of Eduardo and his family. They cooked over a charcoal fire that was constantly hot.

From time of order to time of serving was invariably an hour. If you were in a hurry and asked for the cooking to be speeded up, regardless of promises, it would still take an hour. The wait was compensated for by the pleasure of drinking a cold bottle of Panama while taking in the beauty of the lagoon or conversing with whichever of the three was not working in the kitchen. Santa Flores and Herman were cooking. Ricardo and I were sitting at the bar talking to Cipriano. Whenever I became lost in trying to understand the Spanish, Cipriano came to my aid with a translation.

After a while, the other two got into a prolonged and rapid discussion and, giving up on trying to follow the gist of it, I turned my attention to Ricardo's shoes. They were ankle length and formal, similar to what we used to call chukka boots, a name brought home from India by Brits who served there in the days of the Raj.

India is a spiritual memory I turn to when filling gaps in time. In 1963, I was assigned by the military to attend the Indian Defense Services Staff College, one of two British students sent each year. The college was high in the Nilgiri Hills, more than six thousand feet above sea level.

One Sunday, I set off for a day's trout fishing. Being unable to find anyone willing to join me, I went alone, ignoring the cautions of others.

The river I was fishing led into the mountains. The sides of the valley reached high above me. During the morning, the sun lit the left slopes. The right of the valley remained in shadow.

Dry fly fishing is addictive. You fish a stretch of river and, when you reach a bend, you are instantly tempted to continue and fish the next stretch. You enter a trance and lose count of time and distance. Always there is reason to fish just one more pool.

Well past noontime, I paused to eat a sandwich. Since entering the valley, I had not seen a single person. Now, with my concentration off the river, I became aware of my vulnerability. I was alone and defenseless in a place of deep seclusion. The fear was momentary, banished by a mysterious confidence that overcame my imagination. I relaxed and was so at peace I dozed before continuing my way up the river.

It was late afternoon when I turned to walk back. The sun was low on the left and now shone onto the slope that had been in shadow. When I reached the spot where I had stopped, I sat a moment and contemplated the scene. It was then that I saw the source of my peace. Opposite me, halfway up the hillside, a man sat lotus style. He wore the robe of a sadhu and was motionless. We exchanged no recognition and none was needed. I knew he sensed my gratitude. The experience was the awakening of my spiritual awareness.

My meditation on days more than half a lifetime ago ended when Herman arrived to lay the table. I noted that Ricardo was on his third beer. I had not heard him so talkative nor seen him so confident.

35

Social Tactics

I was on a flight from Sydney to Los Angeles after visiting my newest grand-daughter and her parents who live in Ashgrove, a suburb of Brisbane, the state capital of Queensland.

Staying in Ashgrove made me nostalgic for England. Streets flanked with wide grass verges, people walking their dogs and greeting strangers, parks with swings and boys playing scratch games of rugby football. When the battery in my computer gave out, I turned my thoughts to Pat and our visits to England.

I miss the English countryside. I recalled a particular summer evening when we sat on a rock high above a village of thatched roofs and ancient stone and without a word observed the Sun taking Her leave behind hills across the valley. As the shadow of darkness climbed slowly towards us, we listened to the music of the twilight, the murmured voices of neighbors talking over garden walls, the hoarse bark of a fox, the chorus of rooks settling on the upper branches of the tallest trees. In near darkness, we climbed down to the valley floor walking, between high hedges that flanked the road and made for the lights of the village pub where I ordered a scotch and ginger ale for Pat and a pint of draught ale for me.

Neither Pat nor I are out of the common mould that produces people suited to normal social practices. We lack small talk and in a game of Trivial Pursuit are sure to lose by an embarrassing margin.

I have a coffee mug that I keep on my desk. Inscribed on its side is a quote by Henry David Thoreau, American philosopher, author and naturalist. It reads, "If a man does not keep pace with his companions, perhaps it is because he hears a different drummer. Let him step to the music he hears, however measured or far away." This mug is a treasured possession.

In Bocas, the only certainty is that what is certain will not be so tomorrow. This epitomizes my life. I understand how ridiculous this is in the eyes of my army contemporaries, who, following the traditional pattern, now live in the security and comfort of the English countryside, taking their dogs for two walks a day, tending to their roses and, when the season is right, hunting pheasant and partridge. To them I am irresponsible and doomed to failure.

The flight from Sydney to Los Angeles was scheduled to take thirteen and a half hours. I was in a bulkhead seat with no view of the videos. I could have moved to a seat in the middle of row 74 and immerse myself in movies, but I decided not to do so.

The titles of the movies seldom mean anything to me. Living in the backwater of Bocas, great movies pass us by. Gringos returning from Stateside visits describe the latest sensations, and I list them in my computer, intending to rent the videos when next in Virginia. Somehow, Pat and I never get around to it.

Our being movie illiterate puts us at a disadvantage. Movies and their stars are the standard lifeline of dinner party hostesses faced with a silence. As other guests enthusiastically launch into this harmless topic, we sit back, nodding our heads in a contrived semblance of awareness.

Instead of watching the plane's movies, I continued to read *The Brethren* by John Grisham, which I had started on the flight out.

Being a slow reader, I appreciate a book that moves the story along at a fast pace. I have an attention span of about ten minutes. Novels that dwell for twenty pages on the same scene are unlikely to keep my attention. I tell myself that one day, when my life is less busy, I will read the classics.

Having limited literary taste used to cause me embarrassment. Like the bullies in school, there are pseudo-intellectuals who take a pleasure in exposing my shortcomings. I have developed a counter-attack technique, designed to throw the aggressor off balance.

"What are you reading?" asked our hostess during a dinner party in Virginia.

The question was directed at me. To admit to either John Grisham or Wilbur Smith would have been a humiliating defeat.

The hostess was an unexciting lady whose emotions cross the page like the recording of a heart that has ceased to beat. She is married to a man too timid to speak for fear of letting her down. They have no children, and I do not wonder why.

The lady never rests from seeking to create the impression of being intellectually superior to all present. She does not brook opposition, which she kills with the sting of a hornet. Like most bullies, she has an innate ability to identify easy targets. From the start she had spotted my literary deficiencies. On the evening in question, I had come prepared.

"We are all waiting, Malcolm. Tell us what you are reading."

All faces are turned towards me.

"*Sex, Ecology and Spirituality* by Ken Wilber," I said. I had found the book at our local library's annual sale of seldom-read books and added it to my purchases in the belief that one day its pages might contain an idea for a short story.

I looked at our hostess in apparent expectation of a comment. For the first time she showed discomfort and so I continued, "It is enormous in scope, insightful from beginning to end, and immensely courageous."

An hour before, I had memorized this sentence from the backside of the book's dust jacket. The choice of words belonged to Mr. Michael Murphy, author of *The Future of the Body*. Given the circumstance, I omitted to give Mr. Murphy credit. I left the impression this erudite and concise synopsis was of my own coinage.

I won the moment and absolution from future invitations.

In the early days of our being in Bocas, there were two ladies who rivaled each other for the attentions of the governor of the province. Newly appointed by President Moscoso, Luis Nuques, a banana baron from Changuinola, attended his office in the Palazzo on an irregular basis. To be on friendly terms with the Governor gave the impression you had been accepted into the highest social circle and implied you also could influence policy.

"I had a conversation with Luco this afternoon," our hostess announced at a small dinner party. "I told him that he must do something about getting proper street lighting."

"Oh, did you?" said her rival. "I did not know he was in town. He usually calls me when he is coming to Bocas."

"Oh well, he was just here for the day. He listened very carefully to what I had to say. I told him he also needs to do something about the noise. We need a ban on music after eleven at night, I told him."

"Did he say how Laly is? She is such a darling, and I am very fond of her. We are like sisters, you know."

"No, he didn't mention her. We only talked business. Poor dear, he has so much on his mind."

"I know. I attended his meeting last week."

"Oh, I did not know there was a meeting last week. I did not receive any notice of it." Our hostess looked perturbed.

"No, well, sweetie, you see it wasn't public. It was just for his advisors."

"Oh, I didn't know you are an advisor."

"Well, not exactly, I am sort of ex-officio, if you know what I mean. I had stuck my head around his door just to say 'hi' and he beckoned me in. I sat at the back where he could see me and the others couldn't."

"What was the meeting about?" asked our hostess.

"Actually, it was about garbage. I was able to help him. He was about to agree to what would have been a mistake, and I shook my finger at him and he saw and deferred the decision."

"Oh, tell me more please! I am most interested. You know, garbage is one of my greatest concerns."

"Oh, I would love to tell you, sweetie, but I don't think it would be appropriate to do so. You see, it was a confidential meeting and closed to the public."

A few months later the Governor resigned, citing the pressure of his business as his reason.

36

A Glorious Start to a Day of Trouble

Under Rolando's close supervision, the house was progressing rapidly.

Now, it was the farm that was causing me grave concern. Pat and I had been away for six weeks, attending to business. A week before our return, Virginia had visited Finca Tranquilla to check on its progress and give Ricardo and his helper their pay. That evening she sent me an e-mail asking that I call her.

"Mister Malcolm, I have good news and bad news. Which you want first?"

I felt my stomach sicken. I had become accustomed to this greeting of hers and knew that it was her way of preparing me for something she felt would upset me. Her reasoning was that if I believed there was something good to follow, my upset would be lessened. She knew I would ask to have the bad news first.

"Go ahead! Get it over with! Tell me the bad news."

"I did went to the finca yesterday and it was all dirty. The grass was long and the bush grow tall."

"How bad was it, Virginia?" I asked.

"Pretty bad, Mister Malcolm. I did tell Ricardo he best get it clean before you come or you would be very angry."

"I will be with you in a week, Virg, and then I will see what to do."

"I have some more to tell you."

"Good or bad?"

"Not good, Mister Malcolm. It will make you sad."

My stomach took a second beating.

"Go ahead, Virg. What now?"

"Bianca did have her babies, but they all die."

"How come?" I asked, riding this punch as best I could. "Is Bianca okay?"

"She is sad like you, Mr. Malcolm. I am very sorry. We are all sad."

After this, I forgot to ask for the good news.

On the afternoon of my arrival in Bocas, a man stopped me as I was entering Don Chicho's to say hello to my sister Joanne. I recognized the man as being from Dark Lands. He told me Ricardo had been bragging, saying that now he was the farm manager and he did not have to work and that I would not be able to fire him.

It is not uncommon for an owner to hear ill spoken of his workers by others who would like to take their jobs. However, this was an unusual allegation and it added to my fears.

The next morning I set out early for the farm, intending to be there by seven, the hour at which work supposedly starts. As I headed the boat due south down the main lagoon, the sun's rays were lighting the eastern sky, painting varying hues of crimson on the undersides of thin layers of lateral clouds. In gaps between the clouds, the sky behind had already shed its night and showed a gentle blue.

The sea was calm and the ride smooth. The outlines of Solarte and San Cristobal Islands were mere smudges of dark on the horizon to either side. I used my compass to keep on course, knowing daylight would give me sufficient visibility to find my way before I reached the winding passage through the mangroves that lie between San Cristobal and Buena Esperanza.

I had been agitated and in a hurry to meet with Ricardo, but now I cut back the engine so the boat barely maintained a plane. The splendor of the dawn drove out all other thoughts.

There was no other boat in sight, no sign of mankind. I was Nature's sole audience to this morning's show, and I was sitting in the best seat in the theater. I rejoiced at being alone to interpret the show in my own way, without another's comment to shatter the crystal ball.

By the time I reached the passage through the mangroves, the sun's rays were lighting the hilltops of Isla San Cristobal. Crossing Laguna Bocatorrito, making for the entrance to Laguna Tierra Oscura, I thought of breakfast and of turning east and seeing if Dave and Linda at Green Acres were the early risers they claimed to be. A disturbance in the flat calm of the water close to the mangroves caught my attention. Tarpon were feeding, their characteristic rolling action breaking the surface. I decided to investigate.

I was a hundred yards from a cayucu before I spotted it in the shadows of the mangroves. An Indian of mature age was paying out a line, and I knew then that he had hooked a fish and I was about to witness a duel between man and his prey. I stopped the boat and settled down to watch.

When the Indian ran out of line, the fish began to tow the cayucu, no small feat given that it was a substantial canoe. The combatants crossed from the mainland side of the lagoon entrance to the shore of San Cristobal before the fish tired and the Indian slowly wound the line back around the narrow mid-rift of the plastic bottle that served as his fishing spool. I moved near so as to clearly see the action. When the fisherman felt his prey turn again to attempt a new break for freedom, he kept sufficient pressure on the line to make the fish struggle to gain each yard of separation.

The Indian gave total attention to the contest and showed no awareness of my presence. He repeated the process of give and take many times, each time taking a little bit more than he gave. When he eased his prey to within a few yards, the fish saw the cayucu and the hunter and leaped clear into the air, twisting in an arc while shaking his head in an attempt to rid himself of the hook. As he shook, his massive scales rattled, adding sound effects to the drama. At that point I thought the contest was over and the fish had won, but I was wrong. The fish was still hooked and the Indian, unperturbed, kept the line spinning out until his prey, again exhausted, was yielding to his pull.

The second round of the battle had begun, but now the odds were increasingly in favor of the fisherman as the resistance of the fish weakened and its runs became ever shorter and less forceful.

Still the Indian took his time, patient and confident of the eventual outcome. When the fish and hunter next saw each other, the fish did not leap. Instead, it swam straight for the cayucu and took refuge directly beneath it.

The Indian rose to his feet, standing with perfect balance. In one hand he held a harpoon fashioned from a mangrove root, in the other, the line. The three of us waited in suspense, the fish, the Indian and me. I alternated between wanting the life of the fish to be spared and the Indian to have protein for his family and friends. Reluctantly, I decided the needs of the Indian children came first.

The end came so quickly that I hardly knew what had happened. In one, unbroken movement, the Indian thrust the harpoon and swung his prey up and over the rail of the cayucu. Lying lengthways, the fish thrashed his tail, rocking the cayucu in a ferocious attempt to get at his adversary, but his head was toward the Indian, who, taking up his paddle, struck a series of blows that soon ended all resistance.

Turning to face me, the victor acknowledged my presence by lifting an arm in salute. I raised both my arms above my head in a signal of congratulations and he smiled back, pleased to have had a witness to his victory. Pulling deep with his paddle, he headed for home. When he was at a respectable distance, I restarted my engine and continued on my way.

It was eight-thirty when I reached the finca.

Ricardo was not at the dock to meet me. There was only a nervous and forlorn looking Bianca, her belly hanging slack and her teats swollen and unused.

I assumed Ricardo was working at the back of the finca and had not heard the boat's engine. Walking from the bluff towards his house, I saw signs of neglect. The grass was long and scrub plants were a foot or more high. He had clearly not heeded Virginia's warning.

I stood on the first ridge and, cupping my hands to my mouth, yelled, "Ricardo," in the direction of the far corner of the finca. I bellowed his name a second time in my strongest parade ground voice, expecting to hear an answering, "yaoo, yaoo," the call used by Indians when revealing their whereabouts in the forest. There was no response.

I turned towards his house and saw him standing in the entrance buttoning his shirt. In the shadows behind him was the figure of woman. I walked towards the two of them and saw that the woman was Berta. She had a look of anger on her young face.

"Ricardo, the farm is a mess. What is going on?" I could not stop myself from sounding angry.

"Need more men," Ricardo said. "The farm need two more men. Too much work."

"Why are you not working? It is almost nine?"

"Berta want talk," he said, looking down at his feet.

"Is Berta back to stay?" I asked.

"Yes," was his only reply.

"What happened with Bianca?"

Ricardo told me a confused story of how he had not expected the pups to be born so soon. He had shut Bianca in her little house as usual one night and in the morning found the dead pups.

I walked the farm with Ricardo. What I saw brought back my worst fears. He had been my one hope and I had done all I could to encourage him and to give him a sense of worth and responsibility.

The immediate need was to catch up on six weeks of virtual neglect. Only Ricardo knew the finca well enough to make this happen.

"Ricardo, you are to hire two additional men for two weeks. By the end of that time, the farm is to be totally clean."

He looked relieved.

I kept a close eye on him over the next week. The clean up progressed well. Berta remained with Ricardo, and I let myself believe that there would be a renewal of commitment and the farm would go ahead from this point.

I was troubled about what had happened to Bianca. I heard talk of Ricardo having been seen drinking in Almirante. I suspected that Bianca had been neglected for a day or maybe more, during which time she had been shut alone in her little hut. I envisioned her there in the heat, without water, giving birth to her babies. This image of suffering and neglect sickened me whenever it came to mind.

I had a mixture of emotions, including my own guilt for not having arranged better care for her. I felt anger with Ricardo but tempered it with the realization that Berta's return must have been a distraction. What had happened drew me closer to Bianca, and from then on I spent more time talking to her whenever I was at the farm.

Toward the end of the second week of restoring the finca to a state of cleanliness, I arrived without warning in the mid-morning to be met by Ricardo wearing a neatly pressed dress shirt and pants and looking like a dude. Berta sat at a table beneath the orange tree, her mouth pouted and her eyes downcast. Between her feet, Bianca lay, relishing having her tummy rubbed by Berta's foot.

"Where are you going?" I asked Ricardo.

"I not going," he said, without looking at me.

"Why are you dressed like this?"

He shrugged.

"I can see you are not working," I said.

"I am working. I supervise the workers."

"No!" I said. "It does not happen like that. You work along side them, and you work the same hours. That is how it happens. I want you to start right away."

Ricardo hesitated and glanced over at Berta before going slowly back to the house.

Berta turned to join him, and I heard raised voices.

I stood waiting. Soon, he appeared in his working clothes and without looking at me walked past, heading in the direction of the other workers.

"Wait a minute, please," I called to him.

He stopped and turned, his face expressionless. Again looking down, he focused on the tip of his machete as he poked at the ground between his feet. I kept my distance, conscious of the razor sharp blade.

"If you are going to continue to work for me, you must change your attitude. The farm cannot function with you behaving this way."

"He needs two more men."

Berta's voice came from behind me. I turned and saw that she and Bianca had resumed their place at the table.

"No!" I told her empathically. "We have managed with just two in the past, and it works fine when both are doing their jobs."

I left Ricardo to go to his work and went in search of Lluvia. I would have liked to have Bianca accompany me, but I did not call her. With Berta again rubbing her tummy, I might have suffered rejection and loss of face.

Lluvia was the one friend on the farm I could trust. Together, we walked to the far end of the bluff, myself in the lead and she following behind, nudging my shoulders with her soft muzzle. When I stopped, she came and stood beside me. We stood savoring a cool breeze lifting off the water of the lagoon.

"Don't worry, Lluvia. I won't desert you. We are going to win this battle."

She turned to look at me and I made her a promise.

"Lluvia, I am going to find you a boyfriend. You are young and beautiful. I will find you a boy horse to love you and admire you. You will have babies, and they will grow up to be as beautiful as you and bring joy to us all."

On the way back to Bocas, I called on Eduardo to see if he had a stallion to sell me.

"Yes, I have one stallion you could have. He mighty big. Very fine horse."

"Can I see him now?"

"No, him way back in the jungle. Him horse, he belong to my other son."

"How much do you want for him?"

"How much you pay for Lluvia?"

"One hundred and seventy-five."

"This horse more bigger. Him mighty fine. I speak with Marco."

When I told Rolando and Virginia of my encounter with Ricardo and Berta, Rolando said, "Mr. Malcolm, you don't have to worry. I will find you two good workers. Ricardo and Berta must go."

37

A Lifeline Just in Time

Two days after my troublesome encounter with Ricardo, Rolando and I threw a party for all who had worked on the new house. We were celebrating its completion.

"Mr. Malcolm, at this evening's party, I want that you talk to Andres. I think he would be good on your farm. He have experience with animals, and he is good worker."

Andres Medina Rodriquiez was born in 1968 in Santa Catalina, a remote Indian community at the mouth of the Rio Tonkris, about halfway between Bocas and Colon. A Seventh Day Adventist mission couple, Dennis and Milia Kick were based at the settlement. Milia gave birth to her first son Marlin a few days before Andres came into the world.

The two boys grew up playing together and, when older, became surfing buddies off the beach of gold sand that stretches unbroken for miles along this deserted shoreline.

Andres was the top student in his final year at the mission school. Dennis encouraged Andres to continue his studies and helped him secure a place at the Insituto Tecnico Agrapecuorai de Atolayo, an agricultural college. After college, he married Kasilda, a girl who was born and raised in a village reached by a three and a half hour journey made by cayucu and on foot from Santa Catalina.

Andres and Kasilda came to Bocas looking for work. In previous years, Andres had worked for Rolando building schools for the government on the mainland. He had respect for Rolando for being a just employer. When Rolando had told him he could only offer work for the short term on the completion of my house, Andres had accepted.

Andres is mestizo, part Bugle Indian and part Spanish. He is of average Indian height and therefore shorter in stature than the Afro-Antilleans.

When I talked to him, he looked me straight in the eye. He listened, considered and discussed, and instantly I had confidence in him. He clearly had a thorough grounding in general agriculture and a particular knowledge of animal husbandry. I believed he would take his responsibilities to heart and that with his knowledge and experience would bring to an end our chapter of farm disasters.

Rolando also introduced me to Samuel. Samuel was well suited to be the other worker. Immensely strong, he came with a reputation for physical endurance. Although in his mid-forties and ten years older than Andres, he told me that he did not want the major responsibility and would be happy for Andres to be in charge in my absence.

Rolando had found me a good combination of brains and brawn. I was almost ready to make the change, but first I had to satisfy myself that I was being fair to Ricardo and had given him sufficient chance to reform his ways. Ricardo had worked well for me until the time of the return of Berta. I had trusted him and he had responded to that trust. I returned to the farm.

Berta was sitting at the table looking as defiant as ever.

"Buenas tardes. Como esta?" I gave her the customary afternoon greeting. She did not answer.

"Where is Ricardo?"

Berta nodded her head in the direction of the back of the farm. I did not need to walk far to know that Ricardo had done little during the five days.

I could have given him notice to leave that afternoon, but I needed witnesses. Moreover, I was concerned as to how he might express anger. I needed others with me when telling Ricardo and Berta to leave.

Instead of speaking with Ricardo, I sought out Lluvia. Talking with Lluvia calmed my nerves. Together we walked to the bluff and stood watching the coming of evening. The lagoon was at peace.

The finca is just nine point two degrees north of the equator. Unlike the lingering evenings of the higher latitudes, there is little time between the lengthening of shadows and the closing in of night.

"It's time I was on my way," I told Lluvia. "There is no moon tonight."

When darkness covers the lagoon, its blanket is complete. It will be many years before power is brought to these shores and the lights of homes lend a hand to navigation. Most living around the lagoon go to bed at sunset, lying on mats or strips of cardboard cut from packing cartons. After a day's work in the sun, sleep comes easily. However, not everyone works and those who have spent the daylight hours idle have only lovemaking to while away the ten hours of darkness. It is little wonder the birthrate is high in these parts.

My rule was to be through the mangrove passage between Isla San Cristobal and Buena Esperanza before dark. At night the mangroves appear to have congealed into a single mass, offering no hint of the way through. Even when you have found the opening, the passage makes several turns, each direction being no more than a hundred yards. Navigation by GPS is impossible for a dummy like me.

Halfway across Laguna Bocatorrito, I noticed someone waving from Eduardo's dock. I changed course. Eduardo was waiting for me.

"I think it better you no buy the stallion."

"Why?"

"He no broken properly yet. He mighty strong. I think you not young man enough for him. He bad boy."

"Eduardo, I appreciate your telling me that. I agree it would be dangerous. Lluvia and I will wait for another boy horse."

"You my friend, and friends take care of each other," Eduardo said as I left his dock.

My diversion and conversation had cost me ten minutes, ten minutes in which it had become considerably darker. The entrance to the passage was no longer visible. On the second attempt, I thought I had found it. I moved forward, the engine barely turning, as I shone my flashlight along the walls of green. After five minutes I came up against an impenetrable barrier of thick mangroves. I turned about to find my way back to the starting point.

I tried calling Pat on my cell phone, but the signal was blocked by the hill above me. I imagined Pat, with supper ready, looking out from the terrace, concern beginning to nag the corners of her mind. I had no way of telling her what had happened.

"Please, God, help me," I prayed. "Get me out of this one, and I promise never to be so stupid again."

I had communicated with God more times since coming to Panama than in the previous fifty years of my life. Much of the communication had been emergency calls for help. I hoped there was not an allocation of answered prayers. If there was, I must be close to the bottom of my barrel.

I was angry with myself. It would have been so easy to leave the finca after confirming the justice of firing Ricardo. If I had not stopped to talk to Lluvia, I would have been home in time for a drink on the terrace and then supper. My need for the sympathy of women has frequently led to trouble. My conversation with Lluvia had cost me dearly.

I heard a distant engine. The sound became louder. I turned my engine off, unsure what to do. Valentino, who owns a farm near mine, had men try and force him to stop near here one night. He was convinced they had wanted to rob him.

"God, please make these friendly folks," I prayed.

I turned my engine back on, revving it to increase the sound. When I turned it down, the other engine had been cut off. There was a long silence. My heart was pounding.

"Yaoo, yaoo," the call was from close by.

I hesitated as I weighed the odds and then gave the response, "Yaoo, yaoo!"

The engine started again and the sound came closer and then cut off once more.

I heard men talking. They were on the other side of a wall of mangrove. Again, the engine started and I listened to it as it returned in the direction from which it had come. The sound became faint before increasing once more, telling me that now the boat was on my side of the barrier. I turned on my engine and shined the light towards the noise. A cayuca was coming towards me. In it two men were shielding their eyes from my light. I turned the light to one side.

"You going the wrong way, Mr. Malcolm." It was Eduardo.

"Thank You, God," I said. "I will repay You."

Rolando and Samuel were beside me the morning when we told Ricardo to go. It was a tense meeting. Ricardo looked highly volatile but was clearly taking instructions from Berta. He stood facing the three of us, prodding the ground between us with his machete. His glances to Berta were like those of a quarter-back to his coach. I wondered at the power of Berta, a girl still in her teens.

Whatever the signal Berta gave, Ricardo accepted the fact that we required the two of them to pack their possessions and leave the following morning. Samuel stayed and at once started to apply his machete to the much-needed clearing of the areas around the two houses.

Ricardo and Berta's first stop after their departure was the Changuinola Labor Office, suggesting that this was in Berta's mind when she signaled Ricardo to accept the order to leave the finca. The compensation demands of the two of them were extensive and largely without justification. Virginia negotiated on my behalf, and the Labor Office decided on a payment that was equitable to both parties.

PART III
The Turn Of The Tide

38

The Revival

In the tropics, neglect of animals and land quickly leads to sickness and disorder. Disease and infection are fast acting, and sick animals soon die if not treated and nurtured. Land unattended is taken over by scrub that rapidly establishes ascendancy over other plants.

The reverse is also true when the management is good and the spirit willing. Under the leadership of Andres, our fertile, volcanic soil, ample sunshine and water, and a year-round growing season gave us a rapid revival of health and good fortune.

In the past we had not accorded respect to our animals. Felipe, Ricardo and Ido had no love for them and had neglected to spot their needs beyond food and water. They seldom noticed when an animal was ailing and, when they did, they would not look for the reason. Our record was shameful, and for that I take blame because I should not have started on my goal until I had learned more and could spend sufficient time at the farm.

Kasilda, the young wife of Andres, assumed responsibility for watching over the babies born to our animals and for caring for any animals that showed signs of ill health. Her personal attention had an immediate effect, and deaths of young animals became a rarity.

Under the new regimen, day-old chicks have their drinking water changed every four hours and receive visits every two hours between 2 a.m. and 6 a.m., the hours when the cool of the night make them huddle together and risk suffocation. A light burns in the young chicks' cage to provide warmth. The intensive care of the chicks continues for their first ten days, after which they are out of danger.

When both our sows gave birth to nine piglets, the last little one from each litter was pitifully small. Kasilda took the two of them to live under her house and nurtured them for three weeks. By then, they were strong enough to fend for themselves in competition with their siblings.

Chickens became our main product, following an environmental impact study that showed the enormity of handling the daily excrement from eighty pigs.

We sold our existing pigs and purchased a quality boar and two sows to maintain some pig presence and began purchasing one hundred day-old chicks every three to four weeks. We kept the chickens free-range and fed on corn, coconut and the insects and bugs that they hunt for themselves. Our organic chickens, with their yellow meat, rapidly earned a reputation for excellent flavor and began to command a handsome price per pound, compared to the market price for the white meat of chickens fed commercial meal and supplements and pumped with hormones and antibiotics.

Andres rapidly developed a list of "clients," as he calls them, to whom he supplies chickens on a regular basis. Our fowl family expanded to include Muscovite ducks, geese, turkeys and guinea fowl.

In keeping with our switch from pigs to chickens, maize (corn) replaced plantains as our main crop. We fertilized the soil with the chicken abono (manure) and beans. A visitor from Guatemala gave us the tip to plant a bean at the foot of each maize plant when the plant is three feet tall. After harvesting the maize, the bean plants get plowed into the soil, replacing the nitrogen. With 365 days of growing and no down time, we began harvesting three crops of maize a year. This made attention to soil nourishment of vital importance.

With animal mortality greatly reduced and our sheep and goats producing babies twice a year, our flocks began to grow. I walked the farm, delighted to see the animals grazing beneath the cocoa trees or in the open pasture by the creek. They were helping to keep the undergrowth under control and at the same time fertilizing the soil.

We added to the farm's fruit trees and plants with avocado, papaya, passion fruit, guanabana, (known as soursop in some places) and other fruits often considered exotic in first world countries, such as naranjilla, which makes a delicious juice, and granadilla, a fast growing vine that gives a melon like fruit also good for juicing. Our target was not to market the fruit but to have sufficient variety to provide a ripe fruit at all times of the year.

My run of good luck continued when I came across a shredder for sale. It was battered and rusty, but that was not a problem. All shredders soon look bruised and worn; it goes with their job. As for rust, it was not in the places that mattered; and, besides, most equipment in the rain forest shows some rust.

The shredder became key to our making abono organico (organic fertilizer). We fed the machine chicken poop, the husks of cocoa pods and washed sea grass before transferring the mix to silage pits. We dispensed with artificial fertilizers and obtained an organic certification for our cocoa trees.

Andres built seeding beds waist high off the ground and roofed them for shade. For ground level irrigation during the dry seasons, we set up a system of continual drip leading from tanks suspended on high platforms and gravity fed from a well Andres and Samuel dug at the top of the farm.

Jeff Moore, the redheaded equestrian judge we met on day two of our Bocas venture, told us about the Echo Foundation in Fort Myers, Florida. A Christian organization dedicated to solving World Hunger through science and technology, Echo offers advice and seeds to third world farmers. Pat and I visited the Foundation's experimental farm and purchased packets of seeds for plants suited to growing in tropical climates and a CD entitled, "Ideas for Growing Food Under Difficult Conditions."

The Echo CD told us about quail grass, a spinach-type plant rich in protein and heavily cultivated in Indonesia. Quail grass grows quickly, producing its first harvest of leaves within four weeks. The leaves have no taste when raw but, when boiled for five minutes, become full of the flavor of spinach. Andres, Kasilda and Samuel took a liking to the quail grass, and for the first time were eating a green vegetable on a regular basis.

Following Echo's advice, we chopped up complete quail grass plants and fed them to the chickens, geese and ducks. Other plants introduced to us by Echo were also contributing to the well-being of our animals and the replenishment of nutrients in our soil. Echo is a teacher and adviser to whom we constantly refer in the process of learning. I want one day to take Andres to the Foundation's Global Village to meet our mentors.

I started to fantasize over becoming a vendor of gourmet abono organico to Gringos whose lands were less fertile than the volcanic soil of Tierra Oscura.

"I will be accepting orders for specialized blends," I announced to dinner party guests.

"We will mix to order. The most costly blend will contain bat poop. Bat is the heaviest per cubic inch and contains the highest nutrient value. As you can imagine, bat is the caviar of poop and is relatively rare."

"And where are you going to find bat poop?" I was asked.

"Good question," I said in my most professorial manner. "If you want it in quantity you have to find a cave that is home to a major colony. My problem is that someone else is on to bat poop and is clearing the known caves on a regular basis."

"Do you like the farm?" An observant friend, who had noticed her growing impatience, addressed the question to Pat.

"I have work to do, and I don't have time to be playing," Pat responded.

"I am thinking of erecting some bat houses on the farm, but they will only attract bachelor bats and only in small numbers."

Pat interrupted to say, "Malcolm, the coffee is ready and we all need our water glasses filled."

"Yes, darling. Right away," I said, getting up from the table.

A hundred chickens every three weeks was not going to make one rich, but making profits no longer mattered. My ambition had changed from seeking to become an entrepreneurial dueno (owner) to that of being a campesino, a small time subsistence farmer whose investment in time and stock is broad, protecting against wipeout of a single crop or by animal disease.

If the farm became self-sufficient and organic, then I would have achieved my aim. I could then devote my excess energies to help improve the education environment of the children of the lagoon and of Bocas in general.

I rejoiced in feeling a change coming over me. I had been preaching the need to slow down but had only done so when watching a dawn or sunset. Most of the day my breathing had been shallow and my mind cluttered with the thoughts of things that had to be done immediately.

"Immediately for what?" I asked myself.

"Immediately so that I could start on the next immediate need."

I had come to Panama to step off the treadmill and had climbed back on. With the survival of the farm no longer under immediate threat, my anxiety level fell. My normal breaths reached deeper into my lungs, and I became more reasonable toward Pat and her needs.

39

Visitors

Pat and I were once the owners of a Venetian Style mansion on Snell Island in Tampa Bay in Florida. We sold the property after having enjoyed it for ten years and moved into an apartment above an art gallery that we owned in downtown St. Petersburg.

Owning a comfortable home on the water in Florida has its drawbacks. Apart from the need to constantly work to protect doors and window frames from the ravages of salt, there is the lack of privacy during the months of January and February.

"Hello, Malcolm. This is Ed Steiner. How are you doing?"

"The Henderson's are in Australia for six months. I am the house sitter!" I slammed down the phone.

"Who was that, Malc?" Pat called from her studio.

"I don't know. I didn't listen past him asking how I am doing. It seems the investment salesmen are even targeting folks down here. Funny how they all start with the same opening pitch."

The phone rang again. I lifted the receiver and listened.

"Malcolm, I know it is you. There is only one person with that quirky English accent."

His voice was heavy New York, almost to the point of being theatrical.

"This is Ed. You know, Ed and Elspeth."

The name Elspeth sparked a distant memory but not one I could bring to focus.

"Oh, hi, Ed! Did I cut you off just now?"

"You sure did, buddy, but I wasn't going to let an old friend do that to me. How you doing, then? How's your beautiful bride?"

"Pat's fine," I said. "She is in her studio working."

"And what are you doing? No, don't tell me. Don't make me jealous. Fishing all day, I bet. That's when you are not on the beach eying those bikini-clad beauties."

"No, actually I am working, too. I am writing a newsletter."

"Thought you had retired."

"How is Elspeth and where are you calling from?" I was still trying to place Ed and Elspeth.

"We are still in Port Amboy in the same house. Remember, Elspeth cooked I-talian for Pat, knowing she loves I-talian. We tried to persuade you to stay the night, but you had to go back to DC."

I remembered the meal in spite of the lapse of fifteen years. Ed and Elspeth had bought a painting at the New York Art Expo. Foolishly, we agreed to deliver it on our way home to Georgetown. The meal was a nightmare of soggy pasta, tomato puree and Parmesan cheese that had congealed into lumps. We had suffered heartburn the length of the New Jersey Turnpike while waiting for the antacid to kick in.

"Well, Ed, it is good to hear from you. How is the painting?" I asked.

"Best investment I ever made. Should have bought a hundred. We saw that piece on Pat in *Art and Entertainment* and we knew we just had to track you down. Nice going, buddy."

"Well, Ed, as I said, it is good to hear from you. I will tell Pat you saw her on TV. Sorry about cutting you off; I thought you were a salesman." I trailed off, indicating the end of the conversation.

"Hold it, old friend! Don't leave me yet. We're heading your way. It's bitter cold up here, and we need to see the sun. Thought we would drop by and take a meal off you. Pat's our favorite artist, you know."

"Ed, I am very sorry, but we are off to Panama in the morning and we won't be back 'til May."

Panama is our defensive shield, protecting us from those who would steal our precious time. We are ever conscious of life's hourglass. At our age, the sand runs fast and months pass as weeks once passed. We still have things left to do in our lives, and it pains us to spend time in the company of those with whom we have little in common.

Many who contemplate visiting us in Panama feel justified in planning to stay beyond the three-day limit recommended by Benjamin Franklin.

"Since Panama is so far away, we are going to make the journey worthwhile and spend two weeks with you," they gleefully announce.

"Fine, but Panama is a wonderful country to explore," I hurry to explain. "Having come so far, you must make a side trip over the mountains to the Pacific. It is so different with its long sandy beaches, and you must see the coffee plantations in the foothills, with all the exotic birds and flowers. It would be a shame to miss that."

"No, we'll do that next time. This year we just want to see you guys. That will be enough for us, unless you want to travel there with us."

I am not sure whether it is the free accommodation or fear of traveling alone that prompts this response.

"Have you checked into the Center for Disease Control website to see if there is time for you to complete the series of inoculations you need for Panama?" I ask, omitting to say that the CDC is overly cautious and that no Bocas ex-patriot goes by what it says.

"Look up the CDC recommendations on the Internet," I advise.

"And by the way, this year the sand flies are particularly bad. Their bites can fester, so be sure to bring whatever antibiotic your doctor recommends. Don't worry about snakes. We have killed five Fir de Lance and a couple of Bushmasters on the farm in recent weeks, but if you bring long-legged rubber boots, you should be fine. There has been a case of someone being bitten by a bloodsucking bat, but that was a young boy and he eventually recovered.

"You both are good swimmers, I assume?

"You are but Elspeth isn't, did you say?

"Oh, I see." I pause as though thinking and then continue.

"Well, you'll be fine. There haven't been any shark attacks in ages. If you burn from touching fire coral it will be painful, but you will recover. We can leave Elspeth behind when we visit Old Point. We have not had a problem going through the reef, but it can be dicey if the surf is high. I only take strong swimmers with me when I visit our property out there."

Guests come in a variety of types.

There are those who arrive saying, "Don't worry about us. We'll just fit in. Tell us what we can do to help," and then do nothing but sit on the terrace waiting for me to bring them drinks and ask me what we are going to see today. My role in their eyes is a combination of barman and tour guide and Pat's of housekeeper and cook. We have to keep reminding ourselves that this is their vacation and they deserve a rest.

"Ole! This is better than Cancun!"

They mean this as a compliment. We make no comment, not wishing to hear again the story of their Mexican adventures.

There are others who give us no promises and fit in perfectly, doing their share to make things work without much extra effort on our part. They are a pleasure to show around, and we end up willingly forsaking our work to be with them.

There is a third group who should never venture into the third world. They are disappointed there are no shopping malls, movie theatres or Mexican restaurants. They complain about the heat, the humidity, the insect bites, the uncollected garbage, the line in the post office and the condition of the native dogs. They create a negative atmosphere as they wait out the days until they can get home to the real world.

Then there are our children and, of course, they are different. We are so thankful to them for sparing the time to come all this way that we overlook any shortcomings.

Hamish, my eldest son, brought his wife Jo and their three daughters Emily, Cecily, and Flora from London for a two-week stay.

One morning I organized an outing to Swan Cayo, otherwise known as Bird Island because of its profusion of sea birds. After viewing the island, our plan was to have lunch at Bocas del Drago on the extreme west of Isla Colon.

We were late getting started and, instead of making the trip on the leeward side of Isla Colon, I chose to go out into the open ocean, a shorter route. Hamish and I stood at the controls, and the four girls were seated forward of us.

I threaded our way through the protective reefs and into the ocean swells beyond.

The wind was picking up, but my new boat was exceptionally sturdy. Its twin hulls were driven by 80 hp Yamaha engines. It weighed half a ton and was claimed to be unsinkable. I had no worries about either its capabilities or my own. Anyhow, a little bit of excitement made for a memorable day and stories to be told back home.

"Malcolm, do you think we are wise to be going this way?" asked Jo, her mother's protective instincts coming to the fore.

"It is fine, Jo," I assured her.

"It is always roughest here at the mouth of the bay where the swell is sandwiched between the headlands. When we get around the corner, we will be riding the swell on an angle and make fast and easy progress."

Rounding the headland, I looked for the settled water I had promised but saw only angry seas. A strong crosswind was building substantial waves on top of the swell. I considered turning back, but I felt safer keeping the bow into the weather.

We were making slow progress as we climbed up the swell and over the waves.

"Dad, you are handling the boat very well!" Hamish shouted against the wind.

"Yes, you are, Granddad," agreed Flora, the youngest of the three.

I knew they were only saying this to comfort their mother. The girls were enjoying themselves. They are small boat sailors and used to the water. They have confidence in their Dad; and, if he had confidence in Granddad, then all was well.

The horizon, which had been clear when we set off, was now obscured by a dark mass of clouds. I looked to the other side of us. The shore was a quarter of a mile away. Between the beach and us was the coral reef that runs the entire length of this side of the island. We could hear the roar of the surf. I was thankful we had two engines.

The wind dropped a shade, and I put on some speed.

Heavy rain hit us at the same time the first big wave came over the bow, soaking the girls and Jo. The water rushed on past them and out over the transom. With the rain came increased wind.

"Sorry about that!" I called out.

"It's okay, Granddad," called Cecily. "We needed cooling off."

"We are going to sing hymns to calm Mummy," said Emily, leading her sisters in the English hymn "For Those in Peril on the Sea."

The waves had become larger and more powerful, and each lifted the stern out of the water, leaving the props momentarily whirling in midair. The rain closed in and our visibility decreased. The shoreline was barely visible.

I joined in the hymn singing and afterwards, on a stupid impulse, called out, "This is better than Disney."

"Malcolm, we are not amused," said Jo.

I agreed with her, though I did not tell her so.

"Malcolm, are you aware there are no other boats out here?" asked Jo.

"It's alright, Jo," I called in an attempt to reassure her. "This type of boat is used by rescue services. It cannot sink."

I looked at my watch. We had been battling the sea for almost an hour, and the top of the island was still not in sight. If we had taken the back route, we would have been eating lunch in the peace of the beachside restaurant in Bocas del Drago and, having seen the rough sea ahead of us, given up on the thought of Bird Island. I vowed I would never go out into the ocean again without first checking the weather. This voyage had far passed the bounds of permissible adventure, and that I had involved my grandchildren brought me shame.

"Please, God, this time, more than ever, get us out of this. I will never be so irresponsible again."

The rain lifted and the sky became lighter, revealing the end of the island.

Further out in the still rough ocean, we saw the stark rock of Bird Island. Giant waves were lashing its outer face, sending spumes of white high up its side.

The island is famous as the only home in the world of the Bobo bird and the nesting place of many other bird species. Pat and I had been there in quieter times. On a calm day, the rock, standing far from the land with dark waters all around, takes on a surreal presence. Setting foot on the rock is forbidden, but on the sheltered, leeward side you can move your boat close and watch the endless activity of the sea birds.

We had had too much adventure, and nobody complained when I changed course, leaving the rock well distant on our starboard side, and headed directly for Bocas del Drago. With the sea now following us, I kept the boat on the crest of the wave, and ten minutes later I ordered Jo a double rum.

We had many strangers knock at the door on one pretext or another. Often it was to inquire if we had rooms to rent. Among the other houses of Bocas at that time, ours drew special interest because of its extravagant size and height.

Some of the visitors were helpful, as were the two from Australia who during the construction woke me up to the extent of the house's problems. Others were overeager to point out the faults.

"Back in California, I tell you, I would have the contractor come back, rip up everyone of these tiles and relay them correctly."

"They are that bad?" I asked the stranger who had inquired if the building was a hotel.

"Sure thing, it is a disgrace. I bet if I were to walk around with a stick and tap on these tiles half of them would ring hollow."

I found him a stick and followed behind as he tapped in each room and down the hall. He found only six hollow sounding tiles out of the two thousand, three hundred and three tiles on the ground floor.

"How about upstairs?" I asked. "Would like to do the same upstairs?"

"Look at this corner," he said, ignoring my invitation. "Have you ever seen such sloppy mitering?"

Not having ever made a study of mitering beyond that on a picture frame, I kept quiet. The corner looked pretty good to me.

I thought of giving the gentleman a lecture on the advantages an apprenticed tile layer in La Jolla has over a Bocatoranian, who six months ago was a fisherman.

"If you cannot leave La Jolla behind you, you should not travel to the third world," is what I wanted to say. "Your judgments based on California show a lack of understanding and are unhelpful and even harmful."

40

The School in Laguna Tierra Oscura

My first visit to the elementary school on Laguna Tierra Oscura raised mixed emotions. On one hand, I was alarmed at the sorry state of the school's amenities; on the other, I was delighted to see that even in adverse conditions the children were eager to learn.

The original classrooms were the standard 21 feet by 21 feet. They housed sufficient desks for half the students. The students who did not have a desk sat in the back on benches behind rough, wooden tables. The desks were metal framed, and each had a small wooden platform for writing. Several of the writing platforms were no longer joined to their frames and fell clattering to the floor when the students rose to sing the national anthem.

Even in this bush school, far from roads, electricity, gas mains and piped water, the children's uniforms were immaculate and a tribute to their mothers. The combination of the enthusiasm of the children and the determination of the mothers contrasted with the failure of the government to keep the schools in good condition.

I was thankful to Virginia for making me change from my farm clothes, but I still felt like the one soldier on parade with dirty boots.

On the wall there was a poster with the heading "The Reproductive System of the Female" and beneath a detailed drawing of a girl's body, showing its reproductive organs in enlarged detail.

I thought of the inadequacies of my own sex education, touched on briefly at school when I was already past puberty and had been experimenting on the sly. My parents never spoke of sex to me, leaving the impression it was something of which to be ashamed. I hoped in the next life I am born Latino and grow up to appreciate sex and handle its urges with greater sensitivity than I have this time round.

Tierra Elementary is situated across the lagoon from Finca Tranquilla. Virginia and Andres were with me: Virginia, to assess the school's needs and to translate when necessary, and Andres, as my farm manager, to advise on how we could help with the needs.

Before us was a sea of excited eyes and broad, innocent grins. I dug in my knapsack for my camera, expecting its appearance to occasion a mad scrambling to the front, but the discipline held and the children remained in their places.

"We have a total of eighty-seven students between the three of us," Lilliana, the principal, told me while introducing two other teachers, an older woman and young man.

Lilliana was tall and slim. I judged her to be in her mid-twenties. In keeping with her students, she was immaculate. Her dress was fine, blue denim. On her feet were dark blue, high-heeled shoes. The shoes struck me as inappropriate, given the rough terrain outside, yet they created a touch of elegance, a glimpse of the world beyond the lagoon, a world that those with ambition could subscribe to.

"Where is the third classroom?" I asked.

As I had walked up the slope from the dock, I had noticed only two classrooms, this and the identical one that shared a common wall.

"We make do with that shed." Lilliana pointed to what looked like a cattle shed, open on three sides with a dirt floor. "We have asked for another classroom, but..." she shrugged her shoulders, leaving the sentence unfinished.

"Where do you live?" I asked.

Lilliana pointed to a wooden hut with a roof of aged zinc.

"Where do the others live?" I asked, indicating that I meant the other teachers.

"They live there, too."

"All three of you live in that hut?" I asked incredulously.

"Yes, we live there from Monday to Friday. We go back to Bocas on the weekend."

"Can we take a look inside your house?"

"Yes. Later, if you wish."

It was time for Lilliana to teach the youngest children in the cattle shed classroom. She was practicing the pronunciation of the vowels with them. For many, Spanish was a second language, Guaymi being their native tongue. The children were attentive and for the most part ignored the visitors. A forest of hands shot skywards whenever she called for a volunteer.

"These children are so keen to learn," I remarked to Virginia.

"Of course, Mister Malcolm! All they need is opportunity. They have brains same as you and me, and they want to learn, but it is hard when so little they have. You know, is hard to do homework with ten people living in the hut and there is no light, but still the good ones make it all the way."

"What happens after they graduate from here?" I asked.

"That is the end of schooling unless their parents have the money to pay for them to live in Bocas and go to the high school. Not many do. Maybe one or two a year."

"You mean for the rest school finishes at sixth grade."

"That is right. It is sad but true."

Outside half a dozen men with machetes had arrived and were cutting the grass around the buildings. In a lean-to, an enormous pot was cooking over a charcoal fire.

"On Wednesday's, some fathers come to clean the schoolyard," Lilliana explained.

"And who is doing the cooking?" I asked.

"Two of the mothers," she replied, ushering me in to watch the stirring of a soup made of corn and yucca. I hoped we were not expected to stay for lunch.

"I want to see where you live," I said.

From the outside the hut looked miserable. The wooden sides showed years of patching; and, although someone had once started to paint the walls, the paint had either run out or been misappropriated before the job was half done.

Lilliana led us on to the narrow porch of three planks' width and into the first room. There were two narrow platforms of wood separated by just sufficient space to allow a person to stand. The other sides of the platforms were against the wall. On the platforms were thin, foam mattresses wrapped in sheets. At the head of both mattresses, there was a pillow. Above each bed, clothes were hanging from sagging half-inch PVC pipes strung to the rafters by string.

"Is this where you live?" I asked incredulously.

"Yes. It is where Albertina and I live. Next door is Edgar's room."

"The ceiling leaks?" I asked, looking at light showing through several small holes in the zinc.

Lilliana nodded affirmatively.

I decided not to remark on the gaps in the floors or the lack of glass in the window. I imagined the mosquitoes and sand flies streaming in at night. I wondered why the teachers stayed.

"This is Edgar's room." Lilliana stood back to allow me to look in.

The room was identical to the one shared by Lilliana and Albertina. Edgar's bed was against the outer wall. The floor of the inner half of the room held piles of textbooks.

"It is the only place we have to store them," Lilliana explained.

"You have no light?" I asked.

"We have a kerosene light, but it is not enough to work by. No, we have to do everything during the daylight," Lilliana said.

"And where is your bathroom?"

Lilliana pulled back a stained tarpaulin. Balanced on the edge of the porch was a five-gallon plastic drum with a spigot. The spigot protruded over a wooden floor. Rotting canvas curtains stained with mildew provided a measure of privacy. I decided not to ask to see the toilet. I was already embarrassed.

Back in the first classroom, I asked Lilliana what was the most important need for the school. In my mind it was clearly proper housing for the teachers.

"We need a place for the children to eat their lunch," she said. "The parents are going to help us hold activities to raise money to buy cement. It will take time before we have raised enough to buy the fifty sacks to make the floor."

"And then what? What comes next?"

"We need better drinking water and clean water for the children to wash."

Andres left the room and examined the roof above the two classrooms. I saw him measuring the length of the building, and I knew he was already planning how to catch and store rainwater.

"Do you have a first-aid kit?" I asked as we prepared to leave.

"No, we don't have anything," Lilliana said, shaking her head.

I felt close to tears. This was appalling. In Bocas our concern is the lack of computers. Here, in this bush school, sixteen miles distant, our concern is clean water, a first-aid kit, a place for the children to eat when it is raining and, though Lilliana would not say so, a halfway decent home for the teachers.

Later that day, Virginia, Andres and I took my boat to Almirante. While Virginia went to the pharmacy to choose items to make up a first-aid kit, Andres and I purchased two fifty-gallon water tanks and lengths of PVC piping, the first step in improving the school's water supply.

That evening I described the school to friends.

"And how long do you think that school has been there?" someone asked.

"I don't know. Maybe twenty years."

"And have either the government or the parents done anything about it?"

"Well, the parents are raising money to build a place for the children to eat their meal."

"You think so? I doubt it. Any money they collect will go on beer. They do sweet, F*** all and just wait for a softhearted, evangelical Gringo like you to drop out of the sky. You are causing more harm than good, buster. They will never learn if they think the likes of you are going to save them."

Later that night I talked with Rolando as we sat in Virginia's office drinking a rum and coke.

"Mister Malcolm, I tell you what. How about you tell the school principal that once they have collected enough money for twenty-five sacks, you and I will buy the other twenty-five between us."

"A deal," I said.

The next morning Andres carried our message to Lilliana.

A few months later, Arlene Yaconelli, the pharmacist who had advised me on the dangers of sunstroke and drinking sodas, went shares with me to purchase zinc for a new roof for the teachers' house and to buy wood to repair its walls.

Over the last year the school's facilities have slowly improved through the combined efforts of the Padres de la Escuela (the parents of the school), the education authorities, Finca Tranquilla and a young German who has bought a finca opposite the school. As more Gringos come to make the lagoon their home, hopefully the pace of improvement will move forward proportionally and before long we will manage to fund scholarships to enable some students to attend high school.

When possible, I attend meetings of the Padres de la Escuela. I often see Felipe there. He is always smartly dressed and recently has been sporting designer sunglasses, which he hooks over the front of his T-shirt. We exchange greetings as equals, and anyone who did not know the history would never guess that he once worked for me.

41

Pat and the Old Folks' Home

The old folks' home in Bocas town has a prime location on the north side of the island where, like our new house, it gets an ample share of the breeze coming off the ocean. The home is officially called the Asilo, or the asylum, in part a reflection of the state of the mental health of its aged residents and part the use of the word in its sense of providing a refuge during the battle of life's later years.

The permanent residents usually number less than twenty, a small number and a tribute to the extended family traditions and responsibilities still strong within both the Afro-Antillean and Indian communities.

When a well-fleshed hambone was left over from a Gringo evening designated to raising funds for community welfare, Pat took the bone, made a soup and the two of us delivered it the next day for lunch at the Asilo.

We served the soup to the residents, who sat at two long tables on either side of the dining room. One man chose not to be with the others but to sit on his own at a small table facing a wall on which stood a washbasin that had long ago lost its faucets and was no longer connected to a water supply.

Pat was shocked at the dark and grimy appearance of the halls and dining room. Nobody could remember the last time the walls were cleaned, let alone painted. Green paint, reminiscent of a military barrack room, had suffered water damage and flaked to reveal large patches of crumbling white plaster.

"This room needs a complete redecoration. One day we will do it," said Pat.

That Christmas, one of Virginia's clients who was going to be absent on Christmas Day donated a whole ham to the Asilo. Pat volunteered to cook the ham, and a group of us carried it to the home at midday along with other Christmas foods.

As we served the residents, Pat repeated her proposal for redecorating the dining room and the halls, and Doreen Reynolds, a leading activist of community projects, seconded the idea.

Doreen organized the prep team, of which I was a member. Our task was to scrub the walls. We all contributed to the cost of paint and three days later, when the prep was completed, Pat masterminded the decorating team, giving a liberal degree of choice to the "artists."

The main dining room burst into life with a bright yellow background on which the most popular motif was palm trees with brown trunks and green leaves.

Pat painted an Amish boy sitting on the back of the washbasin, with a leg hanging over either side. The boy is fishing, a reminder to the old man of his own youth. The old man was known not to recognize anyone and never to smile, but after Pat made the painting for him, he would give the slightest of smiles and a hardly perceptible nod of his head when he passed her out walking.

Another of Pat's projects has been the collection of toiletries for the ladies who have the misfortune to be held in the local jail, where soap, shampoo, toilet paper and other feminine hygiene needs are not provided. The soap and shampoo, often leftovers from hotels visited by our friends, find their way from the States to the Bocas jail and play an important part in making existence more bearable for its female occupants.

The contribution of Gringos to the good of the community is considerable and often goes unacknowledged. Often, it comes from a group activity such as the painting of the Asilo or a fund raising evening of dinner and an auction, but much is in the form of individual help given by Gringos to their Panamanian neighbors. Frequently, the most generous are those who can least afford to give, a characteristic of giving that is not limited to just the Gringo community of Bocas.

42

Airport Troubles

Seat 18A on American flight #2131, departing Miami 10:02 a.m. for Panama City was in the second exit row with generous legroom and no restriction on reclining. I felt a smug contentedness. Other than the lawyers traveling first class at their clients' expense, I had one of the two best seats. I could cushion my head against the window pillar and catch up on sleep lost during a night of frequent waking to check the time.

A few rows back sat John, Pat's oldest son. We had met up at the departure gate, he having started his journey in Washington, DC, and I in Tampa. He was traveling light, and Pat had given him art supplies in a blue travel bag of mine to carry as his second piece of checked baggage.

The cabin door had closed, and seat 15B was without an occupant. It could not get much better than that. "Let it roll," I said to myself.

There was a delay. We should have departed the gate at 10:00 a.m. At 10:10 the captain told us there was a departure delay for security reasons. The cabin door had reopened. I thought of Jose Saenz, our "man in Panama,"[1] who would be waiting to meet us.

Five minutes later a voice on the intercom said, "Malcolm Henderson, please identify yourself." I felt a mild panic.

A man strode down the aisle toward me. He was broad shouldered and athletic. His expression was one of determination and showed none of the courtesy typical of airline personnel. "May I see your passport, sir?"

My identity confirmed, the man ordered me, "Collect your hand baggage and come with me. You will not be flying on this flight."

---

1. Jose Saenz was a taxi driver when Pat and I were first introduced to him by Dave and Linda Cerutti on our second visit to Panama. Since then he has gradually expanded his service (www.goldenfrog.net, bocasfrog@yahoo.com) to Gringos and today has more than 1,000 Gringo clients for whom he takes care of almost every need within Panama City and beyond.

The FAA charged me with twenty-two offenses under Title 49, Code of Federal Regulations (49 CFR). On fifteen of the offenses, I received the minimum fine of $250.00, making a total fine of $3,750.00.

This was not my only encounter with airline security. After attending an army reunion in England, Pat and I flew to Baltimore from London to connect with a flight to Richmond, Virginia. In my hand luggage was a briefcase containing security devices given to me by one of my army buddies. I was to test the market in the States. In addition to door, window, and car safeguards, there was a personal alarm that ladies could carry in their purses. It was the size of a bar of soap and made of an indestructible material.

After clearing customs, we made our way to the gate for the Richmond flight. Pat passed through security ahead of me. As my hand luggage reached the center of the x-ray tunnel, an alarm bell of phenomenal strength shattered the nerves of the travelers, the security personnel, the shoeshine man, and nearby vendors. It pounded at us with pulses that reverberated through our bodies.

Along with others, I cursed whomever was responsible and clasped my hands to my ears. Only when I saw my suitcase being abruptly hauled off the belt did I come to the realization that I was connected to this horrific sound.

On a nearby table I opened the suitcase, removed the briefcase, and seized the offending device.

"Turn the damned thing off, for Christ's sake!" howled the security man.

"I'm trying to!" I shouted back, frantically searching for a switch. There was no switch. The object was as solid as a stone washed smooth by centuries of lying on the bed of a fast-moving river.

"Come with me!" yelled the security man. "No, leave your stuff there! Just bring that thing with you!"

I was led to the office of the head of airport security. The door was shut hurriedly behind me, leaving the device and me alone within the confines of a small room. By the time the chief had arrived, I was close to madness. He held out his hand, and I gave him the alarm. He, too, could find no switch.

"Do something about it!" he yelled at me, handing back the alarm.

I put the alarm on the floor and, taking off a shoe, beat it with an intense fury. Putting the shoe back on, I stomped it and it shot out from under my foot like an escaping scorpion and spun across the room to the feet of the chief who was close to losing reason.

"Take that thing out of my office!" the chief screamed.

"Where to?" I screamed back.

"What airline are you on?"

"US Air!"

"Take it to them! They're responsible for you! I'm not!" Opening the door, he thrust me out into the public area. I took off my jacket and wrapped it around the alarm. It helped only slightly as I made my way out of security and headed for the US Air counter.

There were lines of a dozen or more people at each check-in desk. I saw no point taking my problem to the ticket agents. What more could they do that the head of security and I had not already tried? I turned away, resolved to leave the airport and look for a place to bury my cross.

Baltimore Airport has semi-circular arrival and departure roads. Walking out at the departure level, I turned to the left. There were several people approaching me. The alarm had lost none of its strength. Wrapped tightly in my jacket, it still managed a sound impossible to ignore, yet people did; because, in situations such as this, it is easier to pretend unawareness than get involved with what was an unusual and possibly dangerous situation.

The faces of those passing me appeared to be locked in a deep concentration that deprived them of their hearing sense. I realized the comedy of the situation and for a moment thought of thrusting the bundle into the arms of another, like playing pass the parcel at a children's party.

I followed the sidewalk down from the departure level and set off at a brisk pace in the direction of the parking lots. My plan was to leave the alarm under a car and then hasten back in the hope of still catching the flight to Richmond. I changed my mind when I spotted a circular concrete flower garden on the far side of the road. I crossed the road and after checking that no one was watching me, extracted the alarm from my jacket and thrust it deep into waist-high mulch. Undaunted by its new location, the alarm continued its urgent call with barely muted volume.

I dusted off my hands and turned to head back to the terminal. Standing in the shadow of the departure ramp and watching me was a young woman. She, too, turned toward the terminal. I started to run.

At security I was sweating as I retrieved my carry-ons. I was still sweating as I sat in the seat next to Pat. Not even when the plane's wheels had left the tarmac did my fear leave me. I imagined a bomb disposal squad blowing apart the flower garden.

43

Lluvia and I have a Dispute

Lluvia and I ended our ride on the knoll above the new house and looked down the length of the lagoon. There was sufficient breeze to make wavelets slap against the rocks below. The breeze cooled us, and Lluvia gave a snort of approval. Only two days before, there had been a confrontation between us. Now, our confidence in each other was restored.

"This is where I belong," I told her, patting her still sweating neck. "This is peace. This is as close to heaven as you can get in this lifetime."

The air was sweet with the scent of the sea. High above the center of the lagoon, four frigate birds were riding thermals. Wings fixed motionless, they glided effortlessly, seeking thermals that would carry them still higher towards the wispy clouds.

"Lluvia, those birds have it made," I told her. "Playing for hours in the sky and all the while watching the water below, waiting for a fish to swim close to the surface."

Lluvia and I had been inspecting the farm when we had our misunderstanding. We had started from the old house with a slow gallop to the crest of the first hill. There, we had turned to pass behind the corn and through the narrow gate to the pigs. This had become routine, and Lluvia positioned herself for the opening of the gate without prompting from me. The pigs were clean and content, and we set off to inspect the sheep and the goats.

On our way we crossed the new concrete bridge that spans the watery area of the daching crop. When Lluvia first saw the bridge, she dug her hooves in and would only condescend to cross after I had dismounted and walked in front. From that day on she had no fears and seemed to like the change of surface and the clatter of her hooves on the concrete.

The climb up the hill beside the sheep field was steep, and that afternoon it was slippery with mud from the morning's rain. Lluvia managed it well, and after counting the sheep we went down the slope to where the yucca was coming close to maturity. I made a mental note to discuss with Andres how much yucca we would store for feeding the pigs and how much we would take to market.

Previously, we had been worried about rats eating the yucca roots. Andres and Samuel had shown me several roots that had been gnawed by animals they assumed were rats. We thought we had a major problem but, strangely, the damage was not repeated. We decided that snakes had taken care of the rats.

From the yucca, Lluvia and I climbed the hill toward the top of the farm. We rode up beside the plantains, with their long green banana leaves reaching well above our heads.

Just short of the top corner, the grass was a foot or so tall, and here Lluvia came to an abrupt halt, nearly pitching me over her shoulders. She stood snorting, her head down and her legs firmly locked as she stared at the grass.

"Come on, Lluvia. There is nothing to be afraid of," I told her.

She had behaved the same way the last time we came to this spot, and I had dismounted and led her to the cleared ground beyond. I did not want this to become a habit and decided I must help her over this nervousness but to do so without dismounting. There was a tree beside me, and reaching out I tore off the end of a small limb to use as a switch.

"Come on, Lluvia. You have to get over this stupidity," I said, gently switching her right hindquarter.

She moved forward a pace and then retreated. I took her to one side and approached from a different angle. Each time, when a few feet short of the long grass, she refused.

I wanted to win this one. We had sorted out all our other problems to my satisfaction. It was time for me to assert myself one final time. I hit her harder with the switch and prodded her flanks with my heels.

"Go for it, Lluvia," I bellowed.

Lluvia reared up on her hind legs. I held tight with arms and legs. She came down on all fours and then up again, and from the peak of her stand she threw both of us sideways against the trunk of the tree.

I came to on the ground with Lluvia standing over me looking apologetic. A large part of the left side of my face was skinless, and my head felt as if my brains had been peppered with buckshot. I wondered if the damage might prove permanent.

Back on my feet, I patted Lluvia and she nuzzled me. We both knew we had overreacted.

We stayed comforting each other and waiting to see if I would recover sufficiently to remount. As always, I had my little bottle of essential oil of lavender with me, and I dabbed the oil on the open wounds, not giving germs a chance to get going.

We decided it would be better to start back on foot, and I turned to lead Lluvia down the hill. As we walked, Lluvia continually nuzzled my back, asking forgiveness and begging we would still be best of friends.

Before we got to the bridge, my head was clearing sufficiently for me to meet Andres and Samuel from horseback rather than walking home defeated. I wanted to play down what had happened in the hope that it would not become known around the lagoon that Lluvia had twice gotten the better of me.

"What happened to you?" asked Pat when I reached the house.

"Lluvia and I had a little argument."

"You are mad. You are going to kill yourself or, worse, make yourself a cripple for the rest of your life. You must get rid of that horse and, in the meantime, don't ride it."

"It was my fault," I started to explain.

"You better go and take a shower. Supper has been waiting for hours."

The next morning when Joanne saw me, I was again in trouble.

"Lordie me, Mr. Malc, what you gone done now? You been trying to kill yourself?"

Miss Joanne was looking up at me from behind her wooden cash desk, concern replacing her habitual smile.

The left side of my face was swollen and lined with parallel streaks that ran horizontal from the cheekbone to the ear. The bridge of my nose had a lateral cut the shape of the nose bridge on my eyeglasses.

"You gone fallen off that rotten bike of yours? You too old to do these stupid things, Mr. Malc. You get yourself a proper bike, or I buy one for you."

I was embarrassed to be the center of attention. Behind me stood others waiting to pay for their breakfasts.

I parried Joanne's questioning by taking up the subject of my bicycle, a longstanding contention between us.

"If I replaced the missing pedal, someone would borrow my bike. If anyone is thinking of borrowing a bike, they are not going to choose one with only one pedal. I ride it perfectly with just the pedal bar. Anyhow, I did not fall off the bike, Miss Pat walloped me one."

"No, she did not, I say. I don't believe any of that nonsense. What happen, Mr. Malc? I am not taking no money from you 'til you tell me the truth."

"I had an argument with Lluvia." I told her the truth this time. "Lluvia did not want to go to the top of the farm. When she could not throw me, she wrapped me around a tree."

"You get rid of that horse right now, I tell you. You are not to get on that horse again. I don't want you no invalid, all stuck up in a wheelchair or worse. You're no use then. We have need of you. You have plenty more to do."

Two days later I was back at the farm. I had not let Pat know I had no intention of not riding Lluvia. Of the two instances when Lluvia threw me, neither was her fault. The first time, I mounted her with Paco standing at her head, and he made her misbehave. This time, I had no doubt that she had saved us from an encounter with a snake.

"Come, it is time to work," I told Lluvia, and we turned about and entered the cocoa trees. We examined the cocoa pods. They are like small American footballs or English rugby balls. Green at first, they turn a delicate yellow when ready for harvesting. We were looking for pods that had turned black with monilla, a blight that has become common in recent years. From Lluvia's back, I sliced off the black pods with my machete.

Harvesting and marketing the cocoa is only marginally worthwhile. Our cocoa trees have been certified organic; but, even for organic beans, the price at the Cooprativa in Almirante was only forty cents a pound. Before taking the beans to the Co-op we had to shell them from the husks, spread and dry and ferment them, and finally put them in sacks and carry them to Almirante. The time involved and the cost of gas for the boat left us little profit.

"It's the middle man who makes the money," Dave Cerutti said. "We do all the coolie work for a pittance, and he makes deals over lunch in a fancy restaurant and pockets thousands."

44

The Loss of Lluvia

The e-mail message was from Virg. It simply said, "I am very sorry about Lluvia."

The shock of its implication left me shaking at my desk in Mathews. I dialed Virg's office number. The connection seemed to take forever, and all the while I was praying that the news was not what I feared.

"Virg, what happened to Lluvia?" My voice was trembling.

"But, Senor Malc, I thought you knew. She died."

"No, Virg! That cannot be. Tell me you are joking."

"Senor Malcolm, I would not joke on such a sad matter. I thought you knew. I sent you an e-mail two days ago when it happen."

"What happened?"

"She hanged herself."

I could not speak.

"Senor Malcolm, you there?"

"I am here, Virg. I just cannot believe this."

"I know. She was your special friend. That is why I did not want to tell you."

"How did she hang herself?"

"I don't know. Andres called me to say she hanged herself at night and died in the morning. He and Samuel buried her that day. I was with her the afternoon before. I took my nieces to the farm with me and they rode her."

"I am sorry, Senor Malcolm. We are all very sad."

I felt a confusion of emotions, a continuing cycle of grief, anger, guilt and disbelief.

I called Andres on his cell phone. He came through as clearly as when I call him from Bocas.

"Lluvia hanged herself with the rope that tied her to a tree. She was not tied properly. Samuel and I both heard her at four in the night. We cut her free, but she was already very poor. I stayed with her, and she died in the morning. Samuel and I are going to buy you another horse."

"Andres, I cannot believe this. Why was she tied to a tree and not corralled with the sheep? I had told Samuel I wanted her in with the sheep."

"I am sorry."

I felt enormous guilt. I had wasted a life in its prime. I had promised Lluvia a mate and babies and instead given her death. If I had bought Eduardo's stallion and not fussed about being unable to control him, Lluvia would be alive and waiting for my return.

Two weeks ago we had stood on the bluff watching the setting sun. I had rejoiced at our mutual understanding and trust and knew Lluvia felt the same way. We had become the closest of friends.

My disbelief was there every morning when I awoke and then recurred at times during the day. If I took a mid-afternoon nap, Lluvia would appear, and I would again smell the scent of her sweat and feel her nuzzling my shoulder.

I did not want to know where Lluvia was buried. Most would want to visit the grave of a loved one, but somehow not knowing allowed me to feel her spirit in every part of the farm. On my return, Bianca was waiting to greet me. She sensed my grief and stayed close.

True to their promise, Andres and Samuel purchased another horse, a small but strong mare, which came accompanied by her yearling daughter. I could not give a name to these two. Time needed to pass before I welcomed them fully into the farm's family.

A few weeks later, Bianca and I were checking on the state of the cocoa trees when I spotted what I thought was a rock where there had not been one before. Approaching, I saw that it was the skull of a horse, devoid of skin and flesh, an empty casket of bone that had once contained the mind of my friend. Bianca sat on her haunches watching as I said a prayer.

45

Apartment to Rent

I had once said to Pat, "I want to close off the downstairs front room of the house and rent it as an office. We are not using that space, and I feel embarrassed to be living in such a huge house when the majority of Bocas families live in a space no bigger than our downstairs dining area."

"I don't think it's a good idea," she had responded, and I had dropped the subject.

I tried it on her again one day when we were flying back to Panama City from Virginia. I upped the ante by announcing the change as a decision already taken and beyond consideration.

"I have decided to rent the front downstairs as an office. Before we catch the plane to Bocas tomorrow, I want you to help me choose a security door to separate the room from the house."

"Who are you going to rent it to?" Pat asked.

I was surprised by the lack of protest.

"Oh, a doctor, lawyer, some such professional."

Rolando came up with an alternative suggestion.

"I tell you, make it not an office but an apartment. That way you rent it short-term and then, when you know your family are coming, you keep it free for them."

Pat listened to Rolando's suggestion.

"We don't have to do much, Mr. Malcolm. We change the bodega into a kitchen and shut off the apartment from the rest of the house with your security door."

Pat became excited and started designing the kitchen.

I was happy. No longer would I be thought of as the richest man in town. Instead of entering my home through impressive tall front doors, I would be walking to the back of the house via an inconspicuous passageway.

188

With the rent from fifty percent occupancy, the addition to my existing income from pensions and social security would more than balance the cost of maintaining the farm.

The change took place with the minimum of disruption. After a few forgetful occasions of returning to the house and walking up the front steps, we settled down to opening the gate to the passage we share with Tony and Silvia.

Silvia had gradually built this space between our houses into a paradise of tropical plants, some with Spanish names like Banedera Espanola (Spanish flag), with its tall, yellow flowers, and Bouquet de Novia (girlfriend's bouquet), the flowers of which group to look like a bouquet. Others were more familiar to us: petunias, jasmine and begonia. Pat had worked alongside Silvia, contributing her own ideas, but it was Silvia's loving care and innately green thumb that had created this potted garden of exotic shapes and varied colors.

Our reduced living space proved practical. Upstairs at the front were our personal work areas, Pat's studio and my office with its Internet connection to the business back in Virginia. A short walk around the interior balcony of the grand hall and we were in our apartment with its informal dining area on the terrace over the sea. Both the work area and the apartment had ornate security gates which, when closed, separated them from the central area.

The downstairs space facing the sea we used for both formal dining and large gatherings, such as our annual Methodist Christmas party or meetings of volunteer committees.

For the first time, I felt comfortable with our house. Reducing our share of the building fitted our needs and ended feelings of excess.

46

The Snake Man

"Do you know anything about snake bite injections?" I asked Cipriano, while sitting at his bar waiting for lunch.

The frequency with which dead snakes were being produced had caused concern. I could not be sure how many had been killed on Finca Tranquilla, but the presence of many venomous snakes in the vicinity called for a plan of action.

"Do you recommend cutting open the wound and sucking out the poison before applying a tourniquet?" I asked Cipriano, airing knowledge gleaned from a survival book.

"Mister Malcolm, more better you see the bush snake man," said Cipriano.

"But I thought the idea was to rush the victim to hospital in Bocas or Almirante."

"The bush snake man never have anyone die, Mr. Malcolm. I will go to him if snake bite me."

"Where is this man? I need to know where to find him."

"Him live down the lagoon."

Through Tobe, Dave and Linda Cerutti's faithful headman, I arranged to meet Cornelio at Green Acres early one morning and for Tobe to help with the translating.

An Indian of my age, Cornelio Abragro is soft spoken and of gentle manner. His nose is shaped like the beak of an eagle. His black eyes are strong and unblinking as he looks directly into your own eyes. Although he is the only known snake doctor left in our area, he is modest when discussing his skills.

"How many people have you cured?" I asked.

"More than forty."

"Any die?"

"No person I treat die. All better."

"What medicines do you use?"

"I use bush plants. Forty-seven different plants I use. I make mixture of the plants to type of snake. Some plants I have to go far in the bush to find."

"Who taught you?" I asked, expecting to hear him say his father or grandfather.

"El Dios, the Lord. He wants me to know."

I believed him. "Have you taught anyone else?"

"No. No person wants learn."

"What about your children?"

"My son and he wife know some. If I am not at house, they give plant medicine to help 'til I arrive to make the cure medicine."

"Who else can cure snake bites like you do?" Cornelio shrugged his shoulders and looked away.

"Sometimes they call for me from the hospitals in Bocas and Almirante to cure persons doctors cannot cure."

Dave and Linda joined our discussion, and we learned Cornelio was having increasing difficulty finding the plants.

"The ordinary people do not know the plants and cut them down."

Cornelio explained he collects and dries the plants, keeping them at his house, for mixing when the need arises. He told us his medicines are for taking internally.

"If we helped you make a garden close to your house, would the plants grow there?" I asked.

Cornelio told us we would need to recreate the environment of the inner bush, but this could be done. He said that the actual growing area need be no more than ten feet by ten feet.

"Would you then teach others, if we find persons who want to learn?"

He told us he would try.

We went on to talk about the different snakes. The most common is the Fir de Lance, often called the Jumping Snake, for its habit of striking up at its victims. It is feared for its aggressive nature, though supposedly these snakes attack humans only when feeling threatened.

Another common snake is the Bushmaster, known locally as the Sleeping Snake because, unlike most snakes, it does not think to move out of the way of an approaching person.

The Banana Snake is yellow. Living high above the ground in the leaves of banana plants, it is likely to bite humans on the upper part of the body, where the venom is the most potentially lethal.

Not so common, but equally dangerous, is the Coral Snake, so named for its attractive color.

Besides the snakes, there are spiders and large ants whose venom can kill if left untreated. The Arana Negro, the largest and most feared of the spiders, grows to be several inches long and lives in holes in the ground.

"Cornelio says when a person get bitten it is better he is brought with snake," Tobe told us. "He then knows which medicine is best."

This last statement conjured up alarming images of frantic hunting in deep undergrowth for a snake fast slithering to the safety of its home. Snake recognition seemed to be an important part of the survival procedure.

Leaving Green Acres, I took Cornelio to meet Andres. Together, Andres and I promised him fencing materials to protect his future snake plant garden from animals and bags of abono organico to help the plants become established in their new home.

As we said good-bye, Cornelio again looked deep into my eyes.

"El Senor wanted this," he said, and again I believed him.

After Cornelio had planted his garden, I asked if he would create another at Finca Tranquilla and teach Andres and me how to administer the medicines. He agreed to do so, and Andres prepared the ground. On his first visit, Cornelio arrived with the four most important plants. He did not know their names but called the most important plant Snake Bite Medicine Number One. The others had a number according to their place in his mental chart of importance.

"How did El Senor tell you which plants to use?" I asked.

"He shows me in a dream, and when I walk in the forest I recognize the plant and know to use it."

He told us that if someone is bitten we are to quickly boil three, five, or seven of the leaves of each plant and make the person drink the tea. Then we should go and look for him.

For a while most Gringos doubted my sanity as I showed them our snakebite garden and emphasized that it had to be three, five, or seven leaves.

"Snakes don't always inject their venom," informed one friend. "Have you thought that maybe for the forty your buddy claims to have cured, this was the case?"

The doubt lasted until a snake bit a margay, a beautiful jungle cat that had grown up with Dave and Linda since being found as a baby with no mother.

Rapidly, the margay lost consciousness, and her breathing became irregular. All hope was lost until someone remembered Cornelio and rushed to find him.

Cornelio administered a tea. The tea halted the deterioration in the animal's breathing and marked the start of a slow recovery that took many days. First, the skin on the leg where the snake injected the poison turned black. As layers of skin died, the margay licked the dead tissue away until eventually bone and sinew were exposed. Only then did new skin begin to grow.

As to teaching others, it has proved difficult to find students. To learn the skill you need to spend nights at a jungle graveyard communicating with the spirits. Few are able to achieve this communication. There is hope that Cornelio's youngest son will be the next snake man, but there is no certainty that he will succeed.

Cornelio has natural cures for other ailments. For several months I had a damp cough that seemed to come up from my lungs. Tony gave me a Chinese medicine telling me, "You have a cough. You take this. Chinese medicine, it don't always work, so no charge to you."

Tony's medicine did not work; and, when I visited Cornelio to see how his garden was doing, I asked him what plant cured my type of cough. With his machete, he cut a dead piece of vine into six two-inch lengths and told me to boil one piece every six hours and drink the tea. Before the fourth treatment, the cough was gone.

Cornelio's cures use the plants that grow on the mainland shores of the lagoons and are based on Indian lore. On Bastimentos, the Afro-Antillean cures are often different.

"When we was young, our mothers always treat us with bush medicine." Oscar Powell told me on a visit to Old Bank. "We did not have the fancy medicines they have now days."

Oscar is a tall, handsome black man with the body of a heavyweight boxer and the manner of a gentleman. His father died when he was six years old. From that day on, he helped his mother bake bread in the early hours of each morning and then delivered the bread to the households of Old Bank before the start of school. Now in early middle age, he is the owner of a waterside restaurant and respected by all races as a man of integrity and fairness.

"The new medicines don't work as fast as the bush medicine," commented Fulvia, his older sister, who sells basic foodstuffs from a hut alongside Old Bank's three-foot-wide concrete pathway that is referred to as "The Street."

"The body is natural, and the plants are natural medicines," explained Oscar. "The body responds to nature faster than to the modern medicines the government doctor gives you, but the parents, they prefer to go to the clinic and get pill instead of making a tea."

We were gathered in front of Fulvia's opened sales window. There were six of us: myself and Carla, a graduate student of the University of Georgia studying bush medicine; Oscar and Fulvia; and two older men, Randolph Dixon and Ernest Powell, who were our guides. We had just completed a walk of The Street, collecting examples of natural plants that cure.

The Old Bank names for the plants reflect its Afro-Antillean heritage, names such as Ram Goat Dashalang, Single Bible (the aloe plant), Congo Lala, Shoe Black, Guinea Hen, Cowfoot, Man to Man. The cures range from hangovers and the common cold to sweet blood (diabetes), high blood pressure, kidney ailments, blood deficiencies, parasites and a whole lot more.

Most of the plants are made into a tea by the simple process of boiling in water. After a couple of hours of talking bush medicine, I realized that my English perception of what was meant by tea had been typically insular.

"In our young days we drank only teas made from plants," said Fulvia. "There weren't no sodas like we have now. Today, the children, they don't drink the natural drinks. They want their Cokes and their moms let them have them. That is why they get sick."

"The plants, them hard to find now because the people they don't plant them around their house like they used to," Ernesto told us.

"There are other plants we could show you," said Randolph. "But to do so, we would have to go way up into the bush."

"What plants do you have for curing snake bites?" I asked.

"There are no poisonous snakes on Bastimentos, and for that reason we do not have any plants that cure snake bites," said Oscar. "God gives you what you need. We don't need snake cures."

"God gives man plants to heal him, but now man cut down the plants and forget their use," commented Ernesto.

"Old Bank should create a cure garden of all of these plants," I suggested to Carla. "It could become an attraction for all who are interested in natural cures."

"I fear that it might bring the pharmaceutical companies and that they would scoop up all the plants and then patent their medicines," said Carla.

Close to our house in town lives Julieta Downer, whose garden is a pharmacy of natural medicines. Julieta retired from the police force with the rank of lieutenant. Although she is a petite woman, it is said she is capable of bringing to ground the most aggressive of troublemakers and knowing the speed of her movements, I do not doubt this to be true.

Julieta and her husband Juan, who is the General Secretary of the Bomberos and in charge of the station when the Commandant is absent, visited the farm on several occasions, bringing gifts of natural medicine plants to put alongside the snake cure plants. In return, I gave them other plants from our own beds.

Sharing knowledge of natural cures and finding new cures is an unending process. It is also a race against time as the rainforests of the world are systematically destroyed and many plants made extinct.

47

The Banderado

The banderado is the flag bearer. It is an honor to be chosen as banderado.

The Bombero band played at full strength. The first rank of trombones and clarinets were marching three paces behind. On my left danced the Queen of the Fair, a perfectly molded black Venus, who topped me by two inches. On my right, her runner up threw kisses to the crowd. I carried the flag.

We headed the parade. As the banderado, I wore a Guajerbera, the formal Panamanian shirt appropriate for the opening of the Ferria del Mar, Bocas' annual Fair of the Sea.

At least as old as their grandfathers, I was a decaying old fruit wedged between two gorgeously ripe peaches. I imagined how I looked to the watching crowd. A sweaty old man with a protruding stomach supported on stubby legs, half the length of those of the Queen.

My companions flowed forward with perfect rhythm born of Latino genes, their weight shifting effortlessly from hip to hip. They acknowledged the yelps and whistles of the men in the crowd with wide smiles and raised eyebrows.

I moved with stiff, formal steps, my hips frozen and hands clasped to the flag. I tried to appear happy, but in truth was acutely embarrassed.

"This is fun!" I shouted to the Queen. She could not hear over the noise of the band but turned to face me.

Her smile never changed. Her mouth was half open and level with my eyes. I could not avoid looking at it. The pink of her tongue showed between perfect, white teeth. Her lips were moist and ruby red, her skin black. The site of her mouth was fascinating in an erotic and hypnotic way. I had to pull my gaze away and look to the other side.

The runner up was shorter than me by the same amount as the Queen was taller. She was more olive than black and had a child-like innocence mingled with the instincts of a born exhibitionist. Her smiles were spontaneous acknowledgments of the male appreciations. She was enjoying every moment. Unlike the

196

Queen with her Mona Lisa smile, this girl projected her personality with unbridled joy.

"She would make a great night club hostess," Pat had whispered during the judging for the Queen the previous week. I had agreed with her. The girl reminded me of Brigitte Bardot. She was a mulatto version of the French film star I fanaticized over in my youth.

Seeing my awkwardness, Brigitte Bardot's chocolate look-a-like put an arm in mine. She spoke words I could not hear and smiled. The smile did it, a confidential smile, as if we had known each other a long time and had shared secrets.

The effect was electric. I relaxed and slipped unconsciously into the rhythm. My legs unfroze, and I moved forward in unison with my companions. I began to lift the flag up and down to the beat of the drum.

"That's it, Mister Malc," I heard a man's voice call. My confidence grew.

I had been reluctant about accepting the invitation to be the banderado.

"But, Senor Malcolm, it is a great honor to be chosen banderado," Virginia had told me. "Of course, you must accept. If you say no they will not understand and will think you very odd."

The parade over, we attended a banquet. It is the privilege of the banderado to pay for the banquet and to invite some guests, a fact that had not been made known to me until after I had agreed to play the part.

I invited as my guests the parents of the children of the schools on Isla Carenero and Isla Solarte along with Andres and Kasilda and other Panamanian friends. I did not invite any Gringos. I did not want them to see me making an exhibition of myself.

I sat at the head table with the Queen and her two runners up. We were being photographed. The girls were all smiles, but I could only contribute my self-conscious grin. Just last year, I had allowed my dentist to cap my crumbling front teeth with an immaculate row of identical spades. Since then, I have not liked how I look when I smile.

The Bombero band, stoked up on my beer, turned up the volume. Some men were dancing, bent over with their heads to the center and their backsides pointing out like in a football huddle. In spite of the position, they moved with both grace and vigor, arms swinging forward and back.

Their dance was reminiscent of a tribal dance I had witnessed long ago in a remote village in the Northern Territory of Kenya. I was leading a platoon on an expedition to climb a mountain we thought none had climbed before.

The night before starting the ascent, we camped close to a village of mud huts. We were told by the village headman that we were the first white men to visit in ten years. In honor of the visit, the whole village performed a traditional dance.

Their dance completed, the headman indicated it was now our turn. In one of those flashes of inspiration that come to the aide of the desperate, I told the platoon we would dance the Hokey Pokey with our rifles in hand and, after the last Hokey Pokey, let loose a fusillade of shots.

Our performance was met with wild enthusiasm but also the request to borrow our rifles. The headman explained they had a score to settle with a neighboring village that had recently raided, stealing cattle and women.

"Are you going to enter the Miss Panama contest?" I asked the Queen.

She did not hear me, nor did she turn her face to me. I tried again.

"Television," she said out of the corner of her mouth. I looked around and saw a camera directed at us.

After the filming, I excused myself, knowing full well the girls were eager for younger swains. I rejoined Pat, who had been looking after our guests, and together we walked home.

The next morning, Joanne failed to notice me enter Don Chicho's.

"Not talking to me this morning then, Joanne?" I asked, standing full square in front of her cash desk.

"I have no mind to talk to you, Mister Malc, when I see you enjoying yourself with all those girls last night."

"I didn't know you were there."

"I see you on the television, all jumping up and down. I don't know what you will get up to next, Mister Malc."

48

Where Andres Was Born

A taller, fuller surf marked the mouth of the river, making it visible from afar. Either side stretched miles of pale sandy beach, backed by the dark green of the jungle. Close behind, tree-clad volcanic mountains rose steeply, crowding the narrow coastal plain.

"It is the water from the river pushing against the surf that makes the larger waves," Clyde remarked and then continued, "Where the river meets the ocean, a bar of sand forms across its mouth making the entrance hazardous for boats. It will be the same with all the rivers along this coast."

Clyde, a Floridian by birth, describes himself as a "banana man." Some say he is the most knowledgeable man alive as far as bananas are concerned. When I had tentatively asked if he would like to come along for the ride, he had not hesitated to accept, telling me he had never visited this section of the coast.

Besides his banana expertise, Clyde is a deep fund of information on most tropical plants and trees. He has lived in Central America for most of his life and in Bocas, on and off since 1970. He is three months my junior in age but in knowledge and wisdom, far my senior.

I had long planned to visit Santa Catalina in the neighboring province of Veraguas. It was there that Andres was born thirty-four years ago and spent his childhood.

A Bugle Indian, who by the chance of place and date of birth was exposed to a second culture, the influence of the missionaries, Denis and Milia Kick, together with that of his parents, gave Andres an exceptional start in life. I wanted to learn more about the place of his childhood.

Andres and I had loaded the boat with an extra forty gallons of gasoline and at first light collected Clyde from his home on Isla Solarte. With us were Kasilda and her daughter Abegail.

I had given Clyde the wheel as we progressed down the outside of Isla Bastimentos, across the wide opening to the Chiriqui Lagoon and past Punta Valiente and the rocky islet of Tobobe. Andres stood with us commenting on the coast-line, pointing out little communities, their huts barely distinguishable, perched on the edge of the rocky peninsula.

"It is only in September and October and sometimes in March or early April the sea is this smooth," he had reminded us.

After Tobobe, Andres took the wheel. He had been fifteen when he first brought a wooden cayucu with outboard through these seas, carrying passengers and produce from Santa Catalina to Bocas.

"If the sea was bad, the journey could take us fifteen hours. Most times we would set out at two in the morning to take advantage of the quieter seas in the first part of the day."

Three and a quarter hours after collecting Clyde, we had arrived at the mouth of Rio Tonkri.

Andres brought the boat close to the bar. The sand was barely a foot below our twin hulls. We looked for a break in the surf that would indicate the channel. After a false start and backing off, we found a ten-foot-wide gap where the depth was close to four feet. With our engines raised as high as possible without losing power and maneuverability, we passed quickly through the turbulence and into flat river water.

On either bank of the river, people stopped whatever they had been doing and stood watching the progress of the strange boat driven by a well-dressed Indian and carrying two white men. We waved and received cautious acknowledgement.

"For what reason had these visitors traveled so far and what would be the out-come of their visit?" The question was evident in the hesitation to welcome the strangers.

Andres spotted a familiar face and called to the man in Bugle, the language of his tribe, a language so different from that of the Guaymi Indians of Bocas that Spanish was the only means of communication between the two Indian peoples.

A moment more of hesitation and then arms were raised in eager welcome. Questions rang out across the water, and Andres idled the engines as he told of the purpose of our visit.

We moored at a small dock beneath the mission station and, on Andres' advice, awaited the appearance of the headman of the village who would sanction our presence and accord us the official welcome.

The ceremony was short but meaningful to both sides. An important part of local protocol, it was watched by the mission family, who were waiting to be the next to greet us. A third greeting came from Andres' mother, Octavia, and his younger sister, Naomi.

Clive and Hazel Walker and nine-year-old daughter Judith entertained us with chocolate cake and lemonade in the kitchen-come-dining-room of the mission house, a plain but adequate, tin-roofed home set high on posts and surrounded with blue plastic water butts to catch rainwater off the roof.

Protestants from Belfast in Northern Ireland, they were reserved at first, waiting and watching to see what type of people we were.

It had been the same when Pat and I had visited the Shetler family on the shores of Lake Tanzania. As Mennonite missionaries working in the most remote region of that vast country, the Shetler's, who came from Ohio, had experienced previous visitors whose main interest was photographing lions and elephants to impress the folks back home. Only when our questions proved our genuine interest in their work did they open up to us.

The Walker's had relieved the Kick's years previously. They had home-schooled Judith and her older sister, who now attended the mission high school in Chame on the other side of the mountains.

Besides their evangelical endeavors, they were providing advice and know-how on a variety of village projects. Their role in this respect was not dissimilar to that of the Peace Corps, except their commitment to the community stretched for an indefinite time, far more than the two years of a Peace Corps volunteer.

"Andres is running my farm," I told them. "The mission taught him well. Before he joined me, the farm was chaos and full of problems. He has improved it enormously."

"He is very intelligent," agreed Clive. "I always said he would do well."

We were speaking in English, but I could see Andres knew we were speaking well of him.

"Would you like to sleep in our guest house tonight?" asked Clive.

"That is very kind of you," I said. "But Andres has already invited us to stay with his parents."

"Well, if you change your mind and feel you need a higher level of comfort, you are welcome here," said Hazel and before we could answer, she added, "If you come here for supper that would be fine too, whether you stay the night here or not."

The two missionaries and their daughter watched, waiting for our reply. I sensed their loneliness and felt caught in a dilemma. They wanted our company, but our place was with Andres and his family. We had only the one night. I hesitated and looked at Clyde. Maybe he would regret our not accepting this offer.

"Thank you, but we cannot very well desert Andres' family. His parents will have planned on feeding us." It was Clyde who announced our intention.

"Do you get many visitors?" I asked.

"Apart from other missionaries, we do not see many people from outside," Clive told us.

"There was that German couple who came here paddling a cayuco," Hazel reminded him.

"Oh, yes! They came and stayed two days and then went on. Later, they came back and spent another three days."

"When was that?" I asked.

The two looked at each other quizzically.

"About six years ago, wasn't it?" Hazel asked Clive.

"Yes, about six years ago," her husband confirmed.

"When we come back the next time, we would love to take up your offer and stay with you for a couple of days," I said.

"And when will that be?" asked Clive.

"Well, now that we know my boat can do the journey safely, we may make a yearly visit, bringing Andres and Kasilda and the girl back to visit the family. I would like to get to know Santa Catalina and the habits and traditions of the community."

We said our farewells, promising to look in on them the next day on our way out.

The walk to Andres' home was considerably farther than previously implied when we were told the house was at the end of the path of grass kept cleared for the occasional visit of the mission plane.

The start of the landing strip was marked by two up-turned metal gas cans of military heritage placed fifty feet apart. From each can, a line of white, plastic Clorox bottles was spaced evenly up a rolling incline until they disappeared from view over a low ridge some four hundred yards away.

The bottles were held in place by wooden stakes and made excellent markers. The airstrip was a reminder that small planes can land on surprisingly uneven ground, a fact Pat and I had learned when our mission pilot in Tanzania landed in the Ngorongoro Crater for a bathroom break that was thwarted for Pat by the sudden appearance of people from behind every bush.

Clyde and I demonstrated our fitness by setting the pace. Reaching the end of the airstrip would be no problem in spite of the considerable heat of a cloudless but humid day. As we crested the last ridge, we were thankful to see a thatched house ahead and were starting that way when Andres called to us pointing to a narrow path leading into the jungle.

We walked single file, shaded from the sun by tall trees. In exchange for the slight drop in temperature, we had an increase in humidity and started to sweat profusely. We had slowed the pace, ostensibly to allow Clyde to identify plants and discuss them with Andres.

I expected to find a clearing ahead of us and to see Andres' folks waiting to greet us.

The jungle ended at the foot of a steep hill. The path led upwards, footsteps worn into the mud but still slippery from last night's rain.

Our pace became still slower. We climbed with heads down, seeking where to place each step. Our bedrolls seemed to have gained weight.

"I am stopping to take in the view," announced Clyde.

Mentally thanking him for his initiative, I stopped and turned to look behind.

Below stretched the jungle and in the middle distance we could make out the mission house. Beyond was the blue of the ocean and far to the left, a low, dark line that Andres said was the island of Escuda de Veragua, fifteen miles away from Santa Catalina.

Our breathing almost normal, we began climbing again. A few minutes later we saw the top of the hill and the four huts that make up the Medina family compound.

Jasinto, Andres' father, was waiting to greet us. Shorter than either of us by more than a foot, he nevertheless had a powerful presence. Like Cornelio, the snake man, his beak of a nose curved gracefully to end above thin lips. His eyes were dark and clear and looked into you as though able to see who lay behind the veneer of sophistication. After a long moment of eye contact, he smiled and I knew I had his approval.

All four houses were built off the ground and thatched with palm, typical of most Indian houses in Panama. The largest of the four was the cookhouse and, as in many homes around the world, it was here that most of the family passed the day when not working or playing.

Close to the cookhouse, a similar building, but without walls was for visitors. It was square, and along all four sides ran low, wooden benches made of long planks of hard wood supported by squat wooden blocks. Here, any traveler on the footpath to the mountains could pass the night, sleeping on the floor.

The other two houses were each about twenty feet in length and fifteen wide, including an open verandah on one side. On wooden stilts, their floors were eight feet above ground. A thick section of a tree trunk, with wedges cut for steps, served as stairs.

The usual occupants of the first house had vacated, giving up their home to the two of us. This meant that fourteen family members, including Andres and his wife and child would be sleeping in the second house.

We climbed the tree trunk to inspect our quarters and sort our belongings.

The first up, I felt the floor give under my weight.

"Watch out, Clyde," I called. "I don't think this floor is made for the weight of us Gringos."

"It won't give on you," assured Clyde. "It is made of slivers cut from the Jirra palm. It is very strong, even if it feels springy. The walls look as though they are made from the same tree but not so. They have used the Chonta palm for the slats and laid them one on top of another."

We stored our bedding rolls, backpacks and two coolers containing food and filtered water. We had brought with us sufficient supplies to last three days, allowing for the possibility of becoming stranded. We knew what was not used would be welcomed by our hosts. The coolers and backpacks had followed us up the airstrip and through the jungle on a wheelbarrow and then had been carried up the hill by Eduardo, Jasinto's son-in-law, and a friend who happened to be passing by.

Andres and Naomi brought us each a dish of spaghetti in tomato sauce.

"This must be from a can," observed Clyde. "Spaghetti is not on their normal menu. I suspect they purchased it especially for us."

We sat on a bench on our verandah. A breeze from the sea was cresting the hilltop, cooling us to a perfect temperature.

I inspected our quarters. Clyde had already chosen to spend the night on the verandah, and I thought I would do likewise until I saw a queen-sized mattress on the floor of one of the two inner rooms. I tested it out. Every spring beneath my body pressed up into me, but I knew I must spend at least a part of the night on the mattress or disappoint the family. The mattress was placed there in our honor.

After lunch we set off with Andres and Kasilda to walk to the school Andres had attended until the age of fifteen. We had seen it from the boat, half a dozen impressive concrete buildings, easily identifiable because of the cream and dark green paint typical of the Panamanian schools.

On the flat land beyond the mission house, we passed large areas of rice, the plants already a foot tall and verdant. Unlike the rice fields I had seen in China and Japan, there was no elaborate irrigation system constructed of low mud walls. I assumed that, with the amount of rain that falls on the Caribbean Coast of Panama, there was no need for a high maintenance irrigation system.

We followed a path along the riverbank and stopped at a store selling condensed milk, sugar, rice, canned tuna fish and peba, the fibrous fruit of a species of palm. The people were eager to talk to Andres. Kasilda stood smiling shyly, as Andres told of his life on the farm in the distant lagoon. She did not know these people in the way that Andres knew them, because she had been born and raised in Terron, a remote village reached first by paddling a cayucu for two hours up a river and then by walking for another hour and a half.

At the mouth of the River Tonkri, men were fishing from cayucus, riding back and forth across the sand bar, handling their log canoes with the ease of kayakers riding the rapids on the Colorado River. We turned to walk parallel to the beach, along a path shaded with palms.

The school compound consisted of four classrooms, a clinic which served the whole neighborhood, and the only two telephones in the area. There were lines waiting at both telephones but none at the clinic.

"We have students from elementary to tenth grade," an attractive, light-skinned teacher in her late twenties told us.

"What happens after that?" asked Clyde.

"Those that want to continue, and have parents who can afford for them to do so, go to Bocas or to some other place where there is a high school. The others start work."

"Those that go away to high school are gone for a long time?" I asked.

"Yes! Maybe they are gone for the whole year. They stay with other families."

"You like it here?" asked Clyde.

"Yes, it is alright. It is very different from where I come from," the teacher smiled.

"And where is that?" asked Clyde.

"Los Santos. I grew up in a town."

We moved on, aware that our presence was distracting students who were watching from the classrooms.

While the others walked further down the path, I crossed the white sand and, taking off my shirt and pants, strode into the waves. There was no one in sight in either direction. Only the sea birds walked the beach, preoccupied in the search for food. Behind, the jungle hid whoever might be watching.

I plunged into waves, wishing they were stronger and taller as they are at other seasons all along this coast. I imagined Marlin and Andres as young boys riding their boards, competing for the best run of the day but also constantly aware of the other's whereabouts, conscious of the power of the ocean.

I swam parallel to the beach feeling neglected muscles stretch then start to ache, along with the ache of lungs underutilized in recent weeks. If I lived here, I would swim everyday, I told myself. I rolled over, floating on my back, and relished the joy of having this moment all to myself. There was no one to ask for a taste of my cake. The present was mine, all mine.

When the sun moved behind the mountains, we made our way home. As we came near the mission house, shrieks of female laughter came from the river. I changed course to find the cause of the spontaneous joy and came upon several schoolgirls standing chest deep in the water, still dressed in their school uniforms.

"Where do we wash?" asked Clyde, when we crested the hill to the family compound for the second time that day.

"In another river at the bottom of the hill on this side," Andres was pointing in a different direction.

We gathered up our wash things and followed Andres back down into the jungle. The river was twenty feet wide. Overhead, trees from both banks stretched out branches to meet in the middle, creating a complete canopy. The river was of swimming depth. Its bed was stony and the water crystal clear and quite cool. It was the perfect balm for hot, aching bodies.

Andres described his early life, telling us how the river had been a sure source of fish for his family but now was almost barren. Too many had come to catch more than their own need so they could sell to other markets. A friend of his joined us, quietly paddling his cayucu upstream. He told us he had fished all day in both the river and the sea but had caught nothing.

I was reminded of the story of the tourist, who had watched an Indian fisherman return early each morning with four beautiful fish. One morning he asked the Indian, "Why do you always come back when you have caught your fourth fish?"

"Because that is all I need for my family and friends."

"Let me give you a lesson in business. Stay out and catch twenty fish or however many you can catch before the sun goes down. Keep your four and sell the rest."

The Indian made no comment.

The businessman felt a need to take the lesson further. "When you have sold enough fish, you can buy a second cayucu and employ a friend to fish it for you. You will make more money."

"And then what?" asked the Indian.

"Why, if you go on expanding like this, you will become rich and can retire and spend your days fishing."

We heard female voices from high on the bank above us. Kasilda and Naomi were watching us. Soon they came cautiously down to the water and entered fully clothed, quickly moving upstream till at a respectable distance from what we had established as the men's washroom. They talked, catching up on a year of news.

That night Clyde and I ate on our verandah. We had decided to let the family have Andres to themselves. We dined on sardines, graham crackers and crab paté, followed by bananas and oranges. We washed the meal down with apple juice laced with a tot of rum.

"It has been a truly memorable day," Clyde said. "It could not have been more perfect."

"Thank you for agreeing to come," I replied. "Without you here I would have only caught half of what they have been saying; moreover, I would have learned little about the plants."

"I have learned something, too," Clyde said. "All these years I have thought that Bugle and Guaymi had similar languages and that each could understand the other. It was a real surprise to me to know that Andres cannot understand the Guaymi of Bocas."

Our conversation did not last long that night. The day had been rich in new experiences and more physical than either of us was used to. Clyde unfolded his bedding roll on the floor of the open verandah, and I retired to the inner room to do justice to the mattress.

We lay listening to the music of soft-spoken voices coming from the cook-house, a gentle murmur that was like a repeating mantra and conducive to sleep.

It was not long before I half awoke to the splash of water on my face. I tried to ignore it, but the drops were persistent, repeating every few seconds. There was a pattering sound on the roof above that brought me to the realization it was raining, a light but determined rain that gave no hint of giving up.

I pulled the mattress as far as I could to one side and lay back on the edge farthest from the center of the room. I heard the steady beat of raindrops hitting the far side of the mattress, but my side remained dry. I realized the problem lay with the thatch covering the peak of the roof. I wondered how Clyde was making out but, hearing no sound of movement, assumed he was fine.

The sound of chattering now came from the next-door house where all the family was supposedly passing the night. Again, it was far from a disturbing noise, and soon I returned to sleep.

Dawn was halfway there before louder voices than those of last night woke us. This was our wake up call. We had made it known we intended an early start to our voyage back so as to take advantage of the calmer morning seas.

"Why? What is up?" I asked, trying to smile. "There must be some mistake."

"You are to come with me," he said. "You are to get off the plane."

As I struggled to extract an over-stuffed carry-on and computer, he stood ready to pounce should I do something drastic. I was aware of many eyes watching me. Clearly, I was the security problem. I was sweating, and I knew my face was already bright red.

Back in the terminal, my escort identified himself as the head of American Airlines Security, Miami, and took me to a window, below which was a trolley with a caged superstructure. Lying in the middle of the cage was the blue travel bag that John had checked at the Washington ticket counter. As I looked from the window, I saw flight #2131 pull back from the gate and start its journey to Panama City.

"Is that your bag?" the head of security asked me.

"Yes," I admitted. I was about to explain that although it was my bag and had my name on the luggage label it was not part of my luggage and that if he checked the baggage tag he would find the name John Moss, but I changed my mind. I did not want the plane to be called back to the gate and have John go through what had just happened to me.

"What is the hazardous substance that you have in that bag?"

"I don't have any hazardous substance in the bag," I said.

"Did you pack the bag?" There was irritation in my interrogator's voice.

"Yes, I did."

"Well, then, you must know what the substance is."

"May I call my wife? She may know."

Pat answered from her studio in St. Petersburg. "Are you there already, Darling?" she asked.

"No, I have been taken off the flight because there is something hazardous in that suitcase you gave to John. Do you know what it might be?"

"No idea. Where's John?"

"On his way to Panama."

"Wait!" said Pat. "A can of varnish wouldn't be hazardous, would it?"

The hazardous substance identified, I was ordered to remain at the gate until the FAA arrived to take charge of the investigation.

"When do you think I will be cleared to go on to Panama?" I asked the security man.

"I doubt you will be flying American again."

It was 3:00 in the afternoon before the investigation began. It was finished in time for me to catch the 5:18 p.m. American flight to Panama.

Kasilda and a girl named Simona had come to the bottom of our stairs bearing mugs of hot coffee and two large pieces of the fruitcake Pat had sent with us as a gift to the family.

"This must be lowland coffee," said Clyde. "The Indians grow it along this coast. It is quite similar to highland coffee but not the same tree."

"It is most welcome and surprisingly tasty," I commented. "It has a strong, pleasant flavor of the roasting."

After packing our bedding and backpacks, we ventured over to the cookhouse. The whole family was assembled. A wood fire was burning on a bed of ashes that rested on clay contained in a five-foot by three-foot box made of wood. The whole was raised on legs to waist height. Over the fire, a blackened cooking pot was covered by a sheet of zinc on which a second, smaller fire was burning.

Andres saw the subject of our interest.

"I built the fire box," he said with pride.

"What is cooking?" I asked.

"My mother is baking. She is baking bread to sell."

I took time to write down each family member's name.

"How is it that Simona has a different last name?" I asked.

Octavia showed concern at the question. Everyone was silent.

"Because her mother did not want her," Octavia said at last. "She is our family now."

I learned Simona was to be fifteen in three days' time, five years younger than I had thought her to be. Later, I gave her five dollars for her birthday.

A man not of the family had passed the night in the visitors' hut, and this morning I had seen him eating breakfast, sitting alone on one of the benches.

"What do the visitors pay you to stay the night here and be fed?" I asked.

"No, they do not pay. It is our way to share when there is a need. We do not ask for pay. That is our tradition," explained Jasinto.

It was time for us to leave if we were to get a start on the calmer waters of the morning. Later, the wind would pick up and the larger waves would slow our progress.

Our visit had been too short. As we handed our surplus supplies to Octavia and said our good-byes, we promised to return and next time spend more than a day. We had begun to know the family and learn of their ways, but we had only touched the surface of all there is be learned of these people. Spared as they are the ills of competitive lives, I knew there was mutual good to come from sharing our respective experiences.

Our departure from Santa Catalina was marked with the same formalities as our arrival but played in reverse.

First, we stopped by the mission house where Hazel and Judith were waiting, soon to be joined by Clive. We fell into easy conversation, picking up where we left off what seemed like a week ago but was barely twenty-four hours.

Our brief experience with this community had given us an insight into the challenges and sacrifices faced by this family. I wondered which of the two parents had led the way to the point of committing to live far from their own kind in an alien climate, where the comforts of their youth were as yet unheard of. Had God's calling rung equally in both sets of ears or had one been the loyal follower of the other's need for fulfillment?

"You will be back then one day, we hope," said Clive.

I was again aware that all three were watching my face, waiting for an answer. What was it about this family that made us prolong the farewell, to seize each offered opportunity to extend the conversation for just a few more moments?

The simple phrase, "You will be back then one day, we hope," told of a need for the company of those familiar with the world beyond these jungle shores. The gentle asking tone of Clive's voice and his choice of sentence construction carried a profound and touching sincerity.

"We will," I spoke for us both, certain at least that I would fulfill the promise.

We exchanged means of communicating, passing over e-mail addresses and phone numbers.

"We only get to read our e-mail when we go to the mission headquarters, and then it takes us two days to get through it all," Clive said.

"Come and see us in Bocas," I said. "You will be welcome to stay in our house," I added, hoping I was conveying the truth of my words.

Nearly twenty years ago, as the little mission plane lifted off the grass beside Lake Tanzania with Pat and me waving to the Shetler family from its cockpit, we both had feelings similar to saying farewell to our own children. Although Clyde and I had spent no more than two hours in total with the Walker family, I felt a similar loss as we shook hands for the last time and made our way down to the dock, where the headman was waiting to formalize our departure from Santa Catalina.

Nosing our way out through the surf, we breached two waves, the water crashing down on the fore deck, soaking all but Andres and Clyde, who were at the wheel. The sea was no longer smooth. A mild swell was creating waves that we were able to manage in reasonable comfort once we were clear of the river mouth.

We were carrying an extra passenger, Octavia. Octavia, a diabetic in need of treatment, would be spending a month in Bocas, staying with Kasilda's sister on treatment days and at Finca Tranquilla at other times.

I settled the mother, Kasilda and Abegail on the seat in front of the consol and covered them with a tarpaulin. Octavia was obviously in a state of anxiety.

"She is afraid of the sea," Andres told me. "She cannot swim."

In spite of living on small islands or in communities only reachable by sea, some Indians never learn to swim. No one knows for sure how many drown each year. This last year, there was a sad funeral. A mother and her four-year-old were passing from Isla Popa to Bastimentos when a squall descended on them without notice. Before the mother could turn the nose of the little cayucu into the wind, the full force hit broadside, turning it over on its side and spilling mother and child into the sea.

Several hours later the two were found dead in the water. The mother's arms were still wrapped around the child. The two coffins were made of cardboard and buried without markers. What money was collected was given to the father to feed his other children.

Halfway across the run from Santa Catalina to Punte Valiant, we turned shoreward and approached the entrance to the town of Boca de Rio Cana.

"This area is similar to the Florida Everglades," Clyde told us. "I have read about it but never visited. The Rio Cana runs back parallel to the coast. I have seen it on the map. It connects with some lakes that are said to contain manatee."

"There is a big community living at the mouth of the river," Andres said. "They are Guaymi and number as many as six hundred."

"We could take the boat in and visit the lakes," I offered. "It will cost us what is left of the smooth weather and the rest of the journey will take longer, but this is an opportunity we should not miss."

All except Octavia were in favor, and again we crossed a sand bar passing into smooth water. The river was wide and on one shore were many houses and some official looking concrete buildings.

We increased speed and headed up river. Looking back at the community, we saw frenzied activity at the river's edge, and a few moments later three large cayucus filled with men set off in pursuit of us. I told Andres to pull back our speed. One of the cayucus sped past us and then turned, blocking any further progress on our part. I took over from Andres and brought our boat to a halt.

The other two cayucus took up positions on either side. In each, three Indians stood scrutinizing us. They were not returning our smiles and gestures of friend-ship.

"What are you doing?" asked a uniformed official. His manner was that of a less-than-courteous state trooper stopping a suspected drug trafficker.

"We just want to visit the manatee," Clyde and Andres both explained.

"This is an Indian reservation. You cannot visit without permission."

"We did not know. We are sorry," Clyde had become our spokesman. Andres not being Guaymi, this seemed a wise choice.

"You must turn around and leave," the man told us.

"Where can we get permission?" Clyde asked.

"You can only get permission if you pay."

"And how much would that cost us?" Clyde continued.

"Follow me," the official ordered and we did.

We docked, leaving Octavia, Kasilda and Abegail on board to guard our possessions, and made our way through a gathering crowd of spectators. We followed the official along a path that led through a school campus to a one-room concrete building.

The walls of the room were decorated with environmental posters, some of which were yellow with age and others more recent. There were also graphs and studies relating to the manatee. Apart from a small desk and two chairs there was no furniture.

"How much do we need to pay you to visit the manatee?" Clyde asked again.

"You must wait for the boss," the official told us.

We occupied our time studying the graphs and posters.

The boss arrived, a young man with a smile.

"You are welcome," he said. "But you must pay to visit the manatee and you can only go with one of my guides."

"That is fine," said Clyde. "And how much must we pay?"

"Four dollars each."

Assuming we would not have to pay for the child, I pulled out twenty dollars and handed it over.

"You don't have change?" the boss was holding out the note. "You don't have eight dollars?"

Between us, Clyde and I came up with the change and I recovered my twenty.

"Panamanian people don't pay. Only tourists," said the boss.

We made our way back to the boat in the company of the guide. We had already eased our way from the riverbank when a squall hit, coming in fast from the sea. It lashed us with cold rain driven horizontally. The force of the rain stung our cheeks and made us turn away to protect our eyes.

I rigged a tarpaulin over the boat top and we huddled beneath, pressed close in an attempt to keep as much of ourselves dry as possible. The rain tapered off before giving a final burst of fury like the chords of *Beethoven's Fifth* and then all was quiet again.

With our guide aboard, we moved up the river between banks of primary jungle. Clyde called out the names of trees and plants, giving us first the Latin and then the local name. Sometimes Andres added a different name.

Rivers reflect the power of the land through which they pass. The canyons of the Colorado create awe in the mind of man suddenly placed in proportion with nature. This river passing between towering walls of impenetrable green, massed deep and laced with sinister, lesser waterways, was also awe inspiring.

"Well, now I don't have to visit the Amazon," I said.

"That is right," agreed Clyde. "Much of what you are seeing you would find along the Amazon."

We stopped in the first lake and broke open our lunch, sharing Oreos, peanut butter and jam sandwiches and oranges with the others. Our guide relaxed, enjoying our bountiful food and swapping tales with Andres in Spanish. The second lake was just like the first. In neither lake did we find the manatee.

The guide volunteered to take us further up the river at no extra cost, but, looking in the direction of the ocean, I saw thick, dark clouds reaching to high altitudes. If we were to make it back that day, we had to leave immediately. We dropped off the guide at the mouth of the river and, with everyone standing toward the back of the boat, thrust into the surf.

This time we avoided having water come aboard, but when beyond the surf we encountered rough sea. We headed toward Punta Gorda but made considerably slower progress than the day before. Andres steered with caution up each wave, down into the following trough and then up again onto the next crest.

Octavia was lying across the foredeck, buried beneath the tarpaulin. She held Abegail in her arms. Kasilda was sitting above the two of them, holding down the edge of the tarp with her feet. The three of us men stood beneath the bimini, holding fast to its heavy steel supports, our bodies being slung this way and that by a sea that was sending waves at us from two angles, one through the force of swell and the other driven by the wind. At the pace we were moving, it would be several hours before we rounded the western end of Bastimentos and entered the calmer waters of home.

As we approached the small island off Tobobe, I took the controls from Andres.

"Hold on!" I said. "Let's see if this works."

I increased speed to thirty-five thousand revs. We slapped harder still into the next few waves. I could see concern on Andres' face. I pushed the throttles further forward, bringing the revs to forty thousand. The transom rose and the bow leveled, and we began to bridge the troughs, riding from crest to crest. We still took some knocks but far less frequently and none any harder than those we had endured before.

"I have never ridden in a better boat for these seas," called Clyde. "This twin hull makes all the difference."

Andres called a warning, pointing to an area ahead where the sea was highly disturbed as if it were the water in a huge washing machine. I cut back the speed and we had some tense moments until, clear again, I pushed the throttle forward once more and we traveled at speed down the long side of Bastimentos.

"Nothing could have been better," Clyde said later that evening.

"We must do this more often," I said, knowing I had found a man after my own heart.

49

The Journey's End and a New Beginning

When Rolando had finished building the big house in town, he had no immediate project to start. Realizing he would soon be sought after by many to build their homes, I seized the opportunity, borrowed more money, and had him build us a small house at the farm.

Out of respect for Pat's concern regarding snakes, the house was built over the water. It consists of one large room, thirty feet by thirty feet, surrounded by a twelve-foot porch. Wooden concertina doors open wide on the side facing down the lagoon. The windows are shuttered but have no glass. A bathroom with an Electrosan environmental toilet, a shower room and a storeroom are attached on the side closest the shore.

In due course, when I have sold the house in town and have paid off my debts, we will build a snake-proof studio for Pat on the bluff. It will be spacious and have sufficient solar panels to allow her plenty of fans so, when she paints in watercolor on paper, the paper will not become moist from humidity.

For six weeks I lived alone in the house over the water, fashioning six years of notes into the form of this book. The only foreigner on the lagoon, my company was Andres, Samuel and Kasilda who, understanding my need for seclusion, kept their distance until I emerged for my twice-daily walks. Bianca guarded me at night, sleeping on the porch. She took her job seriously, arriving at dusk and staying until Rey, our male guard dog, came looking for her in the morning.

Most evenings, nature provides Finca Tranquilla with a program of visual entertainment. Beyond the far end of the lagoon, the setting sun projects ever changing hues of red and yellow onto the undersides of a kaleidoscope of clouds. In the distance, Indians fish from cayucus in the shadows of the mangroves. At first, the only sound is the cackling of the parrots in the mango tree that stands tall on the shore behind the house. When the light is gone, the parrots hand the stage to the toads that start their repetitive croaking. If the night is clear, I walk onto the knoll where one day we will build Pat's new studio. The stars stand out brightly in a sky untarnished by city lights.

The dawns are no less beautiful. Lingering wisps of mist lace the mountains. The surface of the lagoon is smooth at this time, broken only when a big fish strikes at surface prey or by a passing school of dolphins. By seven-thirty, cayucus with the white-shirt-clad school children head for school, the bigger children at the paddles. It is then either time to start work or to walk the farm and watch the feeding of the animals.

On the evenings when Pat is not with me, Andres and I often sit in conversation. He is half my age but a man of considerable wisdom and intelligence. We discuss on a basis of equality and mutual respect. He calls me Malcolm, having somewhere along the way dropped the formality of Senor. We speak in Spanish and, although it sometimes takes two or three tries before I understand a particular point, Andres is both persistent and patient.

One time Andres told me, "When I lived in Santa Catalina, my friends would laugh because I spent time talking to the old men. Some were eighty and ninety years old. I wanted to hear not only what it was like when they were young but also the wisdom they had gathered over their lifetime."

In turn I told him of my eighty-year-old fisherman friend, Gilbert, and how each morning in Mathews we share experiences over a cup of tea.

"We are fortunate," I said. "We learn from each other and every day add new bricks to our houses of knowledge. It does not matter to me that I am old and will die before many more years pass. You will live on, and in your mind you will carry a part of me."

The town of Bocas has changed considerably over the past six years. Pedestrians no longer rule the road and instead are restricted to walking on the sides of Calle Rev. Ephraim Alphone. There is a profusion of taxis along with the SUV's and trucks of Gringos and of the new middle class of Bocatoranians who have prospered through the town's rebirth. Andino's still exists but is overshadowed by a much bigger supermarket and an excellent gourmet food shop established by an enterprising lady boater who cast anchor and stayed.

Virginia has more than twenty Gringo clients and has commissioned Rolando to build a steel and concrete office on the waterfront that will include an apartment for her own use. Peter is engaged to a Gringo girl from Costa Rica. Tony and Silvia are talking of selling the store and moving back to Colon. Tony no longer sits at the entrance of his shop but is to be found behind the middle of the counter, his face a foot from the screen of a small TV as he watches novellas (soap operas). Joanne is still behind her cash desk.

New Gringos arrive every month, and we old settlers tell them that things are not like they used to be and bore them with tales of our early pioneering when life here was hard. Marilyn and Jerry Johnson have prospered with their real estate business and work so hard that we seldom see them. Others fill their places at our dinner table.

The town's dress code has taken a large step to the left, and bare tummies and short pants are the fashion for many of the local girls. The young ask for cell phones for Christmas, regardless of how they will pay for the calls, and dream of visiting Miami.

After seventy to eighty years of regression, Bocas is fast regaining respect in Panama and beyond. Given its immense physical attraction, its racial harmony, its easy access and lack of hurricanes, the long-term good fortune of the town appears to be assured.

Untouched and unchanged are the twenty-five acres of rainforest that I have named Nu Coin, Guaymi for Buena Agua (Good Water). A red frog stands guard at the waterfall; though, with the passing of six years, I suspect he is not my original friend but a child or grandchild. As long as I own the rights to this piece of land, I will endeavor to protect it from damage by mankind.

As for Laguna Tierra Oscura, it is still a haven of tranquility and hopefully will remain so for the rest of my days.

There is little left to do to complete the self-sufficiency of Finca Tranquilla. We have many animals, rich soil, an abundance of natural fertilizers, and sufficient fruit and vegetables for our own needs. Our water supply is constant and gravity fed from a well we have dug at the top of the farm, and our energy comes from solar panels.

We still need to introduce more green vegetables, plant tobacco for use as a natural insecticide, and convert a swamp into a talapia fishpond.

There is no other farm like ours on the lagoon, but it is my hope that the example of the farm will encourage neighbors to make greater use of the rich soil of the Dark Lands and to bring a variety of nutritious foods into their diets, reducing the starch related diabetes.

Thanks to the will of God, the patience of Pat, the encouragement of my Panamanian friends, the constant attention of Virginia and the skills of Rolando and Andres, I have emerged from the long, dark tunnel.

I know that life in the tropics will continue to produce surprises and that there is no certainty as to the future, but that is how my life has always been and nowadays is the way of much of the world.

The farm will never cease to present opportunities for improvement, and each day I learn something new about the animals and plants that surround us.

The challenge of how to help better the lives of the children of both Bocas and Laguna Tierra Oscura will always be with us, continuing to stretch our minds and resources.

"Dime con quien andas y te dire quien eres." This Spanish saying translates, "Tell me who you walk with, and I will tell you who you are." Maybe it really is true that some of those I call primo in this town share the same Scottish gene. That could be why I feel so comfortable in their company.

I have used up most of my lifetime getting to the point where I accept the teachings of spiritual leaders that you do not have to compete or judge success against the success of others. This acceptance came about over the last six years. If I had not come to Panama and faced its challenges, I would have continued pretending to others that I am more than I am. I would never have learned another language, and I would still be saying that one day I would write a book.

Epilogue

Bocas today has some similarities to Key West in the 1920's. A remote backwater, it offers a new start to those wanting to change course. Shielded from prying eyes and spared the costs of heating bills and car payments, it allows Gringos to pursue their dreams at a relatively low cost. It is possible for a Gringo to hang out in Bocas on the smallest of pensions, while waiting for the genius genes to kick in.

Among the Gringo community are many whose lives, past and present, warrant inclusion in any study of contemporary Bocas. A writer contemplating such a volume would not have to search for material but would face the problem of where to draw the line and how to placate the damaged egos of those who are left out.

In writing my story, I decided I would identify only those who had a direct impact on my journey. This was how it came about that Steve Yaconelli, the man I most admired, did not have mention, along with other notable characters. Although Steve and his wife Arlene were our most regular dinner guests, Steve's days were devoted to teaching scuba diving and mine to the farm. We spoke of our respective addictions, but did not sample each other's world.

Steve's sudden death in a diving accident occurred the day after I had written the last sentence of my manuscript. His death impacted immediately on my own Bocas situation by strengthening the case of those lobbying against my continuing to live in a remote tropical setting, far from the medicine in the United States.

Until then, those of us Gringos who are of senior age had given scant thought to our own demise. Statements of preference for a burn up, a fully-fledged funeral or a clandestine commitment to the waves, were topics that arose after well-lubricated dinners.

Steve was eight years my junior, an athlete who kept in shape by running up hills. He was the fittest of our gang, not given to heavy drinking or smoking. Regardless of what brought about his death, we were all put on notice to do some serious thinking.

Accepting the absence of Steve was made doubly difficult because, of all of us, he was the most amenable and most universally liked. The grandson of a film-maker, Steve, a talented cameraman, had come to Bocas directly from Hollywood with a slew of major films to his credit and a wealth of Hollywood stories with which to titillate our imaginations. He came to Bocas to fulfill his life's ambition to write movie scripts and teach the young to scuba dive.

When entertaining small groups in the townhouse, we seldom move from the terrace over the sea. Never long without a breeze, the terrace has sufficient space for both a casual seating area and a formal round table at which we sit eight in comfort. Steve and Arlene were frequent guests to the point where, like Virginia, they became family, refilling glasses and attending to the needs of other guests. Both had the talent to make the host and hostess relax and enjoy their own party.

At the start of an evening, Steve would be the silent one. Rather than venture into the general conversation, he would give his whole attention to one person, listening to every word and responding with sympathy and understanding.

"He was like a brother," Pat said, on hearing the shocking news of his death.

When we were seated around the dinner table, Steve would listen intently, occasionally interjecting one-line pistol shots of dry humor, without change in his deadpan expression. When the conversation took on the nature of a debate, he would lean back watching each speaker, assimilating the varied opinions, assessing as a professor assesses his students. With perfect timing, he would step into the ring and, with his writer's ability to express with few words, cut to the essence of the subject, which the rest of us, in our eagerness to hear our own voices, had failed to identify.

The unique nature of Steve's contribution to social gatherings has left a hole that cannot be filled by any one of us, however much we try to mirror his style. His example, however, will live on and continue to teach us to be genuine in our caring and attentiveness to others.

No longer could I sidestep question of medical evacuation. Old age shortens the odds against needing emergency treatment to stem a crisis. The two private doctors of our town studied medicine overseas, one in Russia and the other in Cuba, both countries with a high reputation for the training of doctors. Doctors Castillo and Anderson are competent and carry with them years of experience in peculiarities of tropical medicine.

What is missing in Bocas is not in the skill of the doctors and the nurses but the lack of hi-tech medical equipment. The same is true of the regional hospital in Changuinola. The nearest hospital capable of administering MRI's and CT scans is in David, on the other side of the mountains, separated by a thirty-minute flight in daylight hours. At night, when the airport is closed, the journey by boat and ambulance takes six hours.

As an immediate measure, I am arranging for Andres and Kasilda to attend a first aid course. Between us we are preparing daytime casavac plans to the Bocas hospital and then on to the airport and at night via the hospital in Almirante and an ambulance to David. For snake and spider bites, Cornelio is our first call.

"The Mathews County Rescue Squad gets anywhere within the county in five or ten minutes," point out my sensible and responsible friends.

Immediate first aid is what we expect in our western world, a service which will stabilize our situation and deliver us to a hospital where the doctors will assume the responsibility for insuring that technology prolongs our lives regardless of their usefulness.

I am writing this from the rehab ward of a Florida hospital. I am recovering from a massive infection that has nothing to do with Panama and which nearly cost me a leg. Infection is common in Panama, and the doctors in the modern clinics in Panama City and David are of necessity masters of its treatment and have access to the latest diagnostic equipment and antibiotics.

For infections, Pat and I would be as well off in Panama as in the States and possibly more so, since staph infections are a rarity. The attention and time given to the thorough washing of hands by doctors and nurses in Panama reminds me of the habits of my father, and I see him again bent over the basin, making sure that not even the smallest part of his hands were unclean.

Heart attacks and strokes are a different matter. The knowledge that the rescue squad, with its trained cardiac nurse, is only five minutes away is a great comfort.

Life provides options. We trade between security and adventure. To settle down with help close at hand is the safest road, but the lost opportunities to travel the back roads and to learn from those we meet along the way is a high price to pay. The mind needs exercise no less than the other parts of our body, and the challenge of the unpredictable provides an unending stimulus.

Even with the rescue squad reaching us within minutes, there is no certainty that the damage already done would not inflict permanent handicaps. The prospect of being incapable of constructive thought and communication is unacceptable. I have lived three score and ten years, and the borrowed time beyond is conditional on my continuing to be a positive influence on the lives of the young. I do not want to be saved if the graph of my usefulness falls into the negative. When that happens, it is the moment to move aside and make space for others.

The time between independent good health and becoming a vegetable is what concerns me. The cost of assisted living in developed countries often devours family wealth previously intended for the education of descendants. In the poorer countries, the extended family nurtures those who cannot afford outside help. For those who can pay, the cost of the attention of a qualified nurse is minimal.

Far from being considered a burden to the young, the elderly are revered in most third world countries. Instead of being shunted into a corner and disregarded, they remain within the family circle, treasured for their years of experience and the wisdom they impart.

My choice is to make Panama my primary residence in the years left to me. Pat has started to love Panama, though her love is tempered by her desire to play the traditional role of an Italian grandmother. Working out the compromise is our most difficult task.

In the eyes of many, my concern for myself speaks of extreme selfishness. I accept the criticism, but I will not ignore my intuition. I have learned that when I do not listen to my inner voice, my spirit rebels and leads me into trouble. Writing has now become an essential part of my well being, and I have embarked on a new challenge, that of writing a historical romance set in Bocas in the 1920's at the height of its former heyday. To attempt a different genre is a risk, but risks have always been part of my adult life.

The End

Notes to Chapter 1

1. An Explanation of the Racial and Cultural Mix of Bocas del Toro

The Naso Indians, usually referred to as the Teribe, were the original inhabitants of the Bocas lagoons. The Ngobe or Guaymi, as they are more commonly called, lived on Punte Valiente and along the shores of Laguna Chiriqui. Today, the Teribe are only found in the foothills above Changuinola, where they live along the banks of the Teribe River. The Guaymi have spread out and now inhabit most other parts of the province.

The first Europeans known to have visited the area were Columbus and his crew, who sailed into the lagoons in 1502 on the explorer's fourth and final voyage to the New World. Finding a break in the coastline, Columbus had hoped the archipelago covered the entrance to his long sought passage to China. Because the land lacked gold and precious stone, the Spanish took little interest in the area during the years of their colonial rule. They maintained an outpost until 1743, but it was ineffectual and did not deter English and French privateers and pirates from using the shelter of the lagoons to replenish supplies and repair ships.

Two years after disease forced the departure of the Spanish, English settlers established themselves on Isla Colon, exporting mahogany, turtles, tortoiseshell, sarsaparilla and cocoa.

The English encouraged the Miskito Indians to travel south from Nicaragua and used them to capture the Teribe and Guaymi, who were then sold as slaves to Jamaican plantation owners. The Miskito also provided the settlers with protection from the Spanish and the French. The Teribe retreated to the mountains.

At the beginning of the nineteenth century, taxation in Jamaica and the Islands of San Andreas and Providencia drove English and Scottish settlers to Bocas. Some of the settlers brought slaves with them. Prominent among the Scotsmen were Daniel and Todeo Brown. The Brown family is one of many in Bocas today whose roots have mixed origins. Bocas still abounds with local families whose names are typically English or Scottish, but whose genes are now predominantly from other lines; names such as Archibold, Baker, Cooper and Dixon, just to take the first four letters of the alphabet.

In 1855, the railway linking Colon on the Caribbean coast with Panama City on the Pacific was completed and several who were left without work made their way to Bocas, adding to the already existing Afro-Antillean population. More followed in the 1890's after the French gave up on their canal. The banana industry, which had begun in 1880 and was to have a huge effect on Bocas, was in need of labor.

In 1890 the Snyder Brothers from the USA established the first formal banana company that nine years later joined with two other companies to form The United Fruit Company. Added to the racial mix were company officers and engineers from the USA and from Germany and workers from Chiriqui on the other side of the mountain, who had lighter skin and a predominance of Spanish genes.

In the 1890's Chinese merchants arrived to open stores selling all manner of commodities.

In 1903 Panama gained independence from Columbia. By then The United Fruit Company was bringing shiploads of new immigrants from the Caribbean Islands to work on the plantations along the shores of Chiriqui Lagoon and later in the flatlands around Changuinola. These immigrants brought to Bocas their national game of cricket.

The completion of the Panama Canal in 1914 led to a further influx of Afro-Antillean workers, including some whose heritage traced to Martinique and French genes.

The rapid growth of the banana industry brought new business opportunities, and entrepreneurs from Germany, England and France arrived to open stores, establish export businesses, provide water transportation, publish newspapers and in general fill the needs of an increasingly affluent community. Many children were born from mixed race relationships of European fathers and Panamanian mothers.

By 1920 the town was home to five consulates, four newspapers, a soda factory, and a cricket club. San Cristobal, Tierra Oscura, Almirante, Changuinola, and Guabito also fielded cricket teams. A few years later, the town had an airstrip, which was eventually to become a major factor in the growth of the tourist industry.

At the height of the town's prosperity, Panama Disease, a fungus pathogen, invaded the banana plantations of the islands and the shores of the Chiriqui Lagoon, killing the banana plants. United Fruit moved first to Changuinola and then later, still plagued by the disease, to Sixaola. By the 1930's the banana industry was all but dead, leaving thousands without work. Cacao trees were planted in the place of the banana plants, but cacao farming required relatively few workers.

The town on Bocas declined rapidly and only now, with the arrival of tourists, is it starting to revive.

The German community lived at German Point on the south side of the town, and the remnants of what was once an impressive German cemetery evidences their prosperity. The Germans, who had suffered a degree of internment during the 1914 War, were largely put out of business during the Second World War, when most of the men were taken and held prisoner in the Canal Zone. Karl Friese, probably the most successful businessman of the time, took poison and died, rather than submit to the indignity of a second internment.

Evidence of local support for the German Navy was found following a report by Indians of having seen a huge fish in the mouth of the Cricamola River. Upon investigation, a generator was found hidden on the banks of the river, and it was deduced its purpose was to recharge the batteries of a German submarine. In 1942, a German submarine torpedoed and sank the *Sixaola*, a United Fruit Company ship, in the open sea outside the lagoon.

California and Texas have provided many of the most recent settlers and visitors. Others have come from Europe, particularly Italy, and some from South America and Australia. Each year there are new babies born to marriages and liaisons between the white-skinned newcomers and the darker skinned Afro-Antilleans and Indians.

Given this melting pot of genes, and in particular the high percentage of Mestizos, it is understandable why Bocas today is a community largely blind to racial color and free of racial friction.

Author's note

This book is for my children and their children so that they can better understand my maverick behavior and how it is that the small country of Panama became my final destination. Others who read this book do so at their own risk.

Some names have been changed, the names of people who might be embarrassed by what I have written. It has not been my intention to cause embarrassment but to honestly portray this period in the development of Bocas del Toro.

Quoted conversations are based on notes made soon after the occasion in which they occured.

Endorsements

Wow! Did someone say adventure? Henderson's "simple" decision to start a diversified organic farm on the equator in Panama opened worlds for him, and for us. Wasting no time, he gets to know the local indigenous, black, mulatto, and gringo communities; the crocodile, snake, and insect communities too. His friends include a medicine man who cures deadly snake bites with local herbs and an American horticulturalist who advises Chiquita Banana on monoculture cropping. Despite hilarious mishaps—crashing his boat into the dock, wrestling escaped pigs, and having to cut a cast off his leg at the local hospital—this transplanted Brit is determined to succeed, and he does. It's hard to ignore the message that adventures such this are there for the taking, if only we could make that "simple" decision too.

—Jennifer Morgan, author, storyteller, and environmental advocate
  Born With a Bang: The Universe Tells Our Cosmic Story
  From Lava to Life: The Universe Tells Our Earth Story

In Don't Kill the Cow Too Quick, Malcolm describes in detail his pilgrimage through the archipelago of Bocas del Toro, at which he arrived by sheer coincidence and where, in spite of all the adversities encountered, he decided to stay. In doing so, he depicts the renaissance of Bocas. He already feels, thinks, and acts like a real Bocatoreno.
Tito Thomas. entrepreneur, architect and another real Bocatoreno

"A story filled with vivid imagery as this Englishman (Malcolm Henderson) shares his adventure of seeking peace with oneself and building a home in the rainforests of Panana. While the road is far less traveled and the challenges appear never ending, you will be intrigued with the simple beauty of the tropical land and the willingness of the people to share their culture."

Carol R. Lechel
Executive Director/President
READ Association of Saginaw County

A most readable book by a successful businessman who, in seeking occasional escape from life's stresses and strains, discovered his Sangrilla on a rainy, tropical island off the north coast of Panama. I would wager that many who read the book will promptly consult a travel agent concerning flights to Panama City.

Don Baldwin
Retired Editor
St. Petersburg (FL) Times

The fashionable literary genre of narrative writing about radical lifestyle changes has been greatly enhanced by this compelling and hilarious series of vignettes set in a hitherto little-known but stunningly beautiful Central American archipelago. Malcolm Henderson's impulsive decision to buy, at first sight, a house and a tropical rain forest on two neighboring islands, sets in motion an extraordinary chain of events, supported by a cast of memorable characters, brilliantly illustrating the paradox of the western image of paradise in the 21st century. But, equally, it is also a glowing testament to the respect and affection of a quintessentially English gentleman for the multi-faceted and multi-ethnic people of Bocas del Toro as they become bound together on a voyage of self-discovery and personal growth.

Richard Paris
Travel Writer
London